THE LIFE AND TIMES
OF NATHANIEL HALE PRYOR

THE LIFE AND TIMES
OF NATHANIEL HALE PRYOR

Explorer, Soldier, Frontiersman,
and Spokesman for the Osage

Lawrence R. Reno

Published by Turkey Creek Publishing
c/o L.R. Reno
303 E. 17th Ave. #200
Denver, CO 80203

First Edition
6   5   4   3   2   1

ISBN 0-9785327-0-8 (13-digit ISBN 978-0-9785327-0-3)

Library of Congress Control Number: 2006904939

Subject Categories: Lewis and Clark Expedition (1804–1806), Discovery and Exploration—West (U.S.), Frontier and Pioneer Life—West (U.S.), River Life—West (U.S.), History—19th Century

Cover design by LaVonne Ewing, Image Resource.
Text design and composition by D. Kari Luraas, Clairvoyance Design.
Cover art by Nick Calcagno, *Captain Nathaniel Pryor at Trading Post on Pryor Creek*. © Mrs. Betty Lou Harper Thomas, Director of the Mayes County Historical Museum [a/k/a The Coo-y-yah Museum], Pryor, OK.

Printed in the United States of America

CONTENTS

ILLUSTRATIONS

Credit for Front Cover—Nick Calcagno, *Captain Nathaniel Pryor at Trading Post on Pryor Creek*, © Betty Lou Harper Thomas

Art Work Credits

Paintings by Mike Wimmer—Artwork © Mike Wimmer—I Do Art, Inc., www.mikewimmer.com.

Sketches by Richard Florence—Richard Florence Studios, 4725 West 102nd Pl., Westminster, CO 80031.

Sketches by J. Courtney Ralston, 12414 Knox Court, Broomfield, CO 80020.

CHRONOLOGY

1875   Nathaniel Hale Pryor born, Amherst Co., VA.

1882   Charles Floyd born, Jefferson Co., VA (now KY).

1898   Nathaniel Hale Pryor marries Margaret (Peggy) Patton, 17 May.

1803   Louisiana Purchase Treaty between France and U.S. signed in May (approx. 828,000 sq. miles acquired for 15 million dollars, or less than 3 cents per acre); Floyd and Field Brothers conditionally enlisted by Clark on 1 Aug; Pryor, Floyd and 7 others officially enlisted by Lewis and Clark as the "Nine Young Men From Kentucky" 15–20 October; flotilla embarks from Falls of the Ohio on 26 October; Spanish turn over Lower Louisiana to France on 30 Nov at New Orleans; France turns over Lower Louisiana to the U.S. on 20 Dec.

1804   Transfer of Upper Louisiana from Spain to France to U.S. at St. Louis on 9 Mar; Pryor, Floyd and Ordway appointed as Sergeants 1 Apr; Corps of Discovery officially embarks on Expedition from Camp River du Bois on 21 May; Charles Floyd died in vicinity of present-Sioux City, IA, 20 Aug.

1806   Corps of Discovery returns to St. Louis 23 Sep; Pryor discharged 1 Oct.

1807   Pryor reenlists in Army, rank of Ensign 27 Feb, 1st Inf. Reg't.; Clark puts Pryor in charge of combined military and trading party to return Chief Sheheke to the Mandans in May; Pryor's party unsuccessful due to battle with Arikara and Sioux in Sep.

1808   Promoted 1st Lieut., 3 May.

1810   Pryor resigns from Army on 1 Apr; with financial help from Abraham (Albert) Gallatin, Pryor establishes trading post and lead smelter at Toledo Mort, near present Dubuque, IA and Galena, IL.

1811   At Clark's request, Pryor spies on camp of Tecumseh and The Prophet, gives intelligence to Clark and William Henry Harrison; Battle of Tippecanoe on 6 Nov.

1812   Winnebago Indians attack and destroy Pryor's post at Toledo Mort, Pryor narrowly escapes 1 Jan.

1813   Pryor reenlists in Army, rank of 1st Lieutenant in 44th Inf. Reg't. 30 Aug.

1814   44th Inf. Reg't. attached to Jackson's Army in South; Pryor promoted to Captain on 1 Oct.

1815   Battle of New Orleans on 8 Jan; Pryor discharged from Army on 15 June.

1816   Pryor makes way to Arkansas Post, Fort Smith and the Three Forks area on the Arkansas River; establishes trading post operations with business partners; Marries an Osage woman, Ah Sin Ka.

1817–30   Conducts trading operations at posts at Three Forks and at Pryor Creek; assists Osages in negotiations with the U.S. and other Indian tribes; becomes spokesman for the Osages as an unofficial sub-agent.

1831   Pryor finally appointed officially as a sub-agent for the Osages; Pryor dies after long illness on 9 June.

ACKNOWLEDGEMENTS

M y cousin, Anna M. Cartlidge (1906–1987) was an excellent family genealogist who introduced me to the remarkable life of Nathaniel Pryor after his service with Lewis and Clark on the Voyage of Discovery to the Pacific Ocean and back. Anna was a prodigious genealogist with whom I corresponded and traded information in the 1960s and 1970s when I first became interested in the genealogy of the Floyd family. I am related to Pryor as a first cousin, four times removed. Pryor was not only a first cousin of Sergeant Charles Floyd on the Expedition, but he was a first cousin of my greatgreatgrandfather, Charles Stewart Floyd. When I discovered that there had never been a comprehensive biography written about Pryor I determined to fill that gap and to publish it in conjunction with the Lewis and Clark Bicentennial Celebration. Another family genealogist, Thad Kinnaman of Sedan, Kansas also contributed valuable information bringing my side of the Floyd family to the current time. Unfortunately, both Anna and Thad have not survived to see the results of their contributions, but those contributions definitely require sincere thanks and acknowledgement. Two other cousins, James and David Mordy have contributed their thoughts, extensive research and support to this project. Dave has provided invaluable help on the computer. Jim provided an excellent study correcting the paternity of Sergeant Charles Floyd and convinced the National Park Service and the Lewis and Clark Trail Heritage Foundation of their errors in this regard, although it was too late to correct the erroneous information set forth in Stephen

Ambrose's *Undaunted Courage*. Special thanks go to Sharon Long, a forensic anthropologist at the University of Wyoming, who completed the excellent forensic reconstruction of Sgt. Floyd, copies of which are now displayed in several museums. Sally Newkirk at the Carnegie Museum in New Albany, Indiana mounted and presented an excellent Floyd Family exhibit during the Lewis and Clark Signature Event at the Falls of the Ohio in October of 2003. Steve Sehnert, one of my friends from the Denver Mile High Rotary Club has provided very valuable computer assistance by scanning photos and documents and he prepared a Power Point presentation for me.

Mrs. Betty Lou Harper Thomas the Director of the Mayes County Oklahoma Historical Society at Pryor, Oklahoma, is very knowledgeable about the life of Nathaniel Pryor and has been very helpful. Mrs. Thomas commissioned and paid for the painting of Captain Pryor at his trading post on Pryor Creek and kindly consented to my reproduction of it. For the other artwork in this book, I am also indebted to Michael Wimmer for the use of his excellent paintings of the Osage Treaty and of Nathaniel Pryor and Sam Houston; to Robert F. Gordon and the Lewis & Clark Trail Heritage Foundation for *Take the Horses to the Mandans*; to the State Historical Society of Missouri for the sketches of the Osage Warriors and Chief; and to my friends Richard Florence and J. Courtney Ralston for their sketches and drawings. Special credit is due to Oklahoma State Senator Charles Ford and the Oklahoma State Senate Historic Preservation Fund, Inc., who arranged for Michael Wimmer to be commissioned to paint the foregoing paintings that are now hung in the Oklahoma State Capitol.

Other family genealogists who have helped relative to the early life and genealogy of Nathaniel Pryor are Lt. General Pat M. Stevens, IV, Kirk LeComte and Tom Fiske. I am especially thankful to my newly discovered Osage Pryor cousins, Edward Red Eagle, Jr. and Linda Thiry, who contacted me in 2004 and with whom several of us from the Floyd family held a mini-reunion of the Floyd/Pryor families in November of 2004. I am especially indebted to the numerous authors who have chronicled the Voyage of Discovery over the years and particularly during this Bicentennial Celebration of the Expedition. The publications and website of the Lewis and Clark Trail Heritage have provided extremely valuable information. Ken Jessen has provided valuable assistance regarding the many facets of self-publishing. And finally, this book would not have been possible without the editorial assistance and support of my friend Bob Pulcipher, of the *Posse of the Denver Westerners*, the cover design by LaVonne Ewing, layout of the content by Kari Luraas, and the assistance of Becky Pate at Central Plains Publishing.

INTRODUCTION

Some years ago the Lewis and Clark Trail Heritage Foundation published an article by George Yater entitled the "Nine Young Men From Kentucky." It described a group of nine young men among the intrepid group that would be selected to go on the Lewis and Clark Voyage of Discovery. At the request of Meriwether Lewis, William Clark did the initial recruiting and he chose his men carefully. He might have chosen thirty clones of Daniel Boone if such clones had been available, but he did the next best thing. He chose young men who had grown up in the wilderness of Kentucky, already known as the "Dark and Bloody Ground." Some of the men were probably well known to Clark, perhaps as kinsmen, neighbors or associates. The men chosen were practiced in the backwoods arts of survival—traveling by boat and canoe on the streams and rivers, hunting their own food, dealing with wild animals as well as Indians, subsisting on roots and berries, able to navigate or orient their way by the stars or dead reckoning, and so forth. I choose to focus on one of these men, Nathaniel Hale Pryor, in particular, with some attention to his cousin, Charles Floyd. Perhaps as much as any man, Pryor was a bridge between the white man's civilization and the Native American culture. As the reader will see, he participated in both cultures to the fullest extent, in Kentucky, along the Missouri River and over the Continental Divide to Oregon, fighting the British in New Orleans, developing a lead smelter operation and Indian trading post in Illinois, marrying into the Osage tribe

1

and operating trading posts in territories that are now Arkansas and Oklahoma.

Pryor's cousin, Charles Floyd, would no doubt have received equal space in this narrative, were it not for his untimely death at such a young age during the early stages of the Lewis and Clark Voyage of Discovery. Charles had already earned a well-deserved excellent reputation and the respect of the men on the Expedition, as well as that of the Captains.

Following Nathaniel Hale Pryor's third and final discharge from the Army in 1815, he cast his lot with the traders and the Osages in the area around the Three Forks area of the Arkansas River in what is now Oklahoma. He married into the Osage tribe and became their *de facto* negotiator, agent, protector and spokesman. Throughout the last fifteen years of his life he was certainly at the forefront of the western push known to Americans as their Manifest Destiny. In his dealings on behalf of the Osages, he was instrumental in keeping the peace by helping to settle disputes with the other tribes in the area and with the white settlers encroaching into the territory. As a result, his impact upon the early settlement of the Indian Territory that is now known as Oklahoma was substantial. By the early 1820s, it could probably be said that Pryor had traveled more extensively and had probably logged more river miles upon the various important rivers of the West and South than any other person in America. He had traversed the lower Ohio; boated several times on the Mississippi between the mouth of the Ohio and St. Louis; traveled all the way up to the headwaters of the Missouri; then down and back up the Columbia and some of its Idaho tributaries. After returning down the Missouri with the Expedition; he led the ill-fated round trip of 3,000 miles on the Missouri attempting to return Chief Sheheke to the Mandans in North Dakota; traveled several times on the upper Mississippi between St. Louis, Fort Madison and the Galena lead mines; probably traveled on several Southern rivers in his service under Andrew Jackson during the War of 1812, from the Mississippi to Pensacola and back; made several trips between New Orleans and

St. Louis; and then made many trips up and down the Arkansas, Verdigris and Neosho (Grand) Rivers. Throughout, Pryor encountered every sort of difficulty and obstacle, including hostile Indians, the British and the forces of nature.

Nathaniel Pryor left little written history, but his footprints have been quietly memorialized in the geography books and atlases. Perhaps no other member of the Lewis and Clark Expedition has had more places named for him, other than Lewis and Clark themselves. A search of the database of the United States Board of Geographic Names reveals 169 entries for the name of Pryor from Virginia to Oregon. Some of those places were named after Nathaniel's father or other Pryors, however, there are many places or features in Montana and Oklahoma that were clearly named for him. For example, the town of Pryor, the Pryor Mountains, Pryor Creek, and the Pryor Mountain Wild Horse Preserve, all in Montana, as well as the town of Pryor and Pryor Creek in Mayes County, Oklahoma. It is believed that Nathaniel Pryor was the only member of the military unit on the Voyage of Discovery who later married a Native American and who has Native American descendants living today who can trace their ancestry directly to him.

In addition to his travels, Nathaniel Pryor encountered and was influenced by many of the important men and women of his era, especially those involved in the exploration and settlement of our Western frontier. It may generously be said that Pryor met, dealt with, or was affected by the directives of such personages as Thomas Jefferson, General George Rogers Clark, William Clark, Meriwether Lewis, the other men of the Expedition, Sacagawea, Touissant Charbonneau, William Henry Harrison, Andrew Jackson, Sam Houston, Davy Crockett, Thomas Nuttall, General Thomas James, Jesse Chisholm, various Indian chiefs, including Tecumseh, The Prophet, Sheheke, Claremore II, Dutch, and many others. Nathaniel Pryor participated in several of the momentous events between 1803–1831, including the Voyage of Discovery, the Battles of Tippecanoe and New Orleans, and the opening of the American frontier.

As Nathaniel Pryor left no written record of his life, it is clearly impossible to fully flesh out his biography with the rare benefit of detailed recollections of those people who knew and associated with him. On the other hand, the historic events in which Pryor participated and the scraps of information that we do have relative to Pryor and some of the historic personages mentioned above can give us much more than just the skeleton of a biography. This is the life of this important explorer, soldier, trader, mediator, peace maker and loyal friend of the Osage Nation.

1

THE WESTERN FRONTIER

Nathaniel Pryor was born in western Virginia, about 1775, probably in Amherst County, Virginia. His father was John Alexander Pryor and his mother was Nancy Floyd. It had been more than a hundred years since Nancy Floyd's forbears came to the Eastern Shore of Virginia at a place called Hog Island. From the early Virginia plantations the family gradually moved west as the frontier moved west to satisfy the unlimited appetite of white settlers for acquiring more of the Indian land in that part of Virginia which was later known as Kentucky.

Frontier Kentucky

It has been said that there were three different kinds of explorers of early Kentucky on the eve of the American Revolution: the hunters; the would-be settlers; and the surveyors who mapped out the land for owners of large land grants and speculators. John Floyd was one of the early surveyors. He was Nathaniel Pryor's uncle, an older brother of Nathaniel's mother, Nancy Floyd Pryor. The Floyds were a stout pioneer family that adapted readily to the rapidly changing transition of the area from an Indian culture to a white culture. Perhaps the Floyds were aided in their endeavors by being part Indian. Family tradition holds that Nathaniel Pryor's grandmother Abadiah Davis Floyd was descended from an Indian princess Nicketti, the sister of Pocahontas. Another source related that Abadiah was descended from Princess Nicketti, the daughter of Powhatan's brother, Chief Openancanough.[1] Although that ancestry should be considered unproven, the appearance and skin color of many of the early Floyd clan convinced many people that there was an Indian ancestor in the family.

In 1774, along with hunters and settlers who were criss-crossing Kentucky in their explorations, several parties of surveyors visited the Kentucky frontier, including a surveying party headed by Captain, or Colonel John Floyd, as he was later known. Floyd at the time was an Assistant Surveyor of Fincastle County, Virginia. After the death during childbirth of his first wife in 1769, Floyd moved to Fincastle County in 1772, where he taught school and lived at the home of his patron, Colonel William Preston, the Fincastle County Surveyor. Preston taught Floyd surveying and on April 7, 1774, appointed him chief surveyor of a surveying party to survey lands in the western part of Virginia, later to become Kentucky. The purpose of making these surveys was "by virtue of the Governor's warrant for officers and soldiers on the Ohio and its waters." In the field, these parties were continually meeting with other survey groups. Sometimes they would join each other for a time, then split up and go about their separate business. On this trek, Floyd started out with eight men; at one time was in a body of thirty-seven men; and, returned home with just four men. Of course the survey groups encountered bands of Indians, most of whom were hostile and resented the incursion of the whites into their choicest hunting grounds.

In 1779, following an unusual and interesting term tour of duty in the early years of the Revolution, John Floyd became a settler and brought his family to Bear Grass Creek, or Floyd's Landing along the Ohio River, in an area that later became Louisville, Kentucky. John Floyd also brought his brothers, Robert Clark Floyd and Isham Floyd, to the area with their families. John Floyd's sister Nancy and her husband John Pryor (the parents of Nathaniel

Pryor) and their family settled in the same area at roughly the same time and at least by 1782, when John Pryor cast a vote from that area for delegates to the Virginia General Assembly. John Floyd brought out another brother, Charles Floyd, to Kentucky in 1780, with instructions to bring much needed supplies and money following the severely harsh winter of 1779–80. So we judge that young Nathaniel Pryor moved to Kentucky when he was between four and seven years old. In 1783, his father John Pryor received 3 shillings and 3 pence for 18 days service as a spy in the command under General George Rogers Clark during the Revolution. We have not learned the circumstances that led to this payment. John Pryor and Nancy died or were killed before July of 1791, when Nathaniel and his younger brother Robert were "bound out as orphans of the late John Pryor."[2]

Thus, while the American Colonies were engaged in the Revolutionary War, fighting against the British troops, we are able to picture young Nathaniel Pryor, his brothers, and his Floyd cousins, growing up in the wilderness and learning the required skills and tools for survival. They necessarily learned how to track animals and men, how to kill buffalo and other game, how to build and manage canoes and other kinds of boats, and how to deal with friendly or hostile Indians as the case may be.

Perhaps nothing illustrates the skills required of the backwoods frontiersman much better than the way that Daniel Boone and his companions dealt with the Indians' kidnapping of Boone's daughter Jemima and Betsey and Fanny Callaway, in 1776. When Boone discovered that the three girls had been taken by a group of three Shawnee and two Cherokee Indians, he and John Floyd and others set out to recover the girls. Based upon his knowledge of the streams and trails in the area, Boone formed an idea as to which route the Indians had taken and their probable destination. Floyd's party was the first to find the Indians' trail and he and Boone then tracked them for two days over some forty miles. On the second day they came upon the Indians who had stopped long enough to kill and roast a buffalo. Floyd, Boone and the other pursuers were able to spring a surprise attack and recovered the girls without harming them. Boone's woodsmanship relied upon anticipating the thought process of the Indians and then taking bold and decisive action to accomplish the objective.[3] John Floyd was given credit for killing the leader of the kidnappers, Chief Hanging Maw, a Shawnee.[4]

More than two hundred years later, the resourcefulness of Boone and Floyd is still an impressive tale to recount. We can imagine that the telling and re-telling of this same incident by the family made an indelible impression on John Floyd's nephews, Nathaniel Pryor and Charles Floyd, the latter being the son of John's brother, Robert Clark Floyd. Both nephews would later become two of the "Nine Young Men From Kentucky" on the Lewis and Clark Expedition. Boone and Floyd may well have been role models for the next generation of adventurers.

Young Nathaniel Pryor and Charles Floyd would also have been aware that their Uncle John Floyd was something of a swashbuckling hero who suffered an untimely death at the age of 33 when he was assassinated by Indians in Kentucky in 1783. Following his daring rescue of the girls with Boone, Floyd returned to Virginia in the latter part of 1776 where he and others invested in and outfitted the privateer *Phoenix*. Floyd was put in charge of the ship. The *Phoenix* captured a British merchant ship in the West Indies, but then was seized by a British man-of-war off the Virginia coast. Clapped in irons, Floyd was taken to prison in London, where he was tried for piracy, but acquitted. Penniless at the time of his release, he was able to avoid the infamous British press gangs around London and made his way to Paris. There, he met and made a favorable impression upon our Ambassador, Benjamin Franklin. Floyd was able to spend some time with Franklin, who was of great assistance to Floyd and even introduced him to the French Court. Family lore tells the story that Queen Marie Antoinette supposedly gave Floyd a pair of silver buckles for his shoes that he brought back to Virginia. Floyd almost died of smallpox in Paris. He also purchased a beautiful scarlet coat that he brought back with him to Virginia and Kentucky. Returning to Virginia just in time to prevent the marriage of his fiancée, Jane Buchanan, to another man, John married Jane and brought her to Kentucky in 1779.[5] John wore the beautiful scarlet coat at his wedding and at special occasions in Kentucky. On April 10, 1783, he was challenged to a duel and chose to wear the scarlet coat to the event.[6] Unfortunately, the coat made him an easy target when Indians ambushed him, his brother Charles Floyd and another man on their way to the duel. The other man was killed instantly, and John was mortally wounded. Charles was able to keep John from falling off his horse by mounting behind him. They rode to nearby neighbors, but John's wounds were fatal and he died the next day. At the time, John's wife Jane was pregnant with their third child who was born two weeks later and was named for his father. That John Floyd, born in April of 1783, was a first cousin to Nathaniel Pryor and later became Governor of Virginia.

The River Superhighways

During Nathaniel Pryor's youth, as the American Colonists moved west, the Ohio and Mississippi Rivers continued their development until they became the superhighways of their day. The French were in New Orleans at the mouth of the Mississippi and the Spanish were across the Mississippi in Texas. Of more immediate concern to the Kentucky folks in the frontier area were the actions of the British. The complaints and grievances of the American Colonists on the western frontier did indeed play a part in the revolutionary fever of the time. Samuel Eliot Morison calls our attention to the situation after the Boston Tea Party when Kentucky was the next scene of conflict. In 1774, Britain ordered its colonial governors to cease making land grants in areas such as Kentucky not already ceded by the Indians.

This "dark and bloody ground" over which many Indian tribes had hunted but where none dared dwell, was visited immediately after the French and Indian War by Daniel Boone and other "long hunters." They brought back tales of great hardwood forests, blue grass prairies, fertile meadows, and vast herds of buffalo and deer.

... Virginia was engaged in a war with the Shawnee nation, which had never ceded its rights over Kentucky and was rendered desperate by the long hunters killing off the game. Governor Dunmore dispatched two armed parties of volunteers to take possession of the illegally granted lands. After one party had been ambushed by 1500 militia of western Virginia, and these under Colonel Andrew Lewis, on 6 October, defeated Chief Cornstalk of the Shawnee at Point Pleasant, where the Great Kanawha river joins the Ohio. Owing to Sir William Johnson's diplomacy, the Six Nations and the Western tribes left the Shawnee to their fate, and in the subsequent peace negotiations the latter ceded all their Kentucky claims to Virginia. So ended "Governor Dunmore's War."[7]

Also in 1774 Britain passed the Quebec Act, which moved the southern boundary of Quebec down to the Ohio River, for the time being erasing any claims by Connecticut, New York and Virginia to the Great Lakes area later known as the Northwest Territory. The pen may often be mightier than the sword, however it was General George Rogers Clark and his army that eventually reversed the Quebec Act and recovered this area for the United States. The fights in the western frontier could be considered a lingering and drawn out continuation of the Revolutionary War during the period from 1783 to 1815. The British did not abandon the idea of regaining control of the Colonies, or at least the western territories, until after the War of 1812. During this period the British government and the large British trading companies often supported Indians with arms and supplies in their fights with settlers on the western frontier from the Ohio River to the Great Lakes.

On the world stage after the American Revolution, major events in Europe during the last two decades of the 18th century led to the ascendancy of Napoleon and gave rise to the conditions that impelled Napoleon to sell the Louisiana Purchase to the United States. On a smaller stage during this same period, the Kentucky frontier was where young Nathaniel Pryor and his cousin Charles Floyd became well prepared for the explorations of Lewis and Clark triggered by the Louisiana Purchase. They were in transition between two cultures in Kentucky and learned their skills from both cultures. They learned reading and writing, along with things such as boating, hunting, fishing and woodworking. As we shall see, in addition to gathering food, the skills they learned for making boats, clothes and moccasins were critical skills for survival. At some stage during his life, Pryor learned one or more Indian languages. In later years, when he was in Oklahoma among the Osage, he was frequently called on to be an interpreter. Perhaps this language learning began even during his boyhood. Perhaps he started with Indian sign language and developed verbal skills after that. In any event, he developed key communication skills.

The Quest for Exploration After the Louisiana Purchase

The curiosity of President Jefferson to find out what comprised the uncharted lands in the Louisiana Purchase is well known. Jefferson also thought it imperative to establish the American military presence in the new lands in order to keep the Indians in line and to keep the British out. Following the Revolutionary War, there had been continual warfare and problems in what we know as the Northwest Territory and even in the western parts of Pennsylvania and Virginia. The northern border of the fledgling American nation with Canada was not definitely established. According to the original English grants to the Colonies, many of those Colonies, such as Pennsylvania and Virginia claimed land all the way from the Atlantic seaboard to the Mississippi. The borders between some of the states were even in doubt. Thus, Virginia claimed territory immediately south of Fort Pitt and named the area Yohogania County, Virginia. Many Virginians occupied and settled in the area, including the author's paternal ancestors. This dispute was not settled between the two states until about 1785, in favor of Pennsylvania.

The westward movement of the settlers and explorers invariably caused problems with the Indian tribes. Despite provisions in the Treaty of Paris in 1783 requiring the removal of the British military and forts from the Northwest Territory, the British delayed in complying with those terms and frequently even provided overt military assistance to the Indians. This led to crushing defeats by the Indians inflicted upon mainly American militia troops with a little assistance from the small regular army. The defeat of General Josiah Harmar's forces in October of 1790 was near the present site of Ft. Wayne, Indiana. A year later, a larger, but even more ill-prepared force under the command of General Arthur St. Clair was defeated by the Indian confederated tribes on September 17, 1791, about fifty miles south of the present site of Ft. Wayne. This was the worst defeat ever suffered by the American army at the hands of the Indians. St. Clair's army lost almost three times as many soldiers killed in this battle as George Armstrong Custer's Seventh Cavalry lost at the Little Bighorn Battle in 1876.

General Anthony Wayne finally ended the Indians' dominance in this area at the Battle of Fallen Timbers on August 20, 1794, in the vicinity of present-day Toledo, Ohio. Although Wayne's forces defeated the Indians, they continued to resist the white settlers whenever and wherever possible. After Wayne's victory, the Americans negotiated a treaty with eleven of the major tribes in the area. Tecumseh had participated in the Battle of Fallen Timbers, but although other Shawnee leaders signed the Treaty of "Greenville," Tecumseh refused to sign and remained an implacable foe of the Americans. The Shawnees and the tribes allied with Tecumseh gave up their claims to the Northwest Territory. That finally caused the evacuation of the British military forts from the new American territory. The large and strong English trading companies, however, did not evacuate American soil and in their trading operations with the Indians continued to supply arms and other implements of war to the Indians. The two largest trading companies were the Hudson's Bay Company and the North West Company and they were forces to be reckoned with. The impact of the involvement of these companies in Indian affairs in the west is illustrated by the following quotation from John M. Hutchins's pamphlet about Lieutenant Zebulon Montgomery Pike.

"This unwarrantable interference with the Indians, residing within the limits of the United States, was continued by the British from the peace of '83, quite down to the commencement of the late war [of 1812]. During a great part of that time, they kept the Indians in hostility with our western settlements; and when the probability of a new war between the two countries, became very strong, they so excited the savages, as to make a battle with them the necessary prelude to general hostilities. Although this interference with the Indians was not an obvious and ostensible cause of the war; yet it may fairly be considered as a very efficient cause. Much of the resentment against the British which prevailed so strongly in the western states, the primary advocates for the war, may fairly be attributed to this source."[8]

President Jefferson was aware of the exploratory trek of Alexander MacKenzie to the Pacific during the 1790s and Jefferson felt it was very important to send a military mission to the Pacific to "show the flag" to the western Indian tribes and as a warning to the British. The Lewis and Clark Voyage of Discovery left St. Louis on that mission in early 1804.

In 1805, without consulting with Jefferson, Brigadier General James Wilkinson, the commander of the small U.S. Army, dispatched Lt. Zebulon Montgomery Pike on a military mission to explore the sources of the Mississippi River. At the time, Wilkinson was conspiring with Aaron Burr on a venture purportedly to establish a new country in the Spanish territory west of the Mississippi. It has never been established as to whether Burr and Wilkinson intended to acquire the Spanish territory for themselves or for the United States. The duplicitous Wilkinson was also acting as an agent for the Spanish government and was receiving payments from the Spanish for providing information relative to the movements of the American military.

Pike was the commander of the garrison at Fort Kaskaskia and had undoubtedly been there when Lewis and Clark passed there and recruited a few of its soldiers for their Expedition. As a result, Lewis and Clark probably picked the best men from the soldiers at Kaskaskia. Be that as it may, Pike recruited nineteen men from Fort Kaskaskia for his own expedition the following year. Accompanied by two sergeants and seventeen privates, Pike embarked upon his mission from Cantonment Bellefontaine, above St. Louis, on August 9, 1805. Compared to the preparations and equipment of Lewis and Clark, Pike's expeditionary force was sadly deficient. Pike completed the arduous mission, but encountered many difficulties and the mission was certainly not as successful as that of Lewis and Clark.

In the summer of 1806, Pike was ordered to lead a military party to explore the sources of the Arkansas and Red Rivers. This mission again was under the direction of General Wilkinson and without the authority of President Jefferson, although that authority and approval was subsequently granted retroactively.

Part of the reason for this explosion of exploration after the Louisiana Purchase was consummated can be traced to the rapidity and secrecy of the negotiations with France leading to the purchase. The boundaries of the territory purchased were not clearly delineated. Many people at the time assumed that the purchase included all of what would become the state of Texas, which it did not. The Spanish were especially distrustful of the motives of the Americans and even sent out military troops to attempt to intercept the expeditions of Lewis and Clark, which they missed, and of Pike, whom they did locate and probably saved. These important exploration expeditions did report to the nation on the quality of the lands to the west and undoubtedly laid the groundwork and foundation of what would become a nationalistic fever to expand to the west. Thus, John L. O'Sullivan first coined the mantra words of the century when he wrote in the *New York Morning News*:

" our manifest destiny to overspread and to possess
the whole of the continent which Providence has given
us for the development of the great experiment of liberty
and federated self-government entrusted to us."[9]

It was into this crucible of exploration, expansion and advancement that Lewis and Clark selected the two young cousins, Nathaniel Pryor and Charles Floyd to embark upon their great adventure in the West.

Notes

1. Jennings, Kathleen—*Louisville's First Families*, The Standard Printing Co., Louisville, KY, 1920, pp. 153–176, at p. 167. Ms. Jennings did not provide citations, but relied on correspondence between John Floyd and William Preston, the location of which is unknown to this author.

2. Yater, George H.—*Nine Young Men From Kentucky*, We Proceeded On, Lewis and Clark Trail Heritage Foundation, Publication No. 11, May, 1992, p. 6.

3. Cartlidge, Anna M.—*Colonel John Floyd: Reluctant Adventurer*, The Register of the Kentucky Historical Society, 66 (October, 1968), pp. 317–366, at pp. 337-340.

4. *Ibid*, p. 339.

5. Jane Buchanan was the ward of John Floyd's friend and patron, Col. William Preston. Jane Buchanan's mother, Margaret (Patton) Buchanan, was the daughter of the illustrious Col. James Patton of Southwest Virginia, whose sister, Elizabeth (Patton) Preston, was Col. William Preston's mother. Col. James Patton's brother, Capt. John Patton, was the father of Capt. James Patton, the Louisville settler. At page 168 of *First Families*, above, Kathleen Jennings wrote that Jane Buchanan was a "kinswoman of James Patton, the Louisville settler, according to some accounts." Nathaniel Pryor married Margaret (Peggy) Patton, one of the daughters of Capt. James Patton, of Louisville, in 1798, so the grandfathers of Jane Buchanan and Margaret (Peggy) Patton were brothers.

6. The part about the duel may be embellishment in the family myth, as Kathleen Jennings, in *First Families*, above at page 162 wrote that the Floyd party was "riding to the salt works from his station on Beargrass."

7. Morison, Samuel Eliot—*The Oxford History of the American People*, New York, Oxford University Press, 1965, pp. 210–211.

8. Hutchins, John M.—*Lieutenant Zebulon Montgomery Pike Climbs His First Peak: The Army Expedition to the Sources of the Mississippi, 1805–1806*, privately published, Applewood, CO, 2005, p. 5, citing from Robert Breckenridge McAfee, *History of the Late War in the Western Country*, (Lexington, Kentucky, 1816)[1960 Readex facsimile reprint] p. 2.

9. Callon, Milton—*What Most People Don't Know About New Mexico*, 1966 Brand Book of the Posse of the Denver Westerners, International, Johnson Publishing, 1967, Vol. 22, p. 283.

2

SERGEANT CHARLES FLOYD

It seems appropriate that we include a chapter on the short life of Nathaniel Pryor's cousin, Charles Floyd. The participation of Sergeant Charles Floyd on the Lewis and Clark Expedition is well known. He was the only casualty on the Expedition, dying of a "billiose cholick" (probably appendicitis) according to William Clark, on August 20, 1804, in the vicinity of present day Sioux City, Iowa. Captains Lewis and Clark named the Floyd River at that point for him.

Charles Floyd was born in 1782 at or near Floyd's Station, on Beargrass Creek, Jefferson County, Kentucky (then Virginia), one of the four children of Robert Clark Floyd and Lilleyan Hampton.[1] Robert Clark Floyd was a brother of Nathaniel Pryor's mother, Nancy Floyd Pryor. Beargrass Creek eventually grew into the city of Louisville. Two of Robert Clark Floyd's other brothers were John Floyd, known as Colonel John Floyd, and the author's great-greatgreatgrandfather, another Charles Floyd. At the time the area was involved in brutal frontier warfare with the British and Indians. Colonel John Floyd, was the commander of the Jefferson County militia and accordingly was responsible for the defense of the Beargrass Stations and the tiny settlement of Louisville from 1779 to 1783. As such, John Floyd worked closely with General George Rogers Clark and the Floyd family in the area of Virginia

Sgt. Charles Floyd. Author's photo at the Sergeant Floyd Welcome Center, Sioux City, IA.

that was to become Kentucky. He and the other Floyds became very closely associated with the Clark family. There is also some evidence that the Floyds and Clarks had been friends and neighbors in western Virginia previously. After serving as one of the five colonels under George Rogers Clark in Clark's 1780 campaign against the Ohio Indians, John Floyd named his next child George Rogers Clark Floyd, born April 29, 1781.

In 1783, a party of Shawnee Indians ambushed John Floyd and his brother Charles Floyd (the author's greatgreatgreatgrandfather, not to be confused with Sergeant Charles Floyd of the Expedition) in April of 1783. John Floyd was shot and was about to fall from his horse, when his brother Charles, seeing him about to fall, quickly jumped off his own horse and mounted behind John Floyd, holding him in his arms. They rode to safety at the nearby cabin of friends, but unfortunately John Floyd's wound was mortal and he died two days later.[2] Perhaps no other member of the Floyd family had as exciting and varied a career as Colonel John Floyd.[3] At the time, John Floyd was married and his wife was pregnant. The author's greatgreatgreatgrandfather was not yet married, so presumably had Charles Floyd been killed instead of John, the author would not be here today.

In the Appendix to Draper's *The Life of Daniel Boone*, Colonel John Floyd is described as "upwards of six feet high, somewhat slender, straight as an Indian and almost as dark as one, indicative of his aboriginal descent; brilliant black eyes and very black straight hair, presenting altogether a handsome appearance. He possessed a fine natural understanding, great integrity of character, and displayed on all occasions cool, undaunted courage and a heart full of the milk of human kindness. He and his connections suffered greatly from the Indians. Five of his relatives of the Davis family were killed by them ... but he had lived long enough to make a name that shall long remain illustrious in the early annals of the West."[4] That description of Colonel John Floyd would seem to fit many of the Floyds of his generation.

The dark complexion attributable to the Indian heritage of Abadiah (Davis) Floyd was present in many of the Floyd family. Robert Clark Floyd was also dark like his brother John. In 1783 Robert Clark Floyd took Melissa Mayfield to court for allegedly having accused Robert and the family of being of the "Mustic Breed or mixed with Mulatto blood." Ms. Mayfield retracted her statement and filed the following affidavit in the records of the Jefferson County Court in Kentucky:

> "Whereas Certain Malicious persons have propagated a report of my having said that Robert Floyd, and the rest of the family, were of Mustic Breed, or mixed with Mulatto blood, I do hereby Solemnly Swear that I have never reported any such thing, respecting the said family, and the report is altogether false, and groundless. Given under my hand this 3rd day of June 1783. Mylassah Mayfield. Sworn to before me as one of the Magistrates

of Jefferson County on the 3rd June 1783, the above con-
cession was acknowledged by Micajah Mayfield, and at
the request of Robert Floyd, ordered to be recorded.
Teste Mer'th Price, Clk: Jeff. Cur."[5]

In 1791, Robert Clark Floyd and his son-in-law, Thomas Minor
Winn, purchased a farm on the headwaters of Beargrass Creek
in eastern Jefferson County. As more settlers arrived and the
locale became more peaceful, the Robert Clark Floyd family
moved across the Ohio River about 1799 to the new settlement
of Clarksville, Indiana Territory, where Robert Clark Floyd and
his older son, Davis Floyd, ran a ferrying operation crossing
the Ohio River. Davis Floyd was soon elected to the Clarksville
town board.[6]

When Clark County, Indiana (Northwest) Territory, was formed
in 1801, Robert Clark Floyd's son, Charles Floyd, though only
nineteen years of age, was named or elected as the first constable
of Clarksville Township. This indicates that he must have been
very highly respected at such a young age by his neighbors.

Later in 1801, Charles Floyd was awarded a mail contract from
the Postmaster General of the United States to deliver mail from
the Falls of the Ohio area to Vincennes, a distance of about one
hundred miles. His brother-in-law, Thomas Minor Winn, was the
Postmaster at Louisville, so perhaps family contacts were used
to obtain this mail contract. Floyd apparently received an annual
salary of $660, which included extra pay of $60 per year because
of the hazardous route along the Buffalo Trace to Vincennes that
he had to ride, a route beset with bandits and hostile Indians. As
the Floyd Family Exhibit at the Carnegie Center in New Albany,
Indiana, aptly noted: "These two positions—constable and mail
carrier—demonstrated that Floyd could be trusted to exert
authority over other men and handle himself in the wilderness.
For his age, he was undoubtedly a very mature and confident
individual."[7]

In the summer of 1803 when Meriwether Lewis wrote to
William Clark and asked him to "find and engage some good

hunters, stout, healthy, unmarried men, accustomed to
the woods and capable of
bearing bodily fatigue in a
pretty considerable degree,"
Charles Floyd was one of the
first three men selected by
Clark, together with brothers, Joseph and Reuben
Field.[8] August 1, 1803, was
their official commencement
date for service and pay,
although their enlistments
were conditional and were
not confirmed and accepted
until Lewis arrived at Clarksville on October 15, 1803.
After Lewis's arrival, John
Colter was also officially enlisted on October 15, followed
by George Gibson, George

*Sgt. Charles Floyd. Drawn by
Richard Florence.*

Shannon and John Shields on the 19th. Nathaniel Pryor and
William Bratton were officially enlisted on the 20th, the eighth
and ninth men enlisted, thus completing the so-called "Nine
Young Men from Kentucky."[9]

No actual physical descriptions of Charles Floyd or Nathaniel
Pryor exist. However, the words of Stephen Ambrose describing
Lewis and Clark probably describe the two cousins as well as
many of the other members of the Expedition.

> "Each man was around six feet tall, broad-shouldered,
> with the grace of a natural athlete. ... Their bodies were
> rawboned and muscled, with no fat. Their hands were
> big, rough, strong, capable, and confident. Each man was
> long-legged, capable of hiking up to 30 miles a day. They
> (the Captains) knew how to train and command, how to

take the boisterous young frontiersmen and turn them
into well-disciplined soldiers who could be relied upon
in any emergency and who could meet any challenge."[10]

Clark issued a detachment order on April 1, 1804, designating
John Ordway, Charles Floyd and Nathaniel Pryor as sergeants,
equal in rank and pay. In Ordway's case, this was simply a confir-
mation of rank, for he had held it in the Regular Army before he
joined the Expedition.[11] When Lewis issued his first detachment
order on February 1, 1804, he put Sergeant Ordway in command
while Lewis and Clark were transacting business in St. Louis,
until they returned.[12] The military members of the Expedition
were then divided into three squads or messes, with a sergeant
in charge of each.[13]

Captain Clark wrote that Floyd was a "man of much merit." As
instructed by his Captains, Sergeant Floyd kept an uninterrupted
daily journal of the Expedition from May 14, 1804, until August
18, 1804, just two days prior to his death on August 20th. Similar
to the journals of the Captains and the other Expedition members who kept journals, Sergeant Floyd's journal is replete with

*Sgt. Floyd a day or two before death. Author's photo at Lewis & Clark
Interpretive Center, Sioux City, IA.*

misspellings, poor grammar and poor syntax. Floyd made some observations of the land through which they passed and commented on the excellent quality of the soil. On June 7, 1804, he reported seeing Indian pictographs and thought them to be "pictures of the Devil and other things." Floyd's entry of August 7, 1804, is the only detailed report of the desertion of Private Moses Reed. Floyd's poor spelling is illustrated by his report that Reed "Desarte from us with out aney Jest Case", that is that Reed deserted without any just cause. Floyd was also one of the journal writers to report on the two fishing trips shortly before he died. He was even healthy enough on August 15th to go on Clark's fishing trip, where they "Caut 300 and 17 fish of Difernt Coindes" using makeshift seines made from brush.[14] The next day "Cap' Lewis and 12 of his men went to the creek a fishen Caut 709 fish Different Coindes."[15] As these fishing trips would have been in the vicinity of present day Omaha, Nebraska, it is very difficult today to imagine such a bountiful harvest of fish from the Missouri or its tributaries at that point.

Floyd's entire journal has recently been published in a wonderful book entitled *"Exploring with Lewis and Clark, The 1804 Journal of Charles Floyd,"* edited by James J. Holmberg. Each page of Floyd's journal has been photographed, with an easier-to-read typed copy and explanatory notes on the opposite page, together with a 29-page introduction describing "The Life, Death, and Monument of Charles Floyd" and a three page introductory description of Floyd's journal, both written by Holmberg.

The Death of Sergeant Floyd

When Sergeant Charles Floyd died on August 20, 1804, he was buried with full military honors on a high bluff over the Missouri River. The location was about one-half mile below the mouth of a small river that the Captains named for Floyd. The Floyd River at Sioux City, Iowa, still bears his name. His grave was marked with a "Seeder" (sic, cedar) post. Captain Clark's journal entry for August 20 noted the ceremony and Clark wrote that "This

Man at all times gave us proofs of his firmness and Determined resolution to doe Service to his Countrey and honor to himself."

In a fragment of an undated letter quoted by Donald Jackson, Nathaniel Pryor wrote:

> "Our dear Charles died on the voyage of the colic. He was well cared for as Clark was there, my heart is too full to say more [several words illegible]. I will see you soon, your brother, Nat."[16]

We can only speculate as to whether this letter was written while the Corps wintered at Fort Mandan in 1804–05, to be taken to St. Louis on the returning keelboat in the spring of 1805, or was written when the Corps reached St. Louis in the fall of 1806. The reference to the writer's heart being too full would indicate a date closer to Sgt. Floyd's death, but "died on the voyage" sounds like a recap of the entire voyage. Also, his closing "I will see you soon" strongly indicates that this letter was written about the time that Nat reached St. Louis in 1806, when he had only a few days remaining before traveling to Louisville to see his sister. He probably would not have written "soon" while still going upriver on a journey of unknown months, of several thousand miles through unknown territory from Fort Mandan all the way to the Pacific Ocean and then all the way back to Louisville.

When the Expedition returned to the site in 1806, they found that Floyd's grave had been disturbed. William Clark wrote that the grave had been opened and that a Sioux chief had buried his dead son's body in the grave with Sgt. Floyd. Supposedly this was "for the purpose of accompanying him to the other world believing the white man's future state was happier than that of the Savages."[17] The gravesite became a landmark for travelers on land or on the river. The noted artist George Catlin painted the scene from the bluff during the 1830s. The "seeder post" was frequently repaired or replaced. In 1857 a spring flood eroded much of the bluff where Floyd had been buried and part of Floyd's skeleton was exposed. Some of his bones had dropped into the river. A local group retrieved as many of Floyd's bones as possible. The bones were marked and on May 28, 1857, they were reburied in a second grave at a prominent bluff approximately 600 feet east of the original grave.

Floyd's second grave was evidently not well defined or marked and it was apparently forgotten. Souvenir hunters carried off the replacement markers and cattle grazed on the site. It was not until the discovery and publication of his Expedition journal in 1894 that interest in Sergeant Floyd was rekindled. Fortunately, some of the men involved in the 1857 reburial were still living and, on Memorial Day in 1895, they helped locate Floyd's second grave. The grave was opened and the bones were identified. Floyd's remains were reburied again on August 20, 1895, 91 years after his death. This time a marble slab marked the site. The Floyd Memorial Association had been formed on June 6, 1895, and began raising funds for a fitting memorial. Construction of the monument began in May of 1900. Floyd's remains were again removed and were buried at the base of the monument, after measurements were made of his skull and his few remaining bones. The monument was completed on April 22, 1901 and the monument was dedicated on Memorial Day, May 30, 1901.

The monument is a very impressive 100-foot high sandstone obelisk, nine-foot square at the base, second in height in the United States only to the Washington Monument. The bones of Sergeant Floyd were placed in urns and are buried

Floyd Monument, Sioux City, IA.
Courtesy of Sergeant Floyd
Welcome Center, Sioux City, IA.

in the concrete core. The monument cost $12,600 and is certainly the most impressive memorial to have been erected relative to any of the members of the Voyage of Discovery, including the Captains. Dr. Elliott Coues, editor of the 1893 annotated reprint of the 1814 Biddle-Allen edition of the journals from the Expedition, was the speaker at the dedication of the Floyd Monument. In 1960, the U.S. Department of the Interior recognized the monument as the first National Historic Landmark Monument.

By 1895 very little remained of the skeleton of Sergeant Floyd. Fortunately someone at the time had the foresight to take photographs of the skull and lower jaw. These were used to make a plaster cast of his skull. That cast, the photos and the measurements of the surviving bones, were used by Ms. Sharon Long, a forensic anthropologist, to make a forensic reconstruction of Sergeant Floyd in 2000.[18] Complete figures of Sergeant Floyd, using Ms. Long's reconstruction, have been installed at the two museums in Sioux City and in the Carnegie Center in New Albany, Indiana. Ms. Long's reconstruction also verified that Charles Floyd was at least six feet tall.

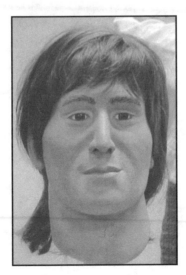

Forensic Reconstruction of Sgt. Floyd. Author's photo.

In the official roll of the Expedition, Meriwether Lewis wrote that Charles Floyd's father "who now resides in Kentucky, is a man much rispected (sic), tho possessed of but moderate wealth." Despite this lack of wealth, the land warrant that Charles Floyd's family received for his service on the Expedition remained in the family until May 1, 1839, when Floyd's youngest sister, Mary Lee Floyd Walton, sold the land warrant to John G. Berry and John T. Winn for $640.[19] It is assumed that John T. Winn was Mary's nephew, the son of her sister, Elizabeth, who had married Thomas Minor Winn. Mary was only about ten years old at the time of Charles's death.

Tributes to Sergeant Floyd

Early travelers and visitors to the site of Sgt. Floyd's burial were obviously moved by the experience. Doctor Chuinard recorded two of the more memorable tributes.[20] H.M. Brackenridge visited Charles Floyd's gravesite in 1811 and paid him the following tribute:

> The place of interment is marked by a wooden
> cross … . The grave occupies a beautiful rising of
> ground, now covered with grass and wild flowers. …
> Involuntary tribute was paid to the spot, by the
> feelings even of the most thoughtless, as we passed by.
> It is several years since he was buried here, no one has
> disturbed the cross which marks the grave; even Indi-
> ans who pass, venerate the place and often leave a
> present or offering near it. Brave, adventurous youth!
> Thou art not forgotten—for although thy bones are
> deposited far from thy native home, in the desert-
> waste; yet the eternal silence of the plains shall mourn
> thee, and memory will dwell upon thy grave![21]

When George Catlin visited the site in 1832, he not only drew a sketch of the bluff and gravesite, but also waxed eloquently, as follows:

> Oh, sad and tear-starting contemplation! Sole tenant of this stately mound, how solitary thy habitation; here heaven wrested from thee thy ambition, and made thee sleeping monarch of this land of silence.
>
> Stranger! Oh, how thy mystic web of sympathy links my soul to thee and thy affections! I knew thee not, but it was enough; thy tale was told; and I a solitary wanderer through thy land, have stopped to drop familiar tears upon thy grave … with streaming eyes I leave thee again, and thy fairyland, to peaceful solitude. My pencil has faithfully traced thy beautiful habitation; and long shall lie in the world, and familiar, the name of "Floyd's grave."

Catlin later used the sketch as the basis for a large oil painting of the site that is now in the National Collection of Fine Arts at the Smithsonian Institution, Washington, D.C. Catlin also used the sketch in his illustrated volume of his *North American Indians*, 1841 (London).

Notes

1. Cartlidge, Anna M.—*Marriages of People Named Floyd*, The Maryland Genealogical Society, Baltimore, MD, 1982, p. 131, citing the will of Lilyan Hampton, Henry Co., VA, Will Book 1:22-23, bequest to "my dau. Lilleyan Flewd." Unfortunately, the early work of N.J. Floyd erroneously attributed the parentage of Sgt. Charles Floyd to Charles Floyd (1760–1828), a younger brother of John Floyd and Robert Clark Floyd. N.J. Floyd's work also omitted any reference to Robert Clark Floyd.

2. At the time of John Floyd's death, his wife Jane Buchanan Floyd was pregnant. The child, John Floyd, was born 14 days later. He

became a very prominent physician, a Congressman and the Governor of Virginia, the only native-born Kentuckian to so serve. His son, John Buchanan Floyd, the grandson of Colonel John Floyd, also became the Governor of Virginia and later was the Secretary of War under President James Buchanan.

3. In 1774, Floyd surveyed lands in Kentucky. Recalled by Col. Preston, he raised a company of men, but arrived at Point Pleasant that evening, just a few hours after that battle. In 1775, he was back surveying in Kentucky. In July 1776, he aided Boone in rescuing Boone's daughter and two other girls from the Indians. Late in 1776, he was in Virginia where he and others invested in the privateer *Phoenix* and he sailed in charge of the ship. His adventures as a privateer are discussed above in the text.

4. Draper, Lyman C.—*The Life of Daniel Boone*, (Ted Franklin Belue, ed.), Stackpole Books, Mechanicsburg, PA, 1998, Appendix, pp. 559–63.

5. Cartlidge, Anna Margaret—*Children and Grandchildren of William and Abadiah (Davis) Floyd*, unpublished manuscript, unpaged, 1968, filed with the DAR, Washington, D.C.; also, Kinnaman, Thad—*Ancestry and Posterity of M.V. Floyd*, unpublished manuscript, Sedan, KS, 1967, p. 4.

6. Davis Floyd was a "long-time friend and associate of the Clarks, including William. He and his father operated a ferry from Clarksville to the Kentucky side of the river in the early 1800s, and he also was a licensed Falls pilot." Holmberg, *Dear Brother*, below, p. 159, n.8. In a letter of 14 Dec 1810 William Clark wrote of several lots in Clarksville that "I purchd. Of Davis Floyd with the Ferry;" also of "lots purchased of D Floyd," and of "a tract purchased of D. Floyed." *Ibid*, p. 251. "A ferry ran between Clarksville and Shippingport (adjacent to Louisville). It would have been the major means of crossing the river in that immediate area, and probably was a profitable business. It most likely was the means by which Clark crossed to Louisville from Clarksville and back. This may be the ferry he mentions buying from Floyd." *Ibid*, p. 253, n. 3.

7. The foregoing information about Charles Floyd is from the Floyd Family Exhibit at the Carnegie Center for Art and History, New Albany, IN, viewed in October of 2003.

8. The Fields were near neighbors of the Floyds, including the author's greatgreatgreatgrandfather, Charles Floyd. Yater, George

H.—*Nine Young Men from Kentucky*, (We Proceeded On, Lewis and Clark Trail Heritage Foundation, May, 1992, WPO Publication No. 11), p. 6. Several authors, including Morris and Ambrose have used the spelling of "Reubin" instead of Reuben. The conflict appears to have been put to rest in favor of "Reuben" in an article by J.I. Merritt, Editor, *Reubin vs. Reuben Field: What's in a name?*, We Proceeded On, Lewis and Clark Trail Heritage Foundation, November, 2005, p. 34. Therein, the article contains a reproduction of Reuben Field's signature, clearly showing the spelling of "Reuben" and that the last name was "Field" and not "Fields."

9. Actually a misnomer as two of the nine men, John Colter and George Shannon, were not from Kentucky, but had accompanied Lewis down the Ohio from Pittsburgh.

10. Ambrose, Stephen E.—*Lewis & Clark Voyage of Discovery*, [Bicentennial Edition: The Filming of an Epic], published by the National Council, Lewis & Clark Bicentennial, ISBN 0-7922-6473-8, p. 42.

11. Appleman, Roy E.—*Lewis and Clark*, (U.S. National Park Service, Washington, D.C., 1975).

12. Ambrose, Stephen E.—*Undaunted Courage*, Simon & Schuster, 1996, pp. 128–131.

13. The memorial at Nathaniel Pryor's gravesite in Pryor, Mayes County, OK, erroneously states that he "was the first volunteer accepted" and that he "served as the Expedition First Sergeant." As discussed in the text, neither claim is substantiated in the records of the Expedition.

14. Holmberg, James J.—*Exploring with Lewis and Clark—The 1804 Journal of Charles Floyd*, U. Okla. Press, Norman, 2005, pp. 90–91.

15. *Ibid.* Only Clark noted the different kinds of fish taken. The modern tendency for fishermen to exaggerate their catches must not be something new. Whereas Clark and Floyd agree closely with the number of fish caught, Whitehouse wrote 386 and Gass wrote 387. Similarly the reported number of fish caught the next day by Lewis's group ranged between 709 and 800.

16. Donald Jackson, ed., *Letters of the Lewis and Clark Expedition, with Related Documents: 1783–1854*, 2nd ed. (Univ. of Illinois Press, Urbana, 1978), Vol. 1, p. 37. Jackson mistakenly described this letter as being "from Charles's younger brother to his sister Nancy." Charles did not have a younger brother and did not have either a

brother "Nat" or a sister Nancy. Jackson also mistakenly wrote that Sgt. Charles Floyd was the son of Charles Floyd (1760–1828), this author's greatgreatgreatgrandfather. Instead, Sgt. Charles Floyd was the nephew of that Charles Floyd, as shown in Appendix A. Charles Floyd (1760–1828) did have a son, Charles Stewart Floyd, who did have a younger brother Nathaniel Wilson Floyd and a sister, Nancy Haws Floyd. The quoted letter, however, must have been written by Nathaniel Pryor, not Nathaniel Wilson Floyd. Only the men on the Expedition would have had first-hand knowledge that Charles was "well cared for" and that "Clark was there." The only man on the Expedition named "Nat" or "Nathaniel" was Sgt. Nathaniel Pryor, whose sister Nancy Pryor married Robert McClelland on August 7, 1792.

17. Moulton, Gary—*The Journals of the Lewis and Clark Expedition*, U. Nebraska Press, Lincoln, NE, 1987, Vol. 8, pp. 349–350.

18. *We Proceeded On*, Feb. 2001, pp. 16–19. Ms. Long, Forensic Anthropologist at the University of Wyoming at Laramie, WY, is related to the author. One of her GreatGreatGrandfathers, John Christian Floyd was the brother of one of the GreatGreatGrandmothers of the author, Caziah Floyd, the wife of Charles Stewart Floyd.

19. Yater, *Nine Young Men*, p. 5.

20. These tributes by Brackenridge and Catlin are found in Chuinard, E.G., M.D.—*Only One Man Died, The Medical Aspects of the Lewis and Clark Expedition*, Lewis and Clark Trail Heritage Foundation, Ye Galleon Press, Fairfield, WA, 1979 (reprinted 1999), pp. 240–241.

21. Chuinard cites Thwaites, Reuben Gold, ed., Early Western Travels, 32 vols, Arthur H. Clark Co., Cleveland, 1905, citing H.M. Brackenridge, *Journal of a Voyage up the River Missouri in 1811*.

3

NATHANIEL HALE PRYOR

Quite a few of the chronicles and journals of the Lewis and Clark Expedition mention Pryor's participation, but it is one of the purposes of this book to tell a more complete story of Nathaniel Pryor, a truly unique and interesting individual who led a varied and exciting life.

Nathaniel Hale Pryor was born in Amherst County, Virginia about 1775, one of the six known children of John Alexander Pryor and Nancy Floyd.[1] John and Nancy Pryor had migrated to Jefferson County, Kentucky (then Virginia) with her Floyd brothers during the Revolution, probably in 1779. John Pryor served in the campaigns under General George Rogers Clark as a spy (scout) and may have accompanied Clark's expeditions against Vincennes and/or Kaskaskia in 1778–79, although that service has not been established with certainty.[2]

Anna Cartlidge documented John Pryor's military service during the Revolutionary War as "Jefferson County, Ky., Militia: County Lieut., 1781; Col. Of M/W (?) Expedition, 1782 (18:279);[3] Major, Clark's Ill., Reg., 1782 (Va. State Library, Series H., Vol. 1, p. 92); May 17, 1783: To John Pryor for 18 days Service as a Spy, 3 pounds, 3 shillings, per Voucher No. 26, Bundle F, Journal of Western Commissioners (26:384);[4] received 1,000 acres on Scaggs Creek, Ky., for 3 years service as Capt. Cont. Line of VA,

Warrant 126 (27:355), Feb. 13, 1783."[5] Because of this service under George Rogers Clark, the Pryor/Floyd family connection to the Clarks was reinforced.

Little more is known about John Alexander Pryor. His ancestry is very sketchy, there are many inconsistencies and it is, at least as of now, totally unverified. We have not determined for certain when or where he was born, although almost certainly he was born in Virginia. The author's cousin, James C. Mordy, of Leawood, Kansas, has recently made a "best guess" as to Pryor's ancestry based upon the following analysis.

On September 5, 1762, a William Pryor acquired 350 acres on the Pedlar River in Amherst County, Virginia.[6] A military "Pension Application of William Pryor of Amherst County, Virginia," probably submitted by a son of the above-mentioned William Pryor, states: "William Pryor of Amherst moved to Great Kanawha [the major west-flowing river across present West Virginia] in 1775." The application asserts that the applicant "was at Point Pleasant later under various commands" [before and during the Revolutionary War] and mentions the applicant having "an <u>elder brother John</u>." (Emphasis added)[7]

The William Pryor who patented the 350 acres was reportedly born in 1727.[8] He reportedly had a brother, John, sons William and Nicholas, and a daughter Susannah.[9] If the first William Pryor's son William was the above pension applicant, as we believe, then son William's "elder brother John" would also be another son of the senior William. Because the senior William Pryor obtained a farm in the Pedlar River valley in 1762 and apparently remained there for at least thirteen years before moving to the Great Kanawha valley in 1775, we believe that his son, John A. Pryor, must have met and married Nancy Floyd in the Pedlar River valley while they were close neighbors there, probably around 1770 to 1772. The Pedlar River valley extends only for about ten miles north of the James River [called the "Fluvanna River" in early documents]. About six miles up this valley is Pryor Creek, still so named today, just to the west of Tobacco Row Mountain.

Thus our analysis concludes that John A. Pryor was a son of the younger William Pryor, the son of the elder William Pryor.[10]

Further that the elder William Pryor was a son of Philip Pryor, who was a son of Robert Pryor, the first Pryor immigrant to America in this line.

Nancy Floyd, wife of John A. Pryor, was a daughter of William and Abadiah (Davis) Floyd. Nancy was probably born about 1754–55, and almost certainly was born in the Pedlar Valley of Amherst County, Virginia. Nancy's father, William Floyd, lived in the Pedlar River valley, on a farm west of Tobacco Row Mountain, for more than forty years—from his 1747 marriage there until 1793, when he and Abadiah moved to Jefferson County, Kentucky. Nancy Floyd's nine siblings were all born on their father William's Pedlar River farm, between 1747 and 1770.[11] Nancy's genealogy, as a member of the Floyd family, is discussed more fully in Appendix A.

It has been reported that a John Pryor was killed in Virginia by Indians in 1780, who took his wife and family captive.[12] This was another John Pryor, as Nathaniel Pryor's father, John A. Pryor, was alive and performing military service in 1781 and 1782 in Kentucky Territory as has been shown above. John A. Pryor was still alive and listed in the 1789 census for Jefferson County, Kentucky.[13]

Similar to the mystery about their births, family genealogists have not been able to determine where or when John Pryor and Nancy Floyd died or where they were buried. We do know that at least six children were born of their marriage, namely: Jane B.; James; Nancy; Eliza; Robert L. and Nathaniel, but we do not know the order of their births. Their names are established by the will of James Pryor, drawn in New Orleans on Christmas Day, 1814, just two weeks prior to his participation in the Battle of New Orleans. His will, probated in Jefferson County, Kentucky, on August 13, 1822, left the sum of $1,000 to his nephew and namesake, James B. Gilly, and the balance of his estate to be divided among his brothers, Robert L. Pryor and Nathaniel Pryor, his sisters, Jane Gilly and Eliza Oldham, and Robert McClelland, the husband of James's sister Nancy, who evidently predeceased James.[14] John B. Gilly, the husband of Jane, was named to be executor of the will.

Presumably both John and Nancy Floyd Pryor must have died before July of 1791, as an entry in the Jefferson County (Kentucky) Court Minutes record on July 6, 1791, indicates that "Robert and Nathaniel Pryor, orphans of the late John Pryor, are to be bound out by the overseers of the poor".[15] Robert and Nathaniel Pryor were "bound out" to an Obadiah Newman, believed to have been a local gunsmith or carpenter. Indians may have killed John A. Pryor some time between his listing in the 1789 census and July of 1791. In a brief biography of Nancy's brother, Col. John Floyd, historian Lyman Draper wrote: "Five of his relatives of the Davis family [his mother's family] were killed by them [Indians]; his brother Joshua [sic, it was Isham], and his brothers-in-law, LeMaster, Asturgus, <u>Pryor</u>, Drake, William and John Buchanan were all victims of Indian warfare." (Emphasis added).[16] Colonel John Floyd had only one Pryor brother-in-law and that was Nathaniel Pryor's father. Anna Cartlidge indicated in her 1968 publication that a John Pryor was listed in the 1810 census for Henry County, KY, but this must have been a different John Pryor in view of the foregoing.

The exact birthdates and birth order of Nathaniel and his five siblings are undetermined.[17] According to the 1791 order in the Jefferson County Court Minutes above, it could be assumed that Nathaniel and Robert were the two youngest children, but perhaps the remaining four children were placed with relatives rather than being bound out, as there were numerous Floyd and Pryor relatives in the Jefferson County area at the time. Their sister Nancy Pryor married Robert McClelland in 1792, so she may have been older than Nathaniel. Jane Pryor did not marry John Gilly until 1808, indicating that she was probably younger. Perhaps Nathaniel and Robert were the oldest children and were "bound out" because they were approaching majority and needed to learn a trade, while this was not deemed to be such an imminent need for the younger children who were then probably living with other family relatives.

On May 17, 1798, Nathaniel Pryor married Margaret (Peggy) Patton, daughter of Capt. James Patton, of Louisville.[18] James Patton brought his wife and three daughters to the Falls of the

Ohio (Louisville) in 1778 with the expedition of George Rogers Clark, arriving on May 27 with twenty other families. The Pattons first settled on Corn Island, where Patton built Fort Nelson. He was a member of the committee that in 1779–80 planned and established Louisville. He then moved to a house in Louisville, where he served with Col. John Floyd as two of its first seven Trustees. In 1780 and again in 1782 he served in Clark's militia forces against the Ohio Indians. After many years of experience, Patton was the first officially appointed Falls Pilot in 1798.[19]

Except for the foregoing, we know very little about the early life of Nathaniel Pryor. It is assumed that Nathaniel's marriage to Peggy Patton was of short duration and that Peggy died before Pryor embarked on the Expedition. In Lewis's letter to Clark of June 19, 1803, Lewis wrote that on his way west he intended to enlist "some good hunters, stout, healthy, <u>unmarried men</u>." [Emphasis added][20] Obviously Lewis was seeking the services of single, unencumbered men. Lewis asked Clark to see if he could find similar men in Clark's nearby area. Reinforcing the conclusion that Nathaniel and Peggy Pryor did not have children and that she had died at least before 1815, is the fact that there is no mention of Peggy or of children of Peggy and Nathaniel in her father's will, dated December 28, 1815.[21] There is a possibility that Nathaniel and Peggy did have one child, as there is some mention of a Nathaniel Miguel Pryor being born to the couple and being raised by one of his aunts. Anna Cartlidge thought that he was probably a nephew, rather than a son. Nathaniel Miguel Pryor did visit Nathaniel Hale Pryor in the Indian Territory during the 1820s, before going to California where he died in the 1850s.[22] This possibility is discussed in Appendix C.

Notes

1. There is some confusion about the birth year for Nathaniel Pryor. Anna Cartlidge used the date of 1772, which date has been used by several subsequent authors citing her work. More recent research

seems to indicate a later date and the author has determined to use 1775. In her 1968 paper, Ms. Cartlidge stated that Pryor was born in 1772, citing vol. 15, p. 255, of the Dictionary of American Biography (Chas. Scribner's Sons, New York, 1934). Volume 15 of that reference has been republished as Volume VIII. In the republished volume, Pryor's birth date is set forth as "c. 1775." It is believed that Ms. Cartlidge must have mistyped or misread the date in her reference.

2. Cartlidge, *Children and Grandchildren*, at p. 32.

3. Perrin, Wm. Henry—*History of Bond and Montgomery Counties, Illinois*, O.L. Baskin, Chicago, IL, 1882.

4. *George Rogers Clark Papers, 1781–1784*, Collections of the Illinois State Historical Library, Vol. XIX, Series Virginia, Vol. IC (1926)

5. Military Warrants, Kentucky, 1782–1793.

6. *Genealogies of Virginia Families*, Genealogy Pub. Co., Baltimore, 1981, Vol. IV, p. 898.

7. Pryor, William—*Pension Application of William Pryor of Amherst County, Virginia*, as found in Harper, Elizabeth Pryor—*Pryor*, pp. 155 and 157. Point Pleasant, site of the famous 1774 battle with the Shawnee Indians, at the junction of the Great Kanawha and Ohio Rivers, was an important strategic military site in the west during the Revolutionary War.

8. Official IGI file of the LDS, p. 12037 (as of 1988).

9. Dayton, Ruth Ward—*Pioneers and Their Homes on the Upper Kanawha*, p. 213; de Gruyter, Julius A.—*The Kanawha Spectator*, as reported by researcher Jim Wood of Beckley, WV, in a letter to Arthur Rainville of February 25, 1987.

10. Natalie Pryor Stephens, in an online posting on January 28, 2003, concluded that John A. Pryor was born in Gloucester County, Virginia about 1737, one of the sons of Samuel Pryor; that Samuel Pryor was born in said county about 1699 and died there in 1766; and that Samuel was the son of Robert Pryor who died in said county in 1755 (nrrkd@aol.com). Ms. Stephens's posting does not contain citations, is undocumented and does not contain discussion. That Samuel Pryor would have been a brother of Philip Pryor, the father of the elder William Pryor in our analysis. Another, family genealogist, in an undated article, wrote that John A. Pryor was descended from the John Pryor reportedly killed by Indians in

1780, the brother of the elder William Pryor in our analysis. See, Fiske, Thomas S.—*The Mystery of Nathaniel Pryor* (undated).

11. See Cartlidge, *Children*, for additional details regarding Nancy Floyd's father William and her nine siblings. Nancy's father William was the Amherst County surveyor and a Captain in the Amherst County Militia before the Revolutionary War. He must have been closely acquainted with his Pedlar River valley neighbors—both the senior William Pryor and his sons, William and John.

12. Harper, Elizabeth Pryor—*Pryor Family Notes*, (collected by Ben Pryor, Griffin, Georgia), Albuquerque, NM, 1987, p. 151.

13. Cartlidge, *Children*, John Pryor paragraph.

14. Middlebrooks, Glenna Parker and Harper, Elizabeth Pryor—*Ancestry of Captain Nathaniel Pryor, The Chronicles of Oklahoma*, Vol. 48, pp. 295–306, 1970, at p. 295, citing Jefferson County, Kentucky, Will Book 2, p. 183; Cartlidge, *Children*, John Pryor paragraph, citing the same Will Book.

15. Yater, George H.—*Nine Young Men From Kentucky*, citing Jefferson County (Ky) Minute Book 3:96, 43. It is this entry that has also convinced the author to use the birth year of 1775, rather than 1772, for Nathaniel Pryor, if born in 1775, would have been no more than 16 years of age at the time of being bound out.

16. Draper, *Daniel Boone*, p. 563. LeMaster was John LeMaster, first husband of John Floyd's sister Jemima, killed in 1781; Asturgus was James A'Sturgus, second husband of John Floyd's sister Jemima; and Pryor was John A. Pryor, husband of John Floyd's sister Nancy. Drake was Joseph Drake, husband of Margaret Buchanan, the sister of John Floyd's second wife, Jane Buchanan Floyd. William and John Buchanan were brothers of Jane Buchanan Floyd and sons of Col. John Buchanan. Cartlidge, *Children*.

17. Cartlidge, in *Children and Grandchildren*, GENEALOGY section lists them as follows: Nathaniel (1772–1831); Nancy (no dates); James (–1822); Robert Lewis (c. 1780–); Jane B. (c. 1787–); and, Eliza W. (1794–). We have concluded that Nathaniel probably was born in 1775 rather than 1772 (see above). Nancy was probably born no later than 1777, as she married Robert McClelland in 1792. Cartlidge, *Children and Grandchildren*, Robert McClelland paragraph, citing Jefferson County, KY, Book I, p. 16, strangely listing "Nancy Pryor; father John Pryor" who would have been deceased

according to our analysis above. As the first child to marry (and the first to die), she may well have been the oldest child. Nathaniel's' sister, Jane B. was probably the youngest, as she did not marry until 1808 when she married John B. Gilly. Cartlidge, *Children*, John B. Gilly paragraph, citing Jefferson County, KY, Book I., p. 61, listing: "Jane Pryor, lawful age" so that she would have been born at least by 1787. Nathaniel's sister, Eliza may or may not be the Eliza McClelland who married Henry Oldham in 1808, and was reportedly born in Georgia in 1794. This would be incorrect in view of the Jefferson County Court records indicating that both of her parents, John and Nancy Pryor, had died prior to July of 1791.

18. Cartlidge, *Children and Grandchildren*, Nathaniel Hale Pryor paragraph, citing Jefferson County, KY, Marriage Book I, p. 30: "Nathaniel Pryor and Peggy Patton; James Patten (sic), consent in writing, May 17, 1798." Either the clerk misspelled "Patton" or it was miscopied. Clearly, his name was Patton, not Patten. See note 19, below, which includes dozens of references to Capt. James Patton, his father, his uncle, and many other Pattons. Capt. James Patton's uncle, Col. James Patton, was an eminent pioneer of southwest Virginia. See, Summers, Louis Preston, *History of Southwest Virginia*, 1746–1786 (J.L. Hill Printing Co., Richmond, VA., 1903, pp. 42–44, 51, 53, 57–58, 82–83.

19. *Captain James Patton of Augusta County, Virginia, and Louisville, Kentucky—Ancestors and Descendants*, from Genealogies of Kentucky Families (Genealogy Pub. Co., Baltimore, 1981, pp. 55–56, 59–64. This article states that Margaret (Peggy) Patton married Nathaniel Pryor, but nothing more about either of them, when or where they married, when or where either of them died, or whether they had any children. In contrast, the article provides extensive information regarding Peggy's sisters Martha (Patsy) and Mary (Polly), including the dates and places of their marriages, of their deaths, and names, birth and death dates for their husbands, children and grandchildren.

20. Ambrose, *Undaunted Courage*, p. 96.

21. Yater, *Nine Young Men*, p. 6, citing Jefferson County Will Book 2:32, Jan. 8, 1816.

22. The possible relationship of Nathaniel Miguel Pryor to Nathaniel Hale Pryor will be discussed more fully in Appendix C.

4

---◆---

PRYOR ON THE VOYAGE
OF DISCOVERY

M eriwether Lewis's wrote to William Clark on June 19, 1803, requesting Clark to accompany him on the exploration venture to the Pacific. Lewis asked Clark to help him "find out and engage some good hunters, stout, healthy, unmarried, accustomed to the woods and capable of bearing bodily fatigue to a considerable degree; should any young men answering this description be found in your neighborhood I would thank you to give information of them on my arrival at the falls of the Ohio; and, if possible learn the probability of their engaging in this service ..."[1]

Clark and the Nine Young Men of Kentucky

After receiving Lewis's letter and agreeing to go on the Expedition, William Clark began interviewing many of the local men who applied to go on the Expedition to the West. In late August, 1803, Clark wrote to Lewis that:

> "The Young men that I have engaged or rather prom-
> ised to take on this experdition are the best woodsmen
> & Hunters, of young men in this part of the Countrey.
> I have had many aplications from stout likely fellows
> but have refused to retain some & put others off with a
> promis of givieing 'an answer after I see or hered from
> you.'"2

At the time, Clark had accepted only three men and those men, accepted conditionally on August 1, 1803, were Charles Floyd and the Field brothers, Joseph and Reuben. That was their official enlistment date and their pay commencement date, although their enlistments were conditional. Floyd and the Fields were not confirmed and accepted until Lewis arrived at Clarksville on October 15, 1803. It is estimated that Clark rejected about one hundred of the local men who applied to him, so Floyd and the Field brothers must have been remarkable young men.

As shown above, Nat Pryor was the eighth or ninth man enlisted for the Expedition. Undoubtedly Clark selected his men because of their superior skills as woodsmen and hunters. Yet Charles Floyd and Nathaniel Pryor may not have been chosen but for the close relationship between the Clark family and the Floyd/Pryor families. John Floyd and John Pryor had served with George Rogers Clark during the Revolution. John Floyd's brothers, Charles and Robert, had also served in the Kentucky Militia around Louisville. After leaving the service, William Clark had moved to Clarksville in early 1803 and already knew Davis Floyd, an older brother of Charles Floyd. Davis was well known in the Indiana Territory and was on the board of the new town. Nathaniel Pryor had married Peggy Patton in 1798 and her father had been one of the first settlers in the area and was also a close friend and associate of George Rogers Clark. Several authors and web sites have indicated that William Clark may have been distantly related to Nathaniel Pryor and Charles Floyd, but the family has not been able to document that relationship. It may be very likely, as the two families resided in the same areas of western Virginia and Kentucky and during the period of 1750 to 1790, the white population of those areas was very small.

Nathaniel Pryor and his first cousin, Charles Floyd, were among the first nine men selected by William Clark for the journey. Floyd's selection may well have been due to the fact that Clark knew of his work as a constable and mail carrier.[3] No physical descriptions of Pryor or Floyd exist, but it has been assumed that they were both about six feet tall, thin, wiry, well muscled and probably of rather dark complexion due to their reputed Indian heritage.[4] Although their selection was probably due to the close association of the Floyds and Pryors with the Clark family it was also due to the fact that they were both raised on the frontier and were accomplished backwoodsmen.

Sergeant Pryor's Service on the Lewis and Clark Voyage of Discovery (1803–1806)

Pryor appears in Lewis's initial "Ohio River Journal," written while en route from Louisville to St. Louis. On November 22, 1803, Pryor became lost while hunting on shore. His disappearance caused some delay, but the party proceeded downstream, firing rifles and blowing horns to get his attention. Pryor was finally seen along the riverbank on November 24th. Pryor "hailed, we passed the river and took him in. he was much fatiequed with his wandering and somewhat indisposed."

After going into winter quarters at Camp River Dubois (now Wood River, Illinois), Pryor, Colter and Gibson were reported as returning to camp on January 16, 1804.[5] This was a point roughly opposite where the Missouri River enters the Mississippi. It was necessary to be on the Illinois side because the purchase of the Louisiana Territory had not been completed and the Spanish controlled the lands west of the Mississippi. Later, as the men prepared for their journey upriver, Pryor was put in charge of the sawing of lumber for the camp and for the construction of the boats.[6]

Lewis, Clark & Seaman. Author's photo at the Lewis & Clark Interpretive Center, Sioux City, IA.

Pryor's service on the Expedition is well documented in the journals of Lewis and Clark. He is mentioned about twice as frequently as Sacagawea. Pryor was considered to be "a man of character and ability" by the Captains. He was frequently assigned special duties of army administration and discipline and often was sent on special missions by the Captains.

On April 1, 1804, as the Expedition prepared to depart from its winter quarters, Pryor, together with his cousin Charles Floyd and John Ordway, were formally appointed as sergeants, "with equal Power (unless when otherwise specially ordered)." They were also directed to maintain journals on the Expedition and evidently did so. The Camp Orders of May 26, 1804 ordered: "The serg'ts ... are directed to keep a separate journal from day to day of all passing occurrences, and such other observations on the country &c. as shall appear to them worthy of notice."

Floyd's and Ordway's journals were eventually published, but Pryor's has never been found. Some authors have indicated that it may have been lost en route to France for publication.

Pryor was evidently "verry sick" at the time of his appointment, as reported by Clark on March 30, and Reuben Field was sent to kill a squirrel to make soup for him. George Shannon was temporarily appointed to perform Pryor's duties while he was sick. The order of April 1st also established the composition of the three squads. Pryor was the Squad Leader of the 1st Squad, comprised of Privates Gibson, Howard, Shannon, Shields, Collins, Whitehouse, Windsor and Hall. Pryor was still sick on April 6th, and the captains directed that "During the indisposition of Sergeant Pryor, George Shannon is appointed (protempor) to discharge the Said Pryor's duty in his squad."

While Lewis was making last-minute arrangements in St. Louis, the Corps of Discovery got underway and left Camp River Dubois on May 14, 1804. Pryor and other members of the permanent party were assigned to the keelboat. The experienced French voyagers manned the two pirogues, along with the additional personnel who would venture only so far as Fort Mandan. Lewis joined them at St. Charles, from where they departed at 4:00 P.M., on May 21st. Pryor and a few men were sent out on June 17, 1804, to get ash timber to make "ores" (oars). Pryor also was an excellent marksman and hunter and frequently went with other hunters to bring back meat for the camp, as on July 20, 1804, when he went out with Joseph Field.

The captains frequently assigned responsibilities of army administration to Pryor. On June 29, 1804, Pryor was appointed as the "Presiding" authority in the court martial of two men from his squad, Privates Collins and Hall, who were charged by Sgt. Floyd with being drunk while on duty. The privates were found guilty and the penalties were severe. Collins received "one hundred Lashes on his bear Back," and Hall received 50 lashes.

The captains issued a Detachment Order on July 8, 1804, governing the "several messes" of the crew on the keelboat. They appointed persons:

"… to receive, cook and take charge of their respective
messes … These Superintendents of Provision, are held
immediately responsible to the commanding Officers for
a judicious consumption of the provision which they
receive; they are to cook … in such manner as is most
wholesome and best calculated to afford the greatest
proportion of nutriment … no man at any time to take
or consume any part of the mess provisions without the
privity, knowledge and consent of the Superintendent. In
consideration of the duties imposed by this order the
Superintendents in future will be exempt from guard
duty, tho' they will still be held on the royster for that
duty … which shall be performed by someone from their
mess; they are exempted also from pitching the tents of
the mess, collecting firewood, and forks poles $c for the
cooking and drying such fresh meat as may be furnished
them; those duties are to be also performed by the other
members of the mess."[7]

Sgt. Charles Floyd died on August 20th in the vicinity of present-
day Sioux City, Iowa. After conducting proper services and his
burial, the captains gave most of Floyd's personal effects to his
cousin, Nat Pryor. A few days later, Pryor commanded one of the
pirogues and was sent upriver to fire the prairie as a precaution-
ary measure.[8]

Throughout the Expedition it appears that the captains placed
a great deal of trust in Pryor's ability and judgment. More than
any of the other Sergeants, Pryor was given special duties and
important missions away from the main body. Evidence of the
confidence placed in Pryor by the captains was shown when he
was directed on August 27th to accompany Pierre Dorion, the
Sioux interpreter, to meet with the Yankton Sioux and to invite
their principal chiefs to visit with the captains. This was actually
the first contact that the explorers made with Indians. Pryor
took kettles, corn and tobacco to the village and returned two
days later with seventy Sioux, including three of their chiefs.
Pryor also provided an accurate description of the village, the

Sgt. Pryor (left) and Sgt. Gass, ladling soup. Author's photo at Lewis & Clark Interpretive Center, Sioux City, IA.

mood and friendly demeanor of these Indians, as well as a description of their tepees. Ambrose wrote that he was probably the first American to describe the "classic Plains tepee."[9] Pryor described them as "handsum, made of Buffalow Skins Painted different Colour, their camps formed of a Conic form Containing about 12 or 15 persons each and 40 in number on the River Jaque of 100 yds wide and deep." Pryor also noted that he had feasted on a fat dog, that the lodgings were snug and that game abounded in the area.[10]

On September 10th, Pryor discovered a salt spring, a very important commodity to have on the Expedition. The next day, he accompanied Lewis on a successful hunting trip.

On September 21st, Pryor may have saved the explorers from a disaster. He was concerned with the rapid erosion of a sand bar on which the Expedition was camped. Clark reported that "the Sand bar on which we Camped began to give way, which allarmed (Pryor), the Serjt on guard ... the Sand was giving away both above & below and would Swallow our Perogues in a few minits, ordered all hands on board and pushed off before part of our camp fel into the river." Five days later, Pryor was sent out with a small detachment of men to locate Lewis who had been off on one of his walking trips for several days. Clark was worried about Lewis's absence and Pryor met him as he returned.

After wintering at Fort Mandan, the explorers proceeded up the Missouri. On June 2, 1805 the party reached a major fork in the River. It was necessary to establish a base camp from which to explore the two rivers in order to determine which was the Missouri. Clark took one party up the south fork, while Lewis, Pryor and five others hiked sixty miles up the north fork. Lewis sent Pryor and Windsor ahead to scout and they reported the northward trend of the river. Lewis concluded from their information that the north fork was going too far north to be the route to the Pacific. Although Clark was somewhat disappointed in the south fork, both he and Lewis concurred that it was the true Missouri. In a show of democratic leadership, the captains let each of their parties voice their opinion as to which fork to take. Although the consensus of most of the men was to go up the north fork, they did agree to be bound by the decision of the captains. Lewis and Clark determined to take the south fork and that did prove to be the correct choice. Lewis named the north fork the Maria's River, "for that lovely fair one", presumably one of his former acquaintances. It is still called the Marias.

Pryor was reported sick on June 25th. Clark treated him with a dose of salts and he recovered quickly. By July 2nd, the Expedition had reached the Great Falls of the Missouri and Pryor and Patrick Gass assisted Lewis in putting together the ill-fated iron boat.[11] Unfortunately, Lewis did not have sufficient materials available to properly seal or caulk the skins covering the frame and the boat sank immediately after it was launched.

On July 9th, Clark wrote that he "passed a butifull Creek on the Std (starboard) side this eveng which meanders thro' a butifull Vallie of great extent, I call after Sgt Pryor, who is a steady valuable and usefull member of our party." Clark, Pryor and seven others began building canoes on July 10th. The next day, one was finished and Pryor took three men in the canoe to bring back meat killed by the hunters. Pryor dislocated his shoulder on July 12, 1805, while carrying some of the meat, an injury that would plague him on the rest of the journey and for the rest of his life. Perhaps the captains were absent-minded, but they named another creek for Pryor on the 21st or 22nd, noting again that he was "a valuable and usefull member of our party."[12]

Clark mentioned Pryor's strained shoulder on July 30th. On August 17th, Pryor helped Clark and a detail build canoes to go downstream from the Shoshone village. On October 9th, Pryor was dispatched with a detail to gather rosin in order to have caulking for the canoes.[13]

After reaching the far west, Pryor volunteered to go with Clark and others on November 17th on a hike along the north shore of the Columbia to see the "main ocean." The sight and the realization that they had reached the Pacific apparently excited all of the men. The small party of explorers had successfully traveled 554 days and 4,132 miles from Camp Dubois. Although they had determined that there was no fabled "Northwest Passage," they had satisfied President Jefferson's mandate of reaching the Pacific Ocean. The Expedition then voted to cross to the southern shore of the Columbia and commenced to build Fort Clatsop. This was an historic ballot, as a woman, Sacagawea, and a slave, York, were permitted to vote with all of the other members of the Expedition. Pryor and Private Gibson, from his squad, were sent out to hunt on December 3rd and returned successfully that night.

It is obvious that Pryor must have had some carpentry skills, perhaps learned when he was "bound out" in his youth. He was frequently put in charge of building forts, stockades, cabins and structures, as well as canoes. During the construction of the fort, Clark wrote on December 10th that "Serjt. Pryor unwell from having his Shoulder out of place." Pryor had dislocated his shoulder again while helping to take down the mast of their boat on November 29th. Lewis treated him, but Clark indicated that the treatment was imperfect.[14] Pryor recovered sufficiently by December 19th for Clark to write that "we dispatched Sjt. Pryor with 8 men in 2 canoes across Meriwethers Bay (today's Youngs

Bay) for boards of an old Indian house which is vacant ... the load of old boards was found to be verry indifferent." Pryor was also one of the men directing the sawing and splitting of the wood brought in for the fort. On January 6th, Pryor was out of the camp on a hunting trip.

On January 8, 1806, Clark led a party consisting of Pryor, Sacagawea, Toussaint, and nine others on a mission to trade for oil and blubber that the Indians had salvaged from a beached whale twenty-five miles south of Fort Clatsop. Private Hugh McNeal, probably searching for female companionship, was lured away from the party at night by one of the nearby Indians. Apparently "it was a Plot to kill McNeal for his Blanket & Clothes." A fight broke out and an Indian woman gave the alarm to the explorers. Pryor led a few men to break up the fight, one of the few instances of a serious dispute between the Indians and the explorers on the journey.

On February 3, 1806, Pryor was sent to retrieve meat killed by the hunters. Private Gibson was missing again, so Pryor led a search party of four men to find him on February 11th. Along the way, the party killed seven elk, but Indian hunting parties in the area relieved them of five of the elk so that they were only able to bring back two. On the 14th, both Lewis and Clark were somewhat alarmed that Pryor's party had not returned, but they did return the next day. On the 22nd Pryor took another party to find and bring back a canoe that had broken loose from its mooring.[15]

Lewis wrote on March 11th about another of Pryor's varied assignments. Pryor had been sent upriver on March 5th to purchase fish from the Indian fishermen. "Sergt. Pryor arrived with a small canoe loaded with fish which he had obtained from the Cathlahmah's for a very small part of the articles he had taken with him. The dogs at the Cathlahmahs had bitten the trong (thong) asunder which confined his canoe and she had gone a dreft. He borrowed a canoe from the Indians in which he has returned. He found his canoe on the way and secured her, untill we return the Indians their canoe, when (the winds permit) she can be brought back." This again demonstrated Pryor's ability to make prompt decisions and to be resourceful in accomplishing his mission. Patrick Gass recorded that some of the fish brought back by Pryor were "ulken and sturgeon."[16] On the 13th, the lost canoe was located and Pryor was detailed to fetch it. He brought it back and also managed on this trip to kill two elk that he also brought back.[17]

All of the party were very impressed with the quality of the canoes made by these coastal Indians. The Indians also placed a high value on their canoes. Thus, on March 17, 1806, when Pryor returned the borrowed Indian canoe, Clark wrote that "Sergt. Pryor ... had also purchased a canoe from those people. For this canoe he gave Captn. Lewis's uniform laced coat and nearly half a Carrot of tobacco. It Seams that nothing except this Coat would induce them to dispose of a Canoe which in their mode of traffic is an article of the greatest value except a wife, with whome it is nearly equal, and is generally given in exchange to the father for his Daughter."

Clark commented on March 20th that the guns of Sgt. Pryor and Drouillard were both out of order and were repaired by John Shields. Shields was the blacksmith and armorer for the expedition and his skill had proved invaluable on many occasions. Lewis had brought along extra locks for the weapons and, according to Clark, "but for the precaution taken in bringing on those extra locks, and parts of locks in addition to the ingenuity of John Shields, most of our guns would at this moment been untirely unfit for use; but fortunately for us I have it in my power to record that they are all in good order."

On the return trip, About April 1, Pryor was dispatched with two men to explore the "Quicksand River" (now the Sandy River). Upon their return, Pryor and his men reported they had explored up the river about 6 miles, towards the mountain now called Mount Hood. On April 10th, Pryor was directed to remain behind until Private Gibson arrived in order to assist Gibson and his men to get his canoes around the whitewater rapids of the Cascades of the Columbia. Nonetheless, the men were unable to prevent the loss of a canoe and a pirogue while trying to navigate those rapids. It was necessary for the men to draw the canoes upstream with cords, which was obviously very laborious.

On April 20th, the explorers arrived at Celilo Falls, the "Great Falls" of the Columbia. The Captains hoped to trade their canoes for horses at that point. Lewis wrote: "set Sergts. Gass and Pryor with some others at work to make a parsel of packsaddles. Twelve horses will be sufficient to transport our baggage with some pounded fish which we intend taking with us as a reserved store for the rocky mountains ... and rid us of the trouble and dificulty of takeing our Canoes further."

About May 15th, Pryor went with the hunters for meat and returned on the 17th with bear meat and its skin.[18] On the 22nd, he was sent to explore Collins Creek, which he did and reported to the captains. On the 23rd Pryor's group killed several deer and then he was sent out again on the 27th to cross the river and procure salmon. He returned not only with salmon, but also with a good stock of roots and bread. Another canoe broke away from the men on the 30th and Pryor was sent after it.

Interestingly, the tomahawk of Sgt. Charles Floyd was carried all the way to the Columbia River watershed, where in 1805 it was discovered missing. Arriving back at the same place the next year on their return trip, the party on June 2, 1806, heard that the tomahawk was in the possession of the nearby Indians. The explorers were then encamped at Camp Chopunnish, on the Middle Fork of the Clearwater River, near the Nez Perce villages at Weippe Prairie, Idaho. In his journal, Captain Clark described the recovery of the tomahawk as follows:

> Drewyer [Drouilliard] arrived this evening with Neesh-neparkkeeook [Cut Nose] and Hohashillpilp, who had accompanied him to the lodge of the person who had our tomahawks. he obtained both the tomahawks principally by the influence of the former of those Chiefs. the one which had been stolen we prized most as it was the private property of the late Serjt. Floyd and I was desirous of returning it to his friends. The man who had this tomahawk had purchased it from the man who had stolen it, and was himself at the moment of their arival just expireing. His relations were unwilling to give up

the tomahawk as they intended to bury it with the deceased owner, but were at length [induced] to do so for the consideration of a handkerchief, two strands of beads, which Drewyer gave them, and two horses given by the Chiefs to be Killed agreeable to their custom at the grave of the deceased.[19]

Clark's emphasis on the importance of recovering Sgt. Floyd's tomahawk clearly demonstrates how deeply Clark was affected by the death of Charles Floyd, as well as the strength of Clark's friendship and almost fatherly concern for Floyd and his family.

When the Expedition split into three groups on July 3rd, Pryor went with Clark's main body to the Yellowstone River. This group had about fifty horses. A party of Crow Indians apparently was following this group and the Crows were well-known horse thieves, although the Plains Indians did not consider this to be theft.[20] The Crows stole twenty-four of the horses from the Clark encampment. Then on July 22nd, Pryor, with Privates George

Robert F. Morgan, Take the Horses to the Mandans *(Authors photo).*
© *Robert F. Morgan and the Lewis & Clark Trail Heritage Foundation, Inc.*

Shannon, Richard Windsor and Hugh Hall, was directed to take the remaining horses overland to the Mandans, to be used as gifts and trade goods. Pryor also carried a letter from Lewis to be delivered to Hugh Heney, (or "Henry") either at the Mandan Villages or at his trading post in Canada, if necessary. Heney was an agent for the English North West Company, a rival of the Hudson's Bay Company. The captains had met Heney during the stay with the Mandans during the winter of 1804–05. The captains were favorably impressed with Heney who had an excellent relationship with the Indians of the Middle Missouri. Lewis and Clark hoped to bring Heney over to the American side. The letter carried by Pryor also requested Heney to accompany Pryor's group to the Sioux and to attempt to convince the Sioux to send several of their chiefs to join Lewis and Clark to be taken to Washington to meet with President Jefferson.[21] This mission for Pryor indicates the great trust and opinion that the captains had for him.

Unfortunately, after Pryor and his party crossed the river, the Crows struck again on the night of the 24th and stole all of Pryor's horses. Pryor obviously knew that his mission could not be accomplished without gifts or horses to trade so he abandoned the overland trip. Interestingly, neither the Clark party or Pryor's small party ever saw any of the Crow Indians, who were reputed to be among the best horse thieves of any of the plains Indians. On July 24, Captain Clark had named another river for Pryor. Many of the names of rivers and creeks have changed over the years, but this one has held up, as Pryor Creek. It joins the Yellowstone River at Huntley, 15 miles northeast of present-day Billings, MT.

Pryor and his men spent the 25th tracking the Crow horse thieves for ten miles on foot. They then gave up the futile and fruitless chase and hiked back to the Yellowstone in the vicinity of "Pompey's Pillar," a large rock outcropping east of present-day Billings that Clark had scaled and named for Sacagewea's baby boy.[22] There, Pryor and his men built two of the bullboats that they had seen used by the Mandans on the river. This involved killing and skinning one or two buffaloes and then stretching the buffalo hides over a framework made from willows. The boats were about seven feet in diameter and sixteen inches deep. Each could carry the four men. Pryor's bad luck continued that night when a wolf bit him while he was asleep in camp. The wolf then attacked Windsor, before George Shannon was able to kill it.[23]

With typical military precaution, Pryor built two of the bull-boats. The men rode in one of them and towed the other in case one of the boats sank.[24] The visibly clumsy craft worked well and Pryor and his men overtook Clark on the 8th of August. Pryor was very impressed with the handling of the bullboats and considered them to be superior to canoes. Again, this demonstrated Pryor's resourcefulness and ability to adapt to difficult situations.

After the entire expeditionary party was reunited, Clark sent Pryor to obtain corn from the Mandans on August 16th. This was done and Clark wrote: "Sent Sergt. Pryor for Some Corn which the Mandans offered to give us, he informed me that they had more Corn collected for us than our Canoes Could Carry, Six load of which he brought down. I thanked the Chief for his kindness."

Sgt. Pryor, Privates Shannon, Hall and Windsor, launching Bull Boat. Sketch by Richard Florence.

While at the Mandan villages on the return trip, Lewis and Clark persuaded Chief Sheheke (or Shahaka, "Coyote" in Mandan; a/k/a "Big White" by the Americans), along with his wife Yellow Corn and their son, to join the Expedition on its return down the Missouri to St. Louis, and then to go with them to Washington to meet President Jefferson.

The website at "Answers.com" under a Wikipedia entry for Nathaniel Hale Pryor describes Sergeant Pryor as "a hefty man with a prominent chin-cleft (or 'pecker tracke,' in the parlance of the day)" and sets forth several additional contributions that Nathaniel Pryor made to the Expedition, without citation of authority and without giving the dates of these events. They include Pryor's removal of a "tenacious kidney stone from deep within Meriwether Lewis's distended urethra." The site also credits Pryor for defending the "honor of Sacagawea as a gaggle of oafish fur traders, armed with blunderbusses and Roofies, attempted to woo the lovely Mandan princess with their breeches around their ankles. Pryor 'whupped 'em with an uglee sticke,' according to the journals of Clarke (sic)." The Journals have some notations that Pryor cooked for the men in his squad. The website expands upon that and recites that: "A competent chef, Pryor fed the entire expeditionary force for a fortnight with a single hardtack biscuit and a spoonful lard, concocting such overlooked menu items as "lard tack," "hard lard," "Snickers bars" and "shut up and eat your own shit, you fat shiny douchebags." Finally, Pryor is given credit for fashioning a collar for Lewis's Newfoundland dog Seaman and for knowing "where to scratch Seaman to get his leg doing that thing that dogs do when they are scratched." Thus we learn a little more about Nathaniel Pryor and that he possessed medical skills, bravery to defend the honor of a woman, the ability to stretch a meager supply of food, a frontiersman's use of raw language and a sense of humor, plus a certain way with dogs. No wonder that both Lewis and Clark considered Pryor to be "a man of character and ability."

After returning to St. Louis, the Corps of Discovery was disbanded and most of the men returned to their families and homes. Pryor's enlistment ended on October 1, 1806. For his service, he received $557.00, which included an additional $278.50 for his "double pay," and a certificate entitling him to a tract of 320 acres to be selected in the Louisiana Purchase land west of the Mississippi.[25] The land warrant was recorded as "satisfied", but as Pryor never settled in the area of the Missouri, it must be assumed that he sold or assigned his warrant.[26] It is interesting to note that Pryor was the highest paid member of the Expedition, other than the Captains. Of course, had Charles Floyd lived, his pay would have exceeded Pryor's due to his earlier date of enlistment.

In October of 1806, Lewis and Clark left St. Louis for Washington, taking with them Chief Sheheke and his wife and son. They also took Rene Jusseaume as an interpreter, together with his wife and son. The party also included several members of the Expedition (Gass, Ordway, Labiche, and possibly Frazier), some Osage chiefs, and Pierre Chouteau, the Indian Agent for the Osages at the time. They all arrived in Washington, by three separate routes, where they were wined and dined for a couple of months.

Notes

1. Ambrose, Stephen E.—*Undaunted Courage*, Touchstone (Simon & Schuster), 1996, p. 98.

2. Ambrose, Undaunted Courage, p. 105.

3. Charles Floyd was the son of Robert Clark Floyd. In 1801, Charles Floyd, at the age of 19 or 20, was appointed as the first constable of Clarksville Township, so William Clark must have known him. The appointment at such a young age testified to his abilities and was probably one of the reasons he was appointed as one of the first sergeants on the expedition. Holmberg, James J.—*Dear Brother— Letters of William Clark to Jonathan Clark*, Yale Univ. Press, 2002, p. 75, n.30.

4. The author's greatgreatGrandfather, Charles Stewart Floyd, a first cousin and contemporary of both Sgt. Floyd and Sgt. Pryor, was

described as being "six feet one, weighed 200 pounds, had light hair". Kinnaman—*Ancestry and Posterity.*

5. Moulton, Gary E.—*The Journals of the Lewis and Clark Expedition,* University of Nebraska Press, Vol. 2, p.157.

6. Moulton, *Journals,* Vol. 2, p. 175.

7. http://www.pbs.org/lewisandclark/inside/npryo.html.

8. Moulton, *Journals,* Vol. 3, pp 8, 11.

9. Ambrose, Stephen—*Undaunted Courage,* p. 162.

10. Moulton, *Journals,* Vol. 3, pp. 21–22.

11. Moulton, *Journals,* Vol. 4, pp. 335–337, 377.

12. Moulton, *Journals,* Vol. 4, pp. 405, 412, 417. One of these "Pryor Creeks" is now Spokane Creek and the other is Beaver Creek, in Broadwater County, Montana. A third creek was named for Pryor in Yellowstone County, Montana and that name is still used today.

13. Moulton, *Journals,* Vol. 5. pp. 116n, 252.

14. Moulton, *Journals,* Vol. 3, p. 243n. Pryor suffered repeated dislocation and Clark, in 1827, reported that Pryor was disabled by "a dislocation of his shoulder when in the execution of his duty under my command."

15. Moulton, *Journals,* Vol. 6., pp. 275–77, 296–7, 336.

16. Moulton, *Journals,* Vol. 10, p. 197.

17. Moulton, *Journals,* Vol. 6, pp. 381–2, 409, 411.

18. Moulton, *Journals,* Vol. 7, 267–8.

19. DeVoto, Bernard—*Journals of Lewis and Clark,* Houghton Mifflin Company, Boston (1953), p. 398; Bakeless, John—*The Journals of Lewis and Clark,* NAL Penguin, Inc., New York (1964), pp. 324–25.

20. One of the websites explained that stealing a horse from another tribe or enemy was one of the four obligatory honors, or *'araxtsi,'* to be attained by any Plains Indian aspiring to become a chief. The Indians did not consider it to be stealing, but referred to it as "taking" or "getting." The first such honor was the *coup,* striking an enemy a non-lethal blow without receiving one from the enemy. The second was to take a bow or weapon from the hands of an enemy without being injured. The third was to become a pipe-owner or raid planner. The fourth was to take a picketed or closely guarded horse from an enemy without being caught. This could

explain the several instances where Indians attempted to "steal" the rifles, knives, tomahawks and horses from the explorers. Material from Joseph Mussulman is at website referred to in note 5, Chapter 5, below.

21. Crosby, Mike—*Joined by a Journey, The Lives of the Lewis and Clark Corps of Discovery*, BLM, 2004, p. 76.

22. Clark inscribed his name on Pompey's Pillar, still the only positive evidence of the Expedition that has been found.

23. Moulton, *Journals*, Vol. 8, pp.285–6.

24. John Clymer's painting of the *Arrival of Sergeant Pryor* indicates that there were two men in each boat and a recent author indicated that two men and their gear went into each boat. Crosby, Mike—*Joined by a Journey*, BLM, 2004, p. 77.

25. Shoemaker, Arthur—*The Many Faces of Nathaniel Pryor*, True West, September, 1988, pp. 48–51, at p. 49.

26. Warrant #4 for 320 acres of land west of the Mississippi River was issued to Pryor for his services and delivered on March 6, 1807, to Meriwether Lewis, who signed for him as the attorney-in-fact for Nathaniel Pryor. Cartlidge, *Children*, at p. 32. Cartlidge noted that a letter from the Hon. A. W. Lamb, of the House of Representatives, dated July 25, 1854, to Mr. Thrusten Polk, states that the warrant was satisfied.

5

PRYOR'S ARMY SERVICE
ON THE FRONTIER

By February 27, 1807, while in St. Louis, Nathaniel Pryor reenlisted in the Army, this time as an officer with the rank of Ensign. He was assigned to the First Infantry at Cantonment Bellefontaine (later designated as Fort Belle Fontaine), located on the south bank of the Missouri, twelve miles north by land from St. Louis. On March 7, President Jefferson appointed Clark as the Agent for Indian Affairs in the new Louisiana Territory, except that Pierre Chouteau was to remain agent for the Osages. On March 9, Secretary of War Henry Dearborn directed Clark to arrange for an escort to return Chief Sheheke and his family, who had returned to St. Louis from their visit to Washington, back up the Missouri to their Mandan village. To carry out Dearborn's directive, Clark selected his trusted former Sergeant, Nat Pryor. This was one of Pryor's first assignments as a new Ensign.

Ensign Pryor Assigned to Escort
Chief Sheheke Home (1807)

When Chief Sheheke and his family returned from Washington with Pierre Chouteau, Nat Pryor met them in St. Louis. To keep costs down, Dearborn suggested that private traders join the Pryor expedition in exchange for trading rights with the Mandans. A large party of soldiers and traders was formed to escort Sheheke and his family back to their Mandan village, some 1700 miles up the Missouri River that Pryor had ascended with Lewis and Clark in 1804 and had then descended down to St. Louis in the late summer of 1806. The Mandan trading party was organized by Pierre Chouteau's oldest son, Auguste Pierre ("A.P.") Chouteau, a recent graduate of West Point, who was only 21 years of age.[1] A.P. Chouteau graduated from West Point in July 1806, ranked fourth in his class. After serving as an aide to General James Wilkinson for a few months, Chouteau resigned his Army commission in early 1807.[2] In addition to the Pryor and Chouteau parties, an Army contingent was also sent along with them to escort several Yankton Sioux who had been visiting in St. Louis back to their villages.

When finally constituted, the Party consisted of about 90 persons. It included Ensign Pryor's military party of himself, two sergeants, eleven privates, and the Sheheke and Jusseaume families. The Yankton Sioux contingent was comprised of 24 Yankton Sioux (18 adults and 6 children), a military escort led by Lt. Joseph Kimball and eight or nine soldiers, and Pierre Dorion's outfit of ten traders headed for the Sioux country. Chouteau's trading party included thirty-two men.[3] Pryor had two of his friends from the Expedition with him. George Shannon was one of the sergeants with Pryor and Joseph Field is believed to have been with the Chouteau party.

Pryor met in St. Louis with Chief Sheheke, his wife Yellow Corn, and their family. The large party of soldiers, traders and Indians was formed at St. Louis and placed under the overall command of Ensign Pryor.[4] The party left St. Louis in two keelboats on May 18, 1807, and proceeded up the Missouri. On September 9th, after proceeding upriver about sixteen hundred miles near the mouth of the Grand River in present South Dakota, they were approached by a large band of approximately six hundred heavily armed Arikara and Sioux Indians (the latter probably Teton Sioux and not Yankton Sioux). The Indians ordered the party to land and trade

Sheheke—"Big White." Drawing by J. Courtney Ralston from painting by Charles Balthazar Julien Febret de Saint Memin, New York Historical Society No. 1860.95.

with them, but Pryor sensed that they were hostile and refused to put ashore. The Indians permitted Pryor's keelboat, which had the soldiers and Indians aboard, to pass, but stopped Chouteau's keelboat, which contained merchandise and had no soldiers aboard to defend it. Chouteau and a few of his men went ashore to talk with Grey Eyes, the Arikara Chief.

Grey Eyes immediately became hostile to Chouteau. A fight started that erupted into a floating battle. Chouteau retreated to his boat and both Pryor and Chouteau headed downstream, beset from both banks by rifle fire and arrows from the Indians. The battle lasted for almost an hour and ended only when a Sioux Chief was killed. Pryor's detachment suffered three wounded, including George Shannon, whose wound was so severe that his leg was amputated after the detachment returned to St. Louis. Chouteau's trading party had four dead and six wounded. Pryor's friend, Joseph Field, may have been one of the men killed with Chouteau. After his return to St. Louis, Pryor filed a 2,200-word report of this incident on October 16, 1807.[5] Pryor then offered to take Sheheke and his family overland to the Mandan villages, but Sheheke refused the offer. Additional details regarding the Pryor-led expedition to return Chief Sheheke and their encounter with the Arikaras may be found in Chapter 9, captioned *Ensign Pryor's Fight*, in a recent Sheheke biography by Tracy Potter.[6]

An interesting sidelight on Pryor's confrontation with the Arikaras and Sioux is that it may have been attributable to the possible perfidy of Manuel Lisa. Lisa was a Spanish trader who had held the exclusive license to trade with the Indians on the Missouri under the Spanish administration of those lands. When the French retook the area, Lisa lost that license and had to share the trade with the Chouteaus of St. Louis.[7] Lisa and a large trading party, including John Colter from the expedition, had preceded Pryor's group up the river by several days. The Arikaras stopped Lisa's party and he was forced to give up part

Sheheke's Wife—Yellow Corn. Drawing by J. Courtney Ralston from painting by Charles Balthazar Julien Febret de Saint Memin, New York Historical Society No. 1860.96.

of his store of guns, ammunition and trade goods. To avoid a more serious attack on his party and to pacify the Indians, Lisa evidently told the Arikaras that another large trading party would be coming up the river with Chief Sheheke aboard and with more trade goods for the Mandans. As the Arikaras were rivals and enemies of the Mandans at the time, the Arikaras wanted to kill Sheheke and his family and this may have caused the immediate hostility to Pryor, Chouteau and their parties. Shortly after the confrontation with the Arikaras, Pryor picked up an Indian woman along the river. She was questioned and from her information, Pryor concluded that Lisa had indeed been treacherous.[8] The woman told Pryor that Lisa had bribed the Arikaras with arms and the information that Pryor's flotilla would be following, loaded with supplies as well as with the Mandan chief. Pryor reported these charges to Clark, but Lisa denied them and they were never verified by anyone other than the Indian woman informant.

Prior to the Louisiana Purchase, Manuel Lisa and the Chouteaus had been bitter rivals in their attempts to monopolize the business of trading with the Indians. After the Purchase, each of them obtained a license to trade with the Indians and their rivalry continued. Later they compromised and they were both co-venturers with Lewis, Clark and others in the Saint Louis Missouri Fur Trading Company. Although Lisa may have treacherously betrayed Pryor's mission, Lisa later proved invaluable to the trade on the Missouri. He remained very loyal to the United States and opposed to the British interests.

Manuel Lisa's trip up the Missouri in 1807 was the first of possibly twelve or thirteen such trading missions undertaken by this successful, picturesque character. He also erected several trading post forts along the Missouri, one of which was between present-day Omaha, Nebraska and Sioux City, Iowa. There he conducted very financially successful operations and also remained on friendly terms with the Indians of the area. Manuel Lisa quickly became one of the major players in the burgeoning beaver fur trade along the Missouri and its tributaries. In refer-

ring to Lisa's post on the Missouri above Omaha, one early
writer wrote that:

> "Lisa spent several profitable winters promoting
> friendly relations with the Indians—an art in which he
> had no superiors—and incidentally reaping a consider-
> able harvest in furs from the natives of western Iowa. In
> all probability no one had an influence over the Indians
> of the Iowa country during the period from 1807 to 1820
> to that of Manuel Lisa."[9]

During the War of 1812, Lisa was made the sub-agent for all the
Indian tribes of the Upper Missouri and his work was very effective in defeating British plans in the West and in resisting the
encroachment of British traders into the area.[10]

The Chouteau family was among the first families to settle in
St. Louis. Auguste P. Chouteau is frequently referred to as the
founder of St. Louis. The Chouteaus became very prominent in
St. Louis shortly after the French regained control of the vast
Louisiana Territory from Spain. For the rest of his life Nathaniel
Pryor would frequently encounter and deal with various mem-
bers of the Chouteau family.

Chief Sheheke was not reunited with his tribe until two years
later in 1809, when a much larger expeditionary force of about 150
men, led by A.P. Chouteau's father, Pierre Chouteau, successfully
returned the Sheheke family to their Mandan village. This second
expedition cost the government about $20,000, which approxi-
mated the total costs incurred by the Lewis and Clark Expedition.[11] Chief Sheheke was later killed in a battle with the Hidatsas
in 1812.[12] An historical marker has been placed at the site of
Pryor's battle with the Arikaras near Grand River, South Dakota. It
commemorates: (1) the stops both in ascending and descending
the rivers by Lewis and Clark, 1804–1806; (2) Nathaniel Pryor's
fight in 1807; (3) the final return of Big White by Manuel Lisa and
Pierre Chouteau, Sr., in 1811 [note the erroneous date]; (4) William
Henry Ashley's fight with the Aricara (sic) in June, 1823; (5) Gen.
Henry Leavenworth's punitive expedition in August, 1823, when

he Aricara's (sic) power was broken; (6) the Atkinson O'Fallon treaty party in 1825 when the first review of U.S. troops in South Dakota was held on the site. The item on the monument pertaining to Nat Pryor reads as follows:

> Here on Sept. 3, 1807
> *ENSIGN NATHANIEL PRYOR*
> Attempting to return Big White
> Mandan Chief to his people was
> Stopped and had 13 casualties in
> The first battle with the Indians
> In South Dakota.[13]

Lieutenant Pryor Assigned to Escort the Clarks to St. Louis (1808)

After the ill-fated Sheheke expedition of 1807, Pryor remained in the army for two and a half more years. As an officer of the First Infantry he was initially stationed at Cantonment Bellefontaine, the first American army post west of the Mississippi River.[14] On May 3, 1808, he was promoted to second lieutenant.[15] Zebulon Pike was also a Lieutenant in the First Infantry and was stationed at nearby Fort Kaskaskia. By 1808, Pike had returned from his two adventurous exploration missions, the first to the headwaters of the Mississippi and the second mission being the better known expedition well into what is now Colorado. As the U.S. Army at the time consisted of less than 4,000 troops spread around the country, Pryor and Pike undoubtedly crossed paths at some time during their military service.

In June of 1808, Meriwether Lewis, Governor of the Louisiana Territory, requested Col. Thomas Hunt to approve a military escort for William Clark, who was bringing his new bride to their new home in St. Louis, together with their three slaves, household furnishings, horses, carriages, supplies, personal baggage, a niece, several other passengers, and some heavy equipment for the Indians, including a horsepower mill, a blacksmith shop and tools.[16] As Commandant of the First Infantry and the Commander of Cantonment Bellefontaine, Col. Hunt sent an escort of twenty privates, and placed Lt. Pryor in charge of the detachment.[17]

Governor Lewis advised Clark by letter of May 29, 1808, that his party would be escorted from the mouth of the Ohio to St. Louis by a military escort to be led by Pryor.[18] In a letter to his brother Jonathan of June 7, 1808, William Clark indicated that he had just heard that "Mr. Pryor and about 20 men with 2 boats is watting [sic] at the mouth of the ohio [sic] for me."[19] Pryor successfully carried out his assignment and Clark's three-boat entourage reached St. Louis safely by July 2.[20]

Lieutenant Pryor Dispatched to Establish Fort Madison (1808)

In the fall of 1807 there were proposals to control the Indians in the area by building two forts and trading posts on the upper Mississippi. The first was to be built near the mouth of the Des Moines River, some 240-river miles upstream from St. Louis. This site was one of the sites for possible forts selected by Lt. Zebulon Pike during his 1805 expedition to the headwaters of the Mississippi River. The other fort was to be built at Prairie du Chien, another 310 river miles upstream. The Sac and Fox Treaty of 1804 had stipulated that trading posts would be established with those tribes.[21] On May 17, 1808, Secretary of War Henry Dearborn wrote to Col. Hunt at Cantonment Bellefontaine to undertake the building of the forts, each to "consist of 30 men to be commanded by discrete, careful officers."[22] Hunt was directed to build a stockade, blockhouse and barracks at each fort.[23]

Upon receiving Dearborn's order, Col. Hunt consulted with Governor Lewis who advised Hunt that he would first send out his most trusted Indian agent, Nicholas Boilvin and a military escort to investigate the situation.[24] Boilvin was the Indian agent at the Sac and Fox village near the mouth of the Des Moines and had been employed in various capacities by the government following the Louisiana Purchase in 1803.[25] This expedition was delayed as Hunt was unable to furnish the escort at the time as Pryor and his men had been dispatched to bring Clark's party to St. Louis.

Later in the summer of 1808, after returning to St. Louis, Clark wrote Dearborn that he would proceed up the Missouri to direct the building of a fort on that river [Fort Clark, that later became Fort Osage], and that: "one other fort is to be built immediately on the Mississippi Some distanc up under the direction of Col. Hunt."[26] Clark proceeded to construct Fort Clark and Col. Hunt sent another detachment of American troops up the Mississippi, to build Fort Madison at a site about 15 miles above the mouth of the Des Moines River. This second detachment was under the command of Lieutenant Alpha Kingsley and his second in command was Second Lieutenant Nathaniel Pryor.[27] Hunt must have thought that Kingsley and Pryor fit the required description of "discrete, careful officers in command."

Governor Lewis sent Nicholas Boilvin along with the detachment to Fort Madison. Boilvin, whom Lewis had described as his most trusted Indian agent, was to provide the Sauk (Sac) tribe with their annuity.[28] Governor Lewis advised Secretary Dearborn that he had promised a sub-agency to Maurice Blondeau, who had previously been in the employ of British merchants, and that "I have promised a sub-agency with the pay of $1.50 per day. This man has more influence with the Sauks and Foxes, or rather possesses their confidence to a greater degree, than any man in the country."[29] Maurice Blondeau quickly shifted his allegiance to the Americans following the Louisiana Purchase and became an important ally for Lewis, Clark, the American cause and Nathaniel Pryor, as we shall see.

The necessity for these forts was not only to protect the influx of American settlers and traders, but also to have a military presence in the area to oppose the encroachment of British traders and possibly the British military. Despite the provisions of the 1782 Treaty of Paris, the British had continued to trade with the Indians in the American territories and had even maintained forts at Detroit and other American territories until well into the 1790s.

The soldiers began the construction of Fort Madison in the fall of 1808. Reports of an impending attack hastened work on the fort, which was sufficiently completed by April of 1809 to permit its occupation. Soon thereafter, Chief Black Hawk and a band of Sac and Fox warriors attempted to take the fort under cover of a war dance, but visibly lighted matches next to a loaded cannon caused them to discontinue their effort and retreat. "Had the Indians obtained an entrance, they would have massacred the whites, Black Hawk stated. Prompt reinforcement of the garrison discouraged any further attempts for the moment."[30]

Nonetheless, throughout Nathaniel Pryor's tour of duty at Fort Madison, and continuing until it was closed in 1813, the troops there were continuously exposed to the threat of Indian attack. From 1809 to 1812 tension mounted as the British, along with Tecumseh and his brother, the Prophet, endeavored to turn the Indians of the Illinois Territory against the Americans.[31] At the time, the Illinois Territory consisted of the present states of Illinois, Michigan, Wisconsin, and parts of Minnesota. Zebulon Pike had picked the site for Fort Madison on his expedition to the headwaters of the Mississippi in 1805, but it proved to be a poor selection. The situation was so bad at Fort Madison in March of 1812, that the factor of the fort reported to Governor Howard that there were so many hostile Indians around the post that the Americans "were afraid to venture more than 200 yards beyond its walls" and added that: "I believe every man of us will perish."[32] The garrison eventually escaped from the Indian encirclement by digging a tunnel to the river and escaping by boats and canoes, burning the fort behind them.

During the next several years, Nicholas Boilvin, who had become the Agent for the Winnebagos, learned of the disturbing activities of British traders in the Upper Mississippi area. A Scottish trader named Robert Dickson "remained fiercely loyal to the British Crown" and was suspected by Clark as being the prime instigator of troubles with the tribes.[33] Boilvin reported that the British were telling the Indians that their American father was too poor to bring them blankets, that the Americans even had to supply their own needs from the British, and that the Americans were preventing the British from supplying the Indians' needs. In February 1811 Boilvin reported that the tribes coming to trade at Prairie du Chien "complain that their American Father does not take sufficient care of them." More significantly, he reported that the British had told the Indians: "soon their English father will declare war against the Americans, and will again take under his protection his beloved red children."[34]

The disparity of trade goods given to the Indians by the British as opposed to the Americans was great. "As long as the British supplied their wants, the Indians, enjoying at best a marginal existence, could not be blamed for visiting [the British posts] in droves." A Sac and Fox warrior receiving from the British "an 'elegant' rifle, fifty pounds of lead for bullets, twenty-five pounds of powder to propel them, and three blankets, ten shirts, and other cloth to cover his nakedness might well be expected to love his British father." And the British generosity was particularly impressive when contrasted with American largess. "The Americans did not profit from the Indians' comparison of the generosity of their two fathers."[35]

Notes

1. Christian, Shirley—*Before Lewis and Clark*, Farrar, Straus and Giroux, New York, 2004, p. 149.

2. *Ibid*, pp.144–45, 149.

3. *Ibid*, p. 150; Barry, Louise—*The Beginning of the West*, Kansas State Historical Society, Topeka, 1972, p. 58, citing several sources.

4. This and the following material taken from an article by Joseph Musselman, at: http://www.lewis-clark.org/CLARK-YELLOWSTONE/PRYOR/ yr 6-sheheke-home.htm.

5. Musselman, *above*, citing Donald Jackson, ed., *Letters of Lewis and Clark Expedition With Related Documents*, 1783–1854 (2nd. Ed., Urbana: Univ. of Illinois Press, 1978) 2:432–38.

6. Potter, Tracy—*Sheheke, Mandan Indian Diplomat, The Story of White Coyote, Thomas Jefferson, and Lewis and Clark*, Farcountry

Press, Helena, MT, and Fort Mandan Press, Washburn, ND (2003), pp. 137–146.

7. The Floyd and Pryor families were united with the Chouteau family in 1825, when Thomas Floyd Smith married Emilie Antoinette Chouteau, a sister of Pierre Chouteau.

8. *The Rivermen, The Old West Series*, Time-Life, Alexandria, VA, 1976.

9. Robeson, George F.—*Fur Trade in Early Iowa*, The Palimpsest, Vol. VI, No. 1, January, 1925, State Historical Society of Iowa, on line, p. 3.

10. *Ibid*.

11. Christian, *Before Lewis and Clark*, pp. 163–68, 175–76; Dillon, Richard—*Meriwether Lewis*, Western Tanager Press, Santa Cruz, CA, at pp. 320–21.

12. Potter, *Sheheke*, pp. 178–79, 184.

13. *The Chronicles of Oklahoma*, Notes and Documents, Vol. 36, p. 473.

14. Shoemaker, *Many Faces*, at p. 49.

15. Foreman, Grant—*Nathaniel Pryor, The Chronicles of Oklahoma*, Vol. 7, pp. 152–165, at p. 152.

16. Holmberg, *Dear Brother*, p. 131; p. 133, n. 4; p. 138, n. 17; Ambrose, *Undaunted Courage*, p. 438.

17. Holmberg, *Dear Brother*, p. 145, n.7; p. 138, n.17.

18. Ambrose, *Undaunted Courage*, p. 438.

19. Holmberg, *Dear Brother*, at pp. 131–132.

20. Holmberg, *Dear Brother*, p. 139.

21. Dillon, *Meriwether Lewis* p. 295.

22. Colter-Frick, L.R. *Courageous Colter and Companions*, Video Proof, Washington, MO, 1997, p. 415.

23. *Ibid* and Dillon, *Meriwether Lewis*, p. 300.

24. Dillon, *Meriwether Lewis*, p. 301

25. Hagen, William T.—*The Sac and Fox Indians*, p. 34.

26. Holmberg, *Dear Brother*, at p. 143. [Clark's spelling].

27. Hagen, *Sac and Fox*, p. 34; Holmberg, *Dear Brother*, p. 146, n. 7; Dillon, *Meriwether Lewis*, p. 312; Cartlidge, Anna—*These, Too, Are Our Ancestors*, unpublished, undated, manuscript received by the author in 1968, at p. 3 (copy filed at DAR Library, Washington, D.C.).

28. Dillon, *Meriwether Lewis*, pp. 300, 307. There is some confusion about "Sauk," "Sac," "Sac and Fox," and other variants. The author will use "Sac" to be consistent, except where quotations use "Sauk." At one time the Sac and Fox were separate tribes, but now they are allied as the "Sac and Fox".

29. Dillon, *Meriwether Lewis*, p. 309. Maurice Blondeau certainly may be one of the more interesting characters in this narrative. Due to the identity of his name, this author assumes that this Blondeau was the son of an early French trader from Montreal named Maurice Blondeau (1734–1809). The elder Blondeau had been one of the original founders of the *Beaver Club* in Montreal, a select group of early entrepreneurs that required experience of trading or trapping in the western French territories in order to be a member. The records of the *Beaver Club* indicate that the elder Blondeau's "first voyage to the interior" was in 1752, and only one of the original founders of the club had an earlier date, that just in 1751. This group competed with the large and strong Hudson's Bay Company ("HBC") and established the North West Company ("NWC") as a competitor to the HBC. At one time, the NWC was outperforming the HBC and the NWC even attempted to take over the HBC. The two companies competed with each other until they finally merged in 1821. At the time of the Louisiana Purchase, the younger Maurice Blondeau was an agent for the NWC at a post along the Mississippi River in the area of Julien Debeque's Mines (present day Dubuque, Iowa). In 1805, Blondeau provided valuable assistance to Lt. Zebulon Pike's Expedition at a time when Pike and his men were encountering extreme difficulties. Blondeau aided Pike by locating two of Pike's men that were lost and was very helpful to Pike as Blondeau spoke the Indian languages. (Iowa History Project, *Making of Iowa*, Chapter 13, *With Pike up the Mississippi in 1805*). Blondeau's subsequent assistance to Lewis, Clark, Pryor and others will be related in the text.

30. Hagen, *Sac and Fox*, pp. 39–40.

31. Hagen, *Sac and Fox*, p. 40.

32. Jones, *William Clark, below*, p. 205; Collins, *Territorial Papers*, 14:534.

33. Jones, Landon Y.—*William Clark and the Shaping of the West*, Hill and Wang, New York (2004), p. 204.

34. Hagen, *Sac and Fox*, p. 41, citing letter of February 11, 1811 from Boilvin to Secretary of War William Eustis, in *Nicholas Boilvin Letters*, 1811–23 (ed. By Marian Scanlan), State Historical Society of Wisconsin; Jones, *William Clark*, pp. 196–97, citing the same letter; Carter, Clarence Edwin ed. *Territorial Papers of the United States*, (Washington, D.C., GPO, 1934–75) 14:438–41.

35. Hagen, *Sac and Fox*, pp. 41–42.

6

NATHANIEL PRYOR JOINS THE "LEAD RUSH"

Pryor must have remained at Fort Madison from the beginning of its construction in September 1808 until the effective date of his resignation of his Army commission, which was April 1, 1810. He may have written and mailed his letter of resignation in late 1809, but it was not accepted until the 1810 date.[1] Upon resigning his commission, Pryor joined the "lead rush" to the area near present-day Dubuque, Iowa, and Galena, Illinois, some 500 miles up the Mississippi from St. Louis.

Pryor's Trading House Near the Galena Lead Mines (1810–1811)

Early in the 18th century the French had discovered valuable lead deposits along the Mississippi in this area and had begun mining operations, utilizing primarily Indian miners that they trained. In 1788 a French Canadian named Julien Dubuque (or "Debeque") acquired the mining rights to approximately 125,000 acres of lead deposits fronting on the Mississippi from the Sac and Fox Tribes, with a grant from the Spanish governor. The

75

Spanish confirmed Dubuque's claim to the lead mines in 1796. Dubuque began mining the extensive lead deposits about eight miles from the Galena River. His mines became known as the "Mines of Spain." Also in 1810, about the same time that Pryor resigned his army commission and went to the Dubuque/Galena area, Pierre Chouteau's second son, Pierre Chouteau, Jr., known as "Cadet," also went to the same area intending to work for Julian Dubuque and manage the half-interest in the lead mines that his uncle Auguste Chouteau had bought from Dubuque in 1804 for $10,848. Although Dubuque died shortly before he arrived, Cadet remained there, overseeing the Indians who Dubuque had used to work the mines, until he returned to St. Louis on May 1, 1813.[2] It is perhaps hard for us to imagine that lead would be a valuable commodity now, but that was certainly the case in the early part of the nineteenth century and these lead mines were very important.

Fur trading on the Mississippi above St. Louis was very profitable and the traders charged high prices to the Indians. George Robeson wrote that:

> "It has been estimated that the 'Ayouwais', (probably the Iowas) a tribe of some eight hundred Indians located about forty leagues up the river 'Demoin' (Des Moines), annually consumed merchandise valued at thirty-eight hundred dollars for which they gave in return six thousand dollars worth of deer skin principally, and the skins of the black bear, beaver, otter, grey fox, raccoon, muskrat, and mink."[3]

In the area around Fort Madison, the American traders carried on a flourishing trade with the Sacs, Foxes and Iowas in spite of opposition by the Sac Chief Black Hawk and the British traders. An 1809 inventory at the "Le Moine Factory" (believed to be at Fort Madison) showed "merchandies (sic), furs, peltries, cash on hand, and debts due" of a value of nearly thirty thousand dollars.[4]

Dubuque and Pierre Chouteau used Indians primarily to work their lead mines. In 1810, it was estimated that the Indians of the area had "manufactured four hundred thousand pounds" of lead that they exchanged for goods. Robeson, in his *Fur Trade in Early Iowa* article noted that Nicholas "Boilvin considered it a good stroke of business if the Indians could be induced to engage in mining as a regular occupation inasmuch as the Canadians, having no use for lead, would probably cease to be competitors." Also, lead "was not perishable and could be transported easily, whereas furs and "peltries were bulky and large quantities spoiled every year before they reached the market."[5]

After leaving the Army on April 1, 1810, Pryor very diligently applied himself to establishing a trading venture and a lead smelter near the Galena lead mines. First, however, he was required to answer collection efforts on a debt he had incurred to St. Louis merchants. Between November of 1809 and March of 1810, Lieutenant Nathaniel Pryor had run up an account of at

Pryor's Note to J. Comegys, July 12, 1810. St. Louis Court of Common Pleas. District of St. Louis, Territory of Louisiana, July Term, 1812, Case No. 67. (Inset of Nathaniel Pryor's signature)

least $28.75 for clothes, cloth and dry good items from Falconer and Comegys. They sought collection from Pryor in July of 1810.[6] Probably to settle the issue, Pryor executed a one-month note on July 12, 1810, to pay $100 to John G. Comegys. This is the first instrument that we have found with the signature of Nathaniel Pryor.[7]

After settling at least temporarily with his creditors in the summer of 1810, Pryor secured a trader's license to trade with the Sac and Fox Indians from his friend William Clark, then the Superintendent of Indian Affairs for the Louisiana Territory.[8] He must also have been negotiating with financial interests to provide funds or trading merchandise for his venture. Pryor proceeded to the Galena area and constructed his trading house on an island in the Mississippi River, near the mouth of the Febre or Fever River (now the Galena).[9] Pryor also built a lead smelting furnace operation near his trading post on the island. He evidently purchased cattle, horses, oxen and other livestock and hired employees.

In all likelihood, Nat Pryor entered into some sort of partnership or financial relationship to be able to have established such a large trading and smelter operation in such a relatively short time. Several early documents indicate that in all probability his financial partner was Abraham Gallatin, the Secretary of the Treasury from 1801 to 1814.[10] Gallatin had been an early speculator in western lands prior to the Revolution and he had assisted Jefferson in plotting the course of the Lewis and Clark Expedition. Gallatin also maintained an interest in the western Indians, so he did have both financial and personal interests in the area. Pryor's Army pay from the Expedition and his subsequent military service would not have been enough to have provided sufficient funds for his trading and smelting establishment. In the Nathaniel Pryor probate proceedings filed in St. Louis after Pryor's death and discussed more fully below, Abraham Gallatin filed a claim in the amount of $5,750.50.[11] The claim referenced a debt incurred by Pryor in 1811 for merchandise valued at $5,750.00. The presence of this claim would appear to conclusively prove that Gallatin financed Pryor's venture at his trading post and lead smelter operation, either as a lender or a partner. As Gallatin was the Secretary of the Treasury in Washington, D.C., in 1810 Pryor would have been required to either go to that city, or to stay in St. Louis to arrange the financing by couriers using the Ohio and other eastern rivers.

The location of Pryor's combined operation was called "Toledo Mort."[12] It was described as being "across the Mississippi River from present day Dubuque, Iowa."[13] Another source has stated that Pryor "operated a lead-smelting furnace at the mouth of the Galena River."[14] Putting the sources together, we believe that Pryor's trading house and lead-smelting furnace were both on an island in the Mississippi, a few miles down river from present Dubuque, Iowa, near the mouth of the present Galena River, by present Galena, Illinois. In September of 1810, Pryor was joined at Toledo Mort by his friend, George Hunt, the former sutler from Fort Madison.[15] Hunt established his trading post a short distance from Pryor's operation.

During the spring of 1811, Superintendent Clark, who was also a Brigadier General in command of the Louisiana Territory Militia, became alarmed when he received information that Tecumseh was attempting to establish a large confederation of Indian tribes with the avowed intention of driving the white settlers from the area and back across the Appalachians.[16] Tecumseh, the Shawnee War Chief, was an imposing looking man with a large hooked nose and a strong chin. He possessed a marked sense of racial pride and firmly believed that the western country should belong to the Indians. This was a view that he had inherited from his father, Pucksinwah,[17] also a Shawnee War Chief, who had been killed at the Battle of Point Pleasant in 1774, trying to drive the white men back in the most serious skirmish of "Lord Dunmore's War."[18] The loss of his father and the American settlers' thirst for expansion into the Indian lands resulted in Tecumseh becoming an implacable enemy of the Americans. The Shawnees under Tecumseh were formidable opponents of the American expansion westward.

Tecumseh was a very able organizer and he had been laboring for years to unite the various Indian tribes from the Great

Tecumseh. Drawing by J. Courtney Ralston, from drawing, Indiana Historical Society, Negative C 6629.

Lakes to the Gulf into a confederation strong enough to force the white man back across the Appalachians. He was aided by his one-eyed brother, Tenkswatawa, also known as Elkswatawa (The Loud Voice), "The Prophet" or the "Open Door," who had acquired a reputation as an orator and conjurer. Originally known to have had an alcohol problem, The Prophet had reformed and regained status among the Shawnees. The Shawnees became convinced that he had supernatural powers when he successfully predicted a solar eclipse. Tecumseh had contacted most of the Indian tribes living in the Great Lakes region and along the Ohio and Mississippi Rivers to try to enlist them into his confederation. At one point, Tecumseh even presented his proposal to the Osage living west of the Mississippi, but they declined to join his confederation.

As early as May of 1807, the two brothers had gathered over 700 braves in a camp near Greenville, Indiana Territory. By the summer of 1811, the gathering of Indians of numerous tribes had grown to several thousand and the community was known as "Prophet's Town." News of Tecumseh's efforts was disconcerting to Superintendent Clark and to William Henry Harrison, Governor of the Indiana Territory.[19] In a letter to his brother Jonathan, Clark wrote that "I think the prophets party must be despursed they do much harm. all to yourself."[20] In the spring of 1811, Clark requested his good friend Nathaniel Pryor to spy upon Tecumseh's camp and to report his observations to Clark and Harrison.[21]

Pryor accomplished the mission assigned to him by Superintendent Clark and reported his intelligence to Clark. The information contained in Pryor's report was so alarming that the Americans decided to act quickly to squelch the uprising before it grew any larger. General (and Governor of the Indiana or Northwest Territory) William Henry Harrison promptly raised an army of one thousand men and marched near Tecumseh's camp on the Tippecanoe River, arriving there on November 6, 1811.[22] Tecumseh was not in the camp as he was on a recruiting trip to the Creeks, Cherokees and Choctaws of Alabama and Tennessee. Before he left, however, Tecumseh had warned his brother to avoid trouble with the whites, as Tecumseh knew that his confederation was not yet strong enough to defeat them. Harrison's quick movement to the area may have been due to his knowledge that Tecumseh was absent. Harrison parlayed with The Prophet late in the day of the 6th and the parties agreed to resume their peace talks the next day.

Perhaps with the hope of making a name for himself as a warrior, The Prophet did not wait for the peace negotiations to resume, but instead led his force, superior in numbers to Harrison's, in a surprise attack against Harrison and his army at 4:00 A.M. on the morning of the 7th. The Prophet, through incantations, trances, and superstitious propaganda, had thoroughly convinced his Indians that he had rendered them invulnerable to the guns of Harrison's troops and that they would be able to emerge victorious and unharmed from the battle. Harrison rallied his troops and the Indians soon found that they were not invulnerable to lead bullets. Although Harrison's army may have suffered more casualties than the Indians, the Battle of Tippecanoe was still a disastrous defeat for the Indians. The Prophet rationalized his defeat by saying that his powers were nullified due to the fact that his wife was menstruating, but The Prophet lost the confidence of the Shawnees after the battle. Tecumseh had been right to advise his brother to avoid a conflict. The rashness of his brother caused the collapse of Tecumseh's confederacy. This battle, plus later American victories over the Indi-

Tenkswatawa (The Prophet), Tecumseh's brother. Drawing by Richard Florence, from painting by Henry Beville, Library of Congress.

ans and their British allies during the War of 1812, finally opened the western frontier to the Americans.

Nat Pryor was not present at the battle of Tippecanoe, but several of his relatives took part. His first cousin George Rogers Clark Floyd commanded the 4th Infantry Regiment during the engagement.[23] Capt. G. R. C. Floyd's adjutant was another first cousin of Nat Pryor. That adjutant was Lieutenant Davis Floyd, the older brother of Sergeant Charles Floyd of the Voyage of Discovery.[24]

One of the unfortunate coincidences at the Battle of Tippecanoe was that a band of Winnebagos had arrived at The Prophet's camp on November 6th. They were returning from a hunting trip in Michigan and they were not yet a part of Tecumseh's confederation. The Winnebagos, a tribe from the area of what is now central and eastern Wisconsin, substantially north and east of the Galena mines, had generally been on friendly terms with the whites and especially with the British. Perhaps their loyalty to the British induced this band to join in The Prophet's attack against the Americans, where the Winnebagos suffered the loss of 25 of their best warriors, as well as the disgrace of a crushing defeat. Although there is some evidence that the Winnebagos may have traded with Pryor at the Toledo Mort area prior to the battle at Tippecanoe, that evidence is suspect.[25]

We do not know whether the Winnebagos somehow learned of Pryor's involvement in the matter, probably from the British, or if they just sought revenge against all Americans, but the Winnebagos did come to Toledo Mort seeking revenge for the loss of their warriors.[26] When William Clark learned of the battle at Tippecanoe, he dispatched Alexander Willard, a government courier and a former member of the Voyage of Discovery, to warn Pryor that he might be in danger. Upon receiving Clark's message, Willard rode north to warn Pryor, but he did not reach Pryor's trading post before the attack of the Winnebagos and found it burned to the ground. Believing Pryor to be dead, Willard continued north toward Prairie du Chien and did not travel back down the river toward St. Louis until later in the spring.[27]

Revenge of the Winnebagos

After reporting his intelligence to Clark and Harrison in the summer of 1811, Nat Pryor had returned to his smelter operation and had not taken part in the battle. It is unknown as to whether or not Pryor and his friend, George Hunt, had heard of the battle at Tippecanoe and it is unlikely that they had. In any event, they were totally unprepared when a large body of Winnebagos, in full war paint and regalia, attacked them on the morning of New Year's Day, 1812, less than two months after Tippecanoe.

The British-controlled Winnebagos attacked Hunt's trading post first. They took Hunt prisoner, but spared his life, evidently thinking that he was British. This would indicate that they were already allied with the British. The Indians did, however, kill Hunt's two American helpers and sacked and burned his store. In the process, they discovered Hunt's stash of whiskey under the puncheon floor of his bedroom and helped themselves liberally to the supply. This gave Hunt the opportunity to slip away and make his escape southward to Fort Madison.

Pryor was at his smelter, accompanied only by a Sac Indian woman who cooked for him.[28] Eight braves took him completely by surprise and made him captive. They also killed his yoke of two oxen. At sundown, the rest of the band of about fifty or sixty warriors joined them. The Indians wanted to kill Nat immediately, but fortunately the Indian woman intervened on his behalf, attempting to convince the Winnebagos that Nat was English and not American. The Indians were not entirely trustful of her because she was not a Winnebago. The Indians retired to feast upon Pryor's yoke of oxen and Hunt's whiskey. Pryor was a prisoner in his own cabin, guarded by at least one brave.

During and after the feast, the Indians continued to debate what to do with their prisoner. The Indian woman secreted herself in a place where she could hear the debate. Finally, she heard that the council decided that she had lied and that the captive was really an American and should be put to death. The woman gave this news to Pryor and then distracted the guard. Pryor was able to overpower the guard, grab his rifle, and hide under a pile of driftwood near the shore. Immediately, the Indians commenced a search for Pryor. Cartlidge wrote that there was snow on the ground so that it should have been easy to track Nat. Perhaps the Indians' senses were dulled by Hunt's liquor. In any event, they milled around, obliterated his tracks and made it possible for Pryor to cross the Mississippi River on cakes of ice and make his way to the Iowa side.[29]

Pryor traveled some fifteen miles down the river in a near frozen condition and finally arrived at the French village where the fur trader Maurice Blondeau resided.[30] Blondeau and the inhabitants of the village were friendly and willing to hide him. Nat was forced to live in the cellar of the house of his rescuers for the remainder of the winter, emerging only infrequently at night. By then, the Winnebagos had learned the identity of their escaped prisoner and were trying to find and recapture him. When Alexander Willard returned to St. Louis, he reported to Clark that Pryor had been killed in the raid. On March 6, 1812, the *New-England Palladium* reported an article from the "Pittsburg (sic), Penn. Paper" as follows:

"General William Clark, of St. Louis, has written to his brother in Louisville, informing that a party of Pouount (sic, Puans) Indians, who reside on the waters of the Illinois river, and who belonged to the Prophet's party, has robbed the trading houses of Mr. G. Hunt and Nathaniel Pryor, Esq. killed Pryor, and two of Hunt's men. Hunt escaped."[31]

Although some authors, including Larry E. Morris in his excellent book *The Fate of the Corps*, have indicated that Hunt and Pryor escaped from the Winnebagos together, this article from the *New England Palladium* in early March indicates that Hunt must have arrived in St. Louis several weeks earlier and before the fate of Nathaniel Pryor was known. No doubt Hunt escaped apart from Pryor. Pryor did not get to St. Louis until later in the spring. A later affidavit made by Maurice Blondeau omits any reference to Hunt having been with Pryor.

In the spring, Pryor accompanied Blondeau on his way down the river to St. Louis, As a precaution, he was hidden under the bales of furs on the boat so he would not be seen from the shore by the Winnebagos or other Indians. For the loss of Pryor's business and property at Toledo Mort, Abraham Gallatin, as attorney in fact for Nathaniel Pryor finally filed a claim with the government in 1826, listing the following items:

30,000 pounds of lead	$1,800.00
500 pounds of mineral ore	75.00
4,000 muskrat skins	1,000.00
300 pounds beaver	750.00
various kinds of cloth and trinkets	868.75
a yoke of oxen, horse, cart & harness	410.00
an anvil, lead molds, salt kettles, knives and powder	279.00
saws, hammers, files, and a vise	<u>34.00</u>
Total	$5,216.75[32]

Gallatin and Pryor did not increase the amount of the claim for the value of Proyr's cabin, the smelter, or for his other livestock and personal property.

This would have been a huge loss for the time, almost ten times the total of $557.00 that Pryor received for his three years of service on the Expedition and about one-half the amount that Auguste Chouteau had paid for a one-half interest in Dubuque's mining operation. As shown by the papers filed in Pryor's probate proceedings, his financial partner in his trading house and smelter operation must have been Abraham Gallatin, also known as Albert Gallatin.[33] Pryor's claim was supported by affidavits from Maurice Blondeau[34] and Francis Boutelier,[35] together with a supporting letter from Clark. The affidavits verified the fantastic tale and escape told by Pryor, although Boutelier's account is seriously flawed as to dates. Boutelier put the attack on January 1, 1813, instead of the prior year. In Boutelier's defense, however, he was only seven years old at the time of the event and his affidavit was not given until 1825. Support for the daring escape of Pryor across the frozen Mississippi is found in an account by Alexander Willard, the man sent by Clark to warn Pryor and Hunt. A few weeks after viewing the burned remains of Pryor's trading house and after his stop at Prairie du Chien, Willard was returning down the river when Indians attacked him. Willard reported to Clark that he was fired on by Indians "as he was carrying messages for Clark on a sleigh down the <u>frozen</u> Mississippi." [Emphasis supplied][36] Willard also discovered the murdered bodies of nine members of an O'Neal family on the Mississippi above St. Louis.[37] It should also be recalled that Meriwether Lewis had spoken very highly of Maurice Blondeau in 1808 when Lewis appointed him to a sub-agency with the Sac and Fox Indians.

After reaching St. Louis by the summer of 1812, Pryor once again had to deal with his debt to Falconer and Comegys, who filed a collection suit against Pryor in the St. Louis Court of Common Pleas. This indicates that Pryor had not paid the $100 note he executed in 1810. On June 17, 1812, Pryor was required to post a bond in the amount of $200 to ensure his appearance in Court during the first week of July. Nathaniel Pryor signed the bond as

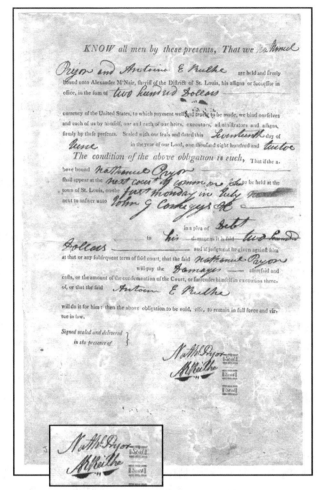

Pryor's Appearance Bond, June 17, 1812. St. Louis Court of Common Pleas, District of St. Louis, Territory of Louisiana, July Term, 1812, Case No. 67. (Inset of Nathaniel Pryor's signature.)

"Nath'l. Pryor." Antoine E. Reilke was on the bond with Pryor.[38] As there is nothing later in the Court documents, apparently Pryor appeared in court as required and the debt was paid.[39]

Although English interference with America's maritime trade on the high seas is usually cited as the main reason leading to the conflict between the countries known as the War of 1812, certainly the activities of the British in the west along the expanding

American borders and settlements was a contributing factor. The English actively fomented unrest among the Indians, hoping not only to stem the increasing tide of western settlement by the Americans, but also hoping to recover part or all of the lands.

After the Battle of Tippecanoe, Tecumseh continued to oppose American expansion into the Indian lands and frequently sought and received covert assistance from the British. During the War of 1812, Tecumseh was commissioned as a Brigadier General in the British Army and led his Indian forces in conjunction with British Army forces. This brought him into a continuation of his conflict with General William Henry Harrison commanding the American forces. Harrison successfully led an American expedition into Canada in 1813 and his forces defeated the combined British and Indian forces at the Battle of the Thames (about 17 miles east of Chatham, Ontario). Tecumseh was killed in the battle. This, plus the Treaty of Ghent after the War of 1812, finally resulted in the British giving up their claims to the area. Without the possibility of British assistance, the remaining Indians acknowledged that the United States controlled the Northwest Territory. Tecumseh's original dream of an intertribal alliance to oust the Americans was finally destroyed.

There is a possibility that Tecumseh's forces allied with the British may have opposed or fought against Zebulon Pike in Canada. Pike had been promoted to Brigadier General at the outset of the War of 1812. Pike was killed on April 27, 1813, leading his troops against the British at Fort York. The retreating British fired a magazine at the fort and Pike was one of the men killed by the rocks and debris of the explosion. The town of York changed its name to Toronto in 1834.

During the War of 1812, Maurice Blondeau remained loyal to the Americans and continued to lend assistance to William Clark. Clark as the Superintendent of Indian Affairs at St. Louis, received a letter from "Indian sub-agent Maurice Blondeau at Peoria" dated July 20, 1813, reporting on the Indians in his sub-agency and the depredations of other Indians in the area. Blondeau was the sub-agent for the Sac and Fox and Miami tribes at the time. In 1815, Blondeau acted as an interpreter for

Clark and helped negotiate treaties with the Omahas and Meskwakis.

George Robeson noted that by 1820, a Doctor Samuel Muir located a trading post on an island opposite the Dubuque mines and it is interesting to speculate if Dr. Muir established his operation on the same island where Hunt and Pryor had been operating in 1810 to 1812. Robeson also mentioned that Maurice Blondeau "maintained a trading house above the mouth of the Des Moines River during almost the entire first quarter of the nineteenth century" and that Dr. Muir and Blondeau "each did a flourishing business."[40]

Notes

1. Colter-Frick, *Courageous Colter*, p. 483; Holmberg, *Dear Brother*, p. 138, n.17; Shoemaker, *Many Faces*.

2. Christian, *Before Lewis and Clark*, pp. 125–26, 215.

3. Robeson, *Fur Trade*, on line, p.2.

4. *Ibid*.

5. *Ibid*.

6. Case No. 69, Court of Common Pleas for the District of St. Louis, Territory of Louisiana. The collection suit was not filed until 1812 and Pryor's 1810 promissory note was an exhibit or evidence in the case.

7. Colter-Frick, *Courageous Colter*, at p. 483 cites Pryor's letter of resignation from the Army in 1809 as having Pryor's signature as "Lieut. Nath'l Pryor," but we have not seen that letter.

8. Colter-Frick, *Courageous Colter*, p. 486. Some authors have indicated that Pryor was licensed to trade with the Winnebagos, but that tribe was located to the North in what is now Wisconsin and it was not located in the Galena area. The confusion may be attributed to an erroneous letter written by Franklin Wharton in 1826. Morris, Larry E.—*The Fate of the Corps*, Yale Univ. Press, New Haven & London, 2004, p. 120. We believe that Pryor was only licensed to trade with the Sac and Fox tribe at this time.

9. Colter-Frick, *Courageous Colter*, p. 486–87.

10. Gallatin's full name was Abraham Alfonse Albert Gallatin, which he shortened to Albert Gallatin after immigrating to the United States. Gallatin (1761–1849) was born in Switzerland and orphaned at the age of nine. He later immigrated to America; was a U.S. Representative to Congress (1795–1801); Secretary of the Treasury (1801–1814); an Envoy and Minister to France (1815–1823); and, Minister to Great Britain (1826–1827). Due to his interest in the Western Indians, he was known as a prominent ethnologist.

11. Missouri State Archives, St. Louis County Case No. 00927, filed in 1833, #C27476. Of course there is also the possibility that the Abraham Gallatin who lent assistance to Nathaniel Pryor was a different person than the Abraham (Albert) Gallatin who was Secretary of the Treasury, but the fact that it is such an unusual name would seem to negate that possibility.

12. Cartlidge, Anna M.—*Trouble at Toledo Mort*, The Filson Club History Quarterly, Louisville, KY, April, 1971, Vol. 45, No. 2, pp. 174–185.

13. *Ibid*.

14. Holmberg, *Dear Brother*, p. 138, n. 17.

15. Cartlidge, Anna M.—*These, Too, Are Our Ancestors*, undated, unpublished paper filed with the DAR, Washington, D.C., at p. 3.

16. Clark did not become Governor of the Louisiana Territory until June 13, 1813.

17. Eckert, Allan W.—*That Dark and Bloody River*, Bantam Books (1995). Tecumseh's father has also been referred to as "Pukusheno" by other authors.

18. Some members of the Floyd family were present at the Battle of Point Pleasant and it is probable that Pryor family members were also present. It should also be noted that some historians have asserted that the Battle of Point Pleasant was actually the opening battle of our Revolutionary War.

19. Foreman, *Nathaniel Pryor*, at. pp. 156–159, quoting the events from a letter to the Secretary of War James Barbour written by Franklin Wharton in 1826, relative to Pryor's claim for recompense from the government and also relative to his possible appointment as agent for the Osages.

20. Holmberg, *Dear Brother*, p. 259.

21. Cartlidge, *Our Ancestors*, at pp. 4–5, Shoemaker, *Many Faces*, at p. 49.

22. This narration and the following description of the Battle of Tippecanoe and of Pryor's travails at Toledo Mort is a composite of information from Cartlidge, *Ancestors*, Foreman, *Nathaniel Pryor*, Shoemaker, *Many Faces*, and the Time-Life Series, various volumes.

23. The name of George Rogers Clark Floyd again emphasizes the close relationship between the Floyd and Clark families.

24. Cartlidge, *Children*, p. 11.

25. Wharton, Franklin—*Letter*, dated February 28, 1826, to Secretary of War James Barbour.

26. Foreman, *Nathaniel Pryor*, cites the following written by William Clark in 1835: "The Winnebagoes who destroyed Capt. Pryor's establishment and took his goods was a party that had been with the Shawnee Prophets Band in the action with Gov. Harrison at Tippecanoe, and who having lost some of their relatives and friends took revenge on the traders on the Mississippi."

27. Morris, *Fate of the Corps*, 120–21.

28. Some authors have written that Pryor and Hunt had Indian wives at their operations at Toledo Mort, relying upon a phrase to that effect in the deposition of Francis Boutelier taken July 5, 1825, and given in support of Pryor's claim for the damages he suffered in the raid. Colter-Frick, *Courageous Colter*, p. 488, and Jones, *William Clark*, p. 204. Boutelier's deposition indicated that Hunt and Pryor <u>escaped with their Indian wives</u>. At the time of the event, Boutelier was only seven years old, so he could only be relying on rumors and tales after the event. I believe it much more likely that Blondeau's deposition or affidavit would have mentioned the Indian wife if there had been one.

29. Morris, *Fate of the Corps*, indicates that Hunt and Pryor escaped together, at p. 121. Cartlidge, in *Our Ancestors*, indicated that Pryor and Hunt escaped separately.

30. Blondeau had evidently lived in the area of Julien Dubuque's mines for several years as Blondeau had met and accompanied Zebulon Pike in late 1805 for part of Pike's exploratory journey up the Mississippi to discover its headwaters. Hutchins, John M.—*Lieutenant Zebulon Montgomery Pike Climbs His First Peak: The Army Expedition to the Sources of the Mississippi, 1805–1806*, privately published, Applewood, CO 2005, pp. 17–18.

31. *New-England Palladium*, March 6, 1812, Vol. 39, Iss.19, Page [1]. Puans was the name used by the French to refer to the Winnebagos.

32. Clark, Wm.—*Missouri Indian Depredations*, 1826, Claim No. 89.

33. Gallatin's financial support of Pryor is also referenced in other affidavits, reports and letters. Cf. Jones, *William Clark*, at p. 206, Dillon, *Meriwether Lewis*, at p. 309, and Colter-Frick, *Courageous Colter*, at pp. 486–87.

34. Colter-Frick, *Courageous Colter*, p. 487. Blondeau's affidavit made on June 27, 1825, in part stated that: "... on the night of the 1st of January, 1812, a party of Winnebago Indians came to the trading house occupied by a Mr. Nathaniel Pryor, the acting Agent for himself and Abraham Gallatin, and burnt the house with a large quantity of goods, lead and furs and peltries ..." Also that: "... after the attack by the Indians, N. Pryor made his escape to the house of deponent ..."

35. *Ibid*, p. 488.

36. Jones, *William Clark*, p. 204. Clark's transmittal letter of the claim reported that: "This claim of Nathaniel Pryor, is for property destroyed and taken from him by a party of Winnebagoes, of the Shawanee Prophet's Party on an island in the Mississippi, to which the Indian title had been extinguished, and at which place Mr. Pryor was regularly licensed to trade with the Sac and Fox tribes." Clark was the Superintendent of Indian Affairs at St. Louis at the time.

37. *Ibid*.

38. The name of Pryor's co-obligor on the bond is somewhat indistinct and could be "Rulhe" or "Rulke."

39. Territory of Louisiana, District of St. Louis, Court of Common Pleas, No. 69, July Term, 1812. All of the court pleadings, evidence and documents are present in this case.

40. Robeson, *Fur Trade*, on line, p. 4.

7

THE WAR OF 1812

There was a strong sentiment of anti-British feeling among the Americans in the Northwest Territory, the Lower Ohio River Valley and along the Mississippi. The people on the frontier were convinced that most of their troubles with the Indians resulted from the machinations of the British who overtly or surreptitiously gave aid, arms and equipment to the Indians. After many of the Indian raids, the settlers reported that they found British arms and equipment on the fields of battle. Although there was also some anti-British feeling on the East Coast, primarily due to the British Navy frequently boarding American ships and interrupting commerce, it was mainly the Westerners who wanted war with Britain. The English were embroiled in their fight with Napoleon in Europe, so did not devote their full attention to fighting the Americans until later in the war. In order to quell the British influence and trading activities in the West, the Americans hoped to conquer Canada and drive the English from North America. There was also support for the war in the Southern states, with the objective being to drive the Spanish from Florida.

Nathaniel Pryor and the War of 1812

Nathaniel Pryor reenlisted in the Army on August 30, 1813, during the War of 1812 as a First Lieutenant in the 44th Infantry Regiment. As such, he would have participated in some of the southern campaigns under the leadership of Andrew Jackson. While the British were winning the war in the northeast, even burning Washington, D.C., Jackson and his men were preserving the American cause in the south and west. The Spanish in Florida, although ostensibly neutral, were assisting the British, as was one faction of the Creeks, the most powerful Indian tribe in the area at the time, in their forays against the American settlers. Tecumseh had visited the Creek Nation prior to the war. When the war started the more warlike of the Creeks, known as the "Red Stick Creeks" due to the red sticks that they carried with them into battles, sided with Tecumseh and the British. The remainder of the Creeks initially attempted to stay neutral. Andrew Jackson was the leader of the western part of the Tennessee Militia. The British furnished money to the Red Stick Creeks, who then used it to buy arms, supplies and equipment from the Spanish in Pensacola. The action between the Americans and the Red Sticks began in the middle of the summer of 1813.[1]

The first battle in this campaign was on July 27, 1813, at the village of Burnt Corn, about eighty miles north of Pensacola. A force of U.S. Militia from Fort Mims in Alabama ambushed a column of Red Sticks, returning from Pensacola. After scattering the Red Sticks, the militia became careless and began looting the camp and packhorses of the Red Sticks. The Red Sticks noticed this, regrouped, attacked and routed the Americans. In reprisal for the ambush, the Red Sticks then turned their attention to Fort Mims, where a number of the neutral Creeks, most of whom were mixed-bloods, had taken refuge.

On August 13, 1813, a Red Stick force of approximately 800 warriors attacked Fort Mims, defended by 175 militia, but in which there were 375 non-combatants. The beleaguered garrison fought well, but was overrun. The warriors then massacred the survivors. 500 people were found dead, most of whom were scalped.

Negroes were not killed, but captured to be slaves for the Red Sticks. Only about 15 people escaped from the massacre. News of the disaster at Fort Mims sent shock waves through the South. No troops could be spared from the North, so the militias from Tennessee, Georgia and the Mississippi Territory were mustered to combat the Red Sticks and their allies from the Upper Creek towns. This brought General Andrew Jackson into the fray.

In October of 1813, Jackson assembled a force of 2,500 Tennessee militia and marched into the Creek territory. On November 3, 1813, Jackson sent a force of about 1,000 dragoons under the command of General Coffee to attack the Red Stick stronghold at Tallushatchee. Coffee encircled the town. The Creek warriors tried to give battle but were forced back into the town where they were trapped and killed. Davy Crockett was serving in the Tennessee militia and was quoted as saying "we shot them down like dogs." 180 warriors were killed, while the Americans suffered five dead and 41 wounded. A week later, Jackson received a request to help some friendly Creeks who were besieged by Red Sticks at Talladega. Jackson hurried his army to the scene where his force of almost 2,000 men suffered 15 killed and 85 wounded, while the Red Sticks had 410 casualties. Jackson was unable to continue the campaign due to the expiration of the enlistments of most of the militiamen and problems with his line of supply. On January 14, 1814, he received about 900 raw recruits with 60-day enlistments and hurriedly resumed his attack.

Jackson attempted to link up with the Georgia militia, but was attacked on January 22, 1814, by a Red Stick force of 400 to 500 warriors near the town of Emuckfaw. Jackson's force of 175 militia, 30 artillery and 200 Creek and Cherokee allies drove off the first attack, but when the Red Sticks quickly resumed the attack, Jackson was forced to withdraw. Two days later, Jackson's column was again attacked as it was crossing Enotachopo Creek. Jackson was able to extricate his force and the estimated casualties from the two battles were 54 Red Sticks killed, while the Americans suffered 24 killed and 71 wounded. Wounded figures for the Red Sticks are not available for the battles where the battles did not result in a clear victory for the Americans, as the Red Sticks quickly removed their wounded.

By March of 1814, Jackson had turned his unruly army of West Tennessee militia into a well-trained and disciplined army. With the addition of Regulars from the 39th Infantry Regiment, Jackson's force swelled to 2,000 infantry and 700 mounted infantry, augmented by 600 Cherokee and Lower Creek allies. On March 26, 1814, Jackson attacked a fortified Red Stick stronghold at "Horseshoe Bend" of the Tallapoosa River in central Alabama. The Red Sticks defended strongly behind heavy log breastworks, but a bayonet charge ordered by Jackson carried the day. Lieutenant Sam Houston distinguished himself by being one of the first men to make it over the breastworks, but received a wound that troubled him for the rest of his life. The battle went on for about five hours, with 550 Red Sticks being killed on the field and another 250 killed during their escape attempting to cross the river. The Americans lost 49 killed and 154 wounded. This complete victory effectively ended the Creek War.

The Creeks were forced to sign the Treaty of Fort Jackson on August 9, 1814. Even though many Creeks had fought alongside Jackson, the Creek Nation was required to cede 23 million acres to the United States, without compensation. Jackson did not distinguish between the Red Sticks and his own allies. Jackson would display much the same view versus the Indians when he ordered his Draconian Indian removals as President in the 1830s. The Cherokees who had fought with Jackson received a grant of 1.9 million acres of the Creek lands.

Between the Battle of Horseshoe Bend and the Treaty of Fort Jackson, Nathaniel Pryor and the 44th Infantry were assigned to Jackson's army. The British, fresh from their victory over Napoleon, as well as their successes against the Americans, were determined to take New Orleans and open the Mississippi to English control and commerce. Although peace negotiations began at Ghent, Belgium in August of 1814, the British hoped to have a brilliant victory at New Orleans and other Southern cities before ratification of any treaty so that their bargaining power would be superior. The first strike by the British was the capture of Pensacola, wresting control of the city from the Spanish on August 14, 1814. The British sought to capture the port at Mobile, defended by a small 130 man garrison from the 2nd Infantry at Fort Bowyer. The garrison acquitted itself well and after 3 days of fighting repulsed the British land force of 130 marines and 600 Indian allies, most of whom were Seminoles. Jackson and his army arrived in Mobile on September 15, 1814, and strengthened the garrison.

Pryor was promoted to Captain on October 1, 1814. He would be known as "Captain Pryor" for the rest of his life. By early November, Jackson's army consisted of about 4,000 troops at Fort Montgomery in Alabama. Jackson marched against Pensacola on November 3rd, arriving there on November 6th. Jackson's force then captured Pensacola on November 7th.[2] Jackson sought the surrender of the city, but his messenger, under a white flag of truce, was fired upon by the British at Fort St. Michael. On November 8th, Jackson attacked with some 3,000 men against a force of British, Spanish and Creeks of about 500 men. There was really only one small battle in the center of the city, won by the Americans. Jackson accepted the surrender of the Spanish and spared the city. The Americans occupied Forts Boyer and St. Michael, but the British remained at Fort Barrancas, which guarded the harbor. Jackson planned to attack that fort the next day, but the British blew up the fort and abandoned it, retreating to their fleet and sailing away. Pryor was present with the 44th Infantry Regiment at Mobile and Pensacola. Davy Crockett and Sam Houston were among Jackson's troops during the Southern campaigns and it is interesting to speculate that Nat Pryor may have served in the army with them.

The Battle of New Orleans

The British then turned their attention to the attack against New Orleans. A large armada and 25,000 veteran troops were dispatched to accomplish this purpose. Facing them, Jackson could count on two or three regiments of regulars, the Creole citizens of New Orleans, Jean Lafitte's pirates (reluctantly accepted by Jackson), Tennessee militia, and a few backwoodsmen who had been summoned from Kentucky and Indiana. Fortunately for the Americans, the British troops suffered heavily from diseases on this mission contracted in the West Indies and lost over half of their force before reaching America. By the time they squared off in the field, the British had 10,000 well-trained troops opposing Jackson's force of approximately 4,000 men.

Jackson, though suffering from dysentery, demonstrated superb generalship in anticipating the moves of the British and positioning his smaller force to best advantage. On December 23rd, the British sent a small force to probe the American lines. Their night attack was against Pryor's 44th Infantry and the British were repulsed. The British then sent a reconnaissance in force on the 28th of December and found that Jackson's left flank, composed mainly of militia units, appeared to be weak. Jackson strengthened and extended that flank, so that when the British attacked again on New Year's Day, the British were met with strong opposition and beaten back. After these preliminary setbacks the British Commander of the expedition, Major General Edward Pakenham, the Duke of Wellington's younger brother, decided to wait until his entire army had arrived. When the battle occurred on January 8, 1815, it was a slaughter of epic proportions. The battle-hardened veterans of the British army suffered some 2,000 casualties (291 killed, 1,262 wounded and 484 captured or missing), including the deaths of their two highest-ranking generals, Major General Edward Pakenham and Major General Samuel Gibbs. Several storied Regiments of the British Army were involved: the 7th, 43rd and 44th Regiments, the 21st North Britain Fusiliers and the Black Watch Highlanders. In inflicting this carnage upon the seasoned British veterans, the rather motley collection of Americans suffered 13 dead, 39 wounded and 19 missing for a total of only 71 casualties.[3] Under the superb direction of Andrew Jackson, all of the various American units had acted cohesively together and it was a major victory for the long rifles of the Americans, firing from entrenched positions, over the muskets of the British, who advanced in Old World military precision over open ground.

During the Battle of New Orleans, Pryor and his 44th Regiment were in the center of the American line, together with the sharpshooters from Kentucky and Tennessee. It is speculative to wonder if the Floyd family held an extended family reunion in New Orleans. At least six members of the closely related Floyd, Pryor and Tuley families were present. Definitely present with Nat Pryor were his brothers, James Pryor and Robert Lewis Pryor, who had rafted down the Mississippi with the Kentucky contingent, together with Pryor's cousins Nathaniel Floyd, Thomas Floyd Smith and William Floyd Tuley. One may also wonder if Nat Pryor had the opportunity to converse with his cousin, Davis Floyd, the older brother of Sgt. Charles Floyd of the Voyage of Discovery, who may have been present. Other cousins and family who were probably present were George Rogers Clark Floyd, John Wesley Floyd, Robert McClelland (a brother-in-law of Nat Pryor), William Churchill Myrtle, George Lawson Rogers, William Preston Tuley and John Withers Winn.[4]

After their defeat at New Orleans, the British persisted in their efforts in the South and undertook a campaign against Fort Bowyer again, commanding the entrance to Mobile Bay. Jackson had strengthened the garrison to a force of 370 men. The British landed a force of approximately 1,000 men and began a siege of the fort on February 11, 1815 incurring some 25 casualties. Fortunately the British commander offered terms of surrender to the Americans on February 12th and the American commander wisely accepted the terms and surrendered the fort without a battle. Remaining American troops in the area began preparations to hurry to Mobile to recapture it, but on February 13th, a British ship arrived off of Mobile Bay with the news that the Treaty of Ghent had been signed. Fort Bowyer was subsequently returned to U.S. control.

The importance to the United States of the victory at the Battle of New Orleans cannot be overemphasized. Although certainly the British knew that peace negotiations were being conducted at Ghent, Belgium, no one in the New Orleans area knew the results of those negotiations. The parties signed the Treaty of Ghent on December 24, 1814, but of course it would take several weeks for the news of the signing to reach America and as shown above, that notice didn't arrive until February 13, 1815. The luminaries signing the treaty for the United States were John Quincy Adams, Henry Clay, James A. Bayard, Sr., Jonathan Russell and Albert Gallatin. By its terms, the treaty was not to be effective until ratified by both countries, which did not occur until February 16, 1815. The effective date of the Treaty of Ghent therefore became February 18, 1815. Had the British won the Battle of New Orleans, it is possible that the terms of the treaty could have been modified to permit the British to continue their presence in the area below Canada. By their victory at New Orleans, the Americans finally put an end to British incursions into the American territories, and secured control of the entire Ohio-Mississippi-Missouri watershed, between the Appalachians and the Rocky Mountains.

Notes

1. This, and the following information regarding the Southern campaign of Andrew Jackson is primarily from the on-line source, *Wikipedia*, the encyclopedia.
2. Preceding and following information from *The Frontiersmen, The Old West*, Time-Life Books, Alexandria, VA, 1977, pp. 207–225.
3. The casualty figures for both sides are from Remini, Robert V.—*The Life of Andrew Jackson*, First Perennial Classics ed., HarperCollins Publishers, New York, (2001).
4. Cartlidge, *Children*, various pages, under individual names.

8

ARKANSAS TERRITORY
AND THE OSAGE

Nat Pryor was honorably discharged from the Army on June 15, 1815. He was about forty years of age, but not yet ready to settle down. His whereabouts for the next couple of years are not definitely known, but he must have reached Arkansas and the Indian Territory (now Oklahoma) by at least 1817. As will be shown below, one of his Osage daughters asserted that she was 24 years of age on September 1, 1842, when she was baptized. Allowing for the nine-month gestation period, this would place Pryor in the area of the Osages at least by December of 1817.

After the War of 1812 ended with the Battle of New Orleans on January 8, 1815, there were jobless ex-soldiers and other restive movers who wanted to settle somewhere. Some came overland to the Arkansas River region from Kentucky, Tennessee and points east. Some others came upriver in keelboats, canoes and other river craft from New Orleans. In addition to trappers, hunters and settlers, there were renegades, outlaws, gamblers and representatives from every spectrum of society.[1]

Captain Pryor to the Arkansas
and Indian Territories (1817–1819)

We do not know where Capt. Pryor was discharged from the service. If he was not discharged from a post close to St. Louis, then he probably worked his way up the Mississippi from New Orleans. In any case, a few months after being discharged, he came to where the Arkansas empties into the Mississippi and headed up the Arkansas. About 20 miles up from the mouth of this river was a settlement called Arkansas Post, where Pryor stayed for a time. It was here that he entered into a trading partnership with Samuel B. Richards.[2] On April 22, 1817, Pryor, Richards and George R. Sampson acquired title to certain land at Arkansas Post.[3] Whether Richards and Pryor conducted business at Arkansas Post is unknown, but fairly soon after forming their partnership they moved and established a trading house at the Three Forks area in present northeast Oklahoma.[4] In their *History of Oklahoma*, Thoburn and Wright have the following:

> "Nathaniel Pryor ... was another influential trader who established his business at Three Forks. Having received an honorable discharge from the United States Army in 1815, <u>he soon afterward</u> went into partnership with Samuel B. Richards, obtaining a license to trade at the mouth of the Verdigris. ... [Emphasis added][5]

The Three Forks region is so-named as the Verdigris and the Grand (Neosho) Rivers enter the Arkansas here at almost the same place, near the present-day city of Muskogee. Although the Grand River remains as the name of this river in Oklahoma, it is called by its Osage name, the Neosho River, upstream in Kansas. The Three Forks area "long was 'farthest west' in the Indian country for daring traders and trappers who in the early years plied their trade under the guns of Fort Gibson."[6] Considering that Pryor moved there in about 1817 and Fort Gibson was not built until 1824, this again illustrates the intrepid nature and character of Nat Pryor. In the 1820s and 1830s, Three Forks was the head of navigation on the Arkansas, which then carried more water than today. It was navigable on its lower 680 miles for steamboats, barges, and keelboats during four or five months of the year.[7]

At Three Forks, Pryor encountered the Osage Indians. For generations, the Osages had claimed hunting rights in most of what is now eastern Oklahoma and western Arkansas. They had fought many battles over this area with the Caddos in the east and the Pawnees in the west. In 1810, further pressure was exerted by the Cherokees who moved into Arkansas and then began drifting into the Osage hunting grounds.[8] Pryor aligned himself with the Osage tribe and particularly with the band of Osage Chief Claremore II, also called Clermont, the "Town Builder."

The Osage Nation

At the time of the Louisiana Purchase, the Osage Nation was probably the largest, most powerful and most war-like Indian Tribe west of the Mississippi River.[9] Between 1500 and 1800, the Osage had gradually expanded their territory so that they controlled a vast area of the west. As shown by the accompanying map, the area included most of what we now call Missouri; most of Arkansas; the southern half of Kansas, the northern part of Oklahoma; and even into southeastern Colorado. They had successfully resisted French and Spanish attempts to settle in their area, although they did have strong trading relationships with the French and Spanish. As the Osage historian Louis F. Burns aptly noted:

> "In a one hundred twenty-five year period, 1678–1803, the Osages performed a feat no other American Indians duplicated. They stopped the westward expansion of the Euro-American peoples and simultaneously tripled the size of their own domain."[10]

By 1803, the Osage Nation was comprised of about 20,000 individuals. Due to their expansionist tendencies, the Osages were

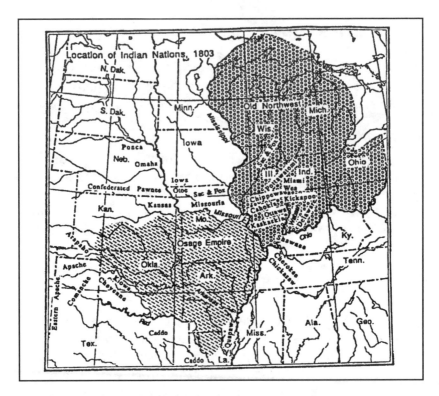

*Osage Domain compared to the Old Northwest Territory, circa 1800.
Louis F. Burns,* A History of the Osage People, *Ciga Press, Fallbrook, CA
(1989), p. 177.*

almost constantly at war with the neighboring tribes of Missouris,
Pawnees, Kansas, Sac and Fox, Apache, Comanche, Cheyenne,
Kiowa, Caddo, Quapaw and others. That the Osages more than
held their own attests to their bravery, strength and domination.
In the eighteenth century, the Osages had even crossed the Mississippi and ventured eastward to participate with the Indian
coalition of tribes that inflicted the disastrous defeat upon General Arthur St. Clair's American Army at the Wabash River in
present-day Indiana in 1791.[11] The Osages evidently did not participate in the Indians' defeat of General Josiah Harmar's army in
1790 or in the subsequent defeat of the confederated Indian
tribes by the troops of General Anthony Wayne at the Battle of
Fallen Timbers in 1793.

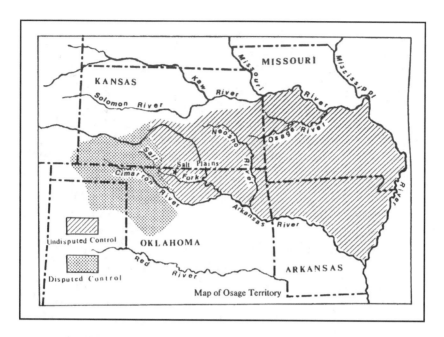

Osage Territory, circa 1800. Louis F. Burns, Osage Indian Customs and Myths, *Ciga Press, Fallbrook, CA (1984), p. xii.*

After the Louisiana Purchase was completed, officials in Washington were well aware of the necessity to keep the Osages on friendly terms with Americans so that they would not ally themselves with the British who were still active both east and west of the Mississippi River with trading companies and even a military presence. The importance of the Osages is emphasized by the fact that they were the first Indian delegation from west of the Mississippi to be invited and received by President Jefferson in Washington. Lewis and Clark set out from above St. Louis in May of 1804. Prior to their departure, Lewis sent a delegation of Osage Chiefs east to Washington. President Jefferson welcomed the Osage delegation of twelve chiefs and two boys, escorted by Auguste Chouteau, in Washington on July 12, 1804. The people in Washington were amazed by the size of the Osage men. Navy Secretary Robert Smith described them as "… the most gigantic men we have ever seen … ."[12] Jefferson even wrote that "They are the finest men we have ever seen."[13] At the time, the average height of the Osage male was six feet two or three inches, with some men being as much as seven feet tall.[14] The Osage were aware of the advantages that size gave them in the hunt and in war and practiced a modified form of selective breeding to insure this height and size. To emphasize their size, the Osage men wore their hair in roaches on ceremonial and special occasions.[15] This was in contrast to most of the Plains Indians who wore their hair in long braids or loosely hanging down over their shoulders and backs. The roach was similar to a Mohawk, but taller. It was a strip of hair standing straight up "in the middle of the head with the rest of the head shaved clean. Porcupine hair and deer tail were used to make the roach stand up straight."[16]

The tribal name of the Osage is actually "Wa-Zha-Zhi," but the French pronounced that as "Osage" and the Spanish and

Osage Roach and Spreader, Drawing by Richard Florence from photo in Art of the Osage, *St. Louis Art Museum and Univ. of Washington Press, 2004.*

Americans continued that name. It is not the purpose of this book to give a detailed description of the tribe and readers interested in the Osage Nation are referred to the excellent books by Louis F. Burns and Lawrence J. Hogan listed in the Bibliography. The Osage Nation had a complex organizational structure made up of two (sometimes three) bands, divided into 24 clans. Although there is some tribal lore to the effect that they were originally from East of the Mississippi, no proof of that has been discovered. The Osages are "Siouxian-speaking Indians, belonging to the Dhegiha group" and their "nearest kindred tribes are the Omaha,

Ponca, Quapaw, and Kaw."[17] Each of these tribes easily understood the language of the others.

The Osages were deeply religious, which surprised and astonished many of the early missionaries, explorers and settlers, who considered all Indians to be savages without religion. The Osages worshipped a single God, Wa-kon'-da. The Osages offered prayers to Wa-kon'-da at sunrise, noon and sunset, with the ritual being that men, women and children would stand outside their lodges or tepees to pray.

As Plains Indians, the Osages relied upon the plentiful buffalo for their existence, although they did raise some crops, generally, beans, corn and squash. They were not nomadic, but lived in established villages except during their semi-annual buffalo hunts in the spring and fall. The buffalo filled most of their needs, as buffalo provided "food; robes for warmth in winter; hides for tepees, parfleches, clothing, cooking pots, ornaments, and boats; and horns, bones, sinews, and hoofs for weapon points, implements, tools, fluid and glue."[18] As in the case of other Plains Indians, the advent of the horse being brought to the area by the Spanish greatly altered the Indians' way of life. No longer were they required to hunt buffalo by the old "buffalo trap" method. The Indians were now able to range farther in search of the buffalo and to hunt them more effectively from horseback. The Osages excelled in horsemanship and quickly adapted to this more mobile form of hunting. The presence of horses also permitted the tribes to create larger tepees. Before the horse, the size of the tepee was limited as they were generally transported by dogs dragging a travois. Although the travois was still used, the horse was able to drag a considerably bigger load. The large tepees of the Osages were said to be unexcelled by most observers.

When the French began settling along the Mississippi River during the eighteenth century, the Osages quickly began to trade with them. The Osages traded furs, hides, and their captured Indian prisoners to the French in exchange for woolens, "blankets, cloth, silk ribbon, beads, knives, axes, kettles, guns and metal goods."[19] As a result, the Osages became one of the first of the Plains Indian tribes to obtain and use the guns of the white men, giving them a considerable advantage over their neighbors. The Osages used their firearms to enlarge their territory and to capture Indians from other tribes to be traded into French slavery. In the first years of the nineteenth century, the Osages entered into a mutual trading relationship with the Chouteaus of St. Louis, which was near the main Osage villages in Missouri and Arkansas. This was the situation at the time of the Louisiana Purchase and, initially, the relationships did not change and the Americans merely took the place of the French and Spanish.

Unfortunately, the Osages proved to be poor negotiators with the Americans at the bargaining table. Between 1804 and 1850, in four of eight treaties entered into by the Osages with the United States, the Osages ceded at least 96,800,000 acres to the United Sates for compensation of just over five cents an acre.[20] These were prime lands in Missouri, Arkansas, Kansas and Oklahoma. Usually, by the terms of the treaties, the Osages received little or no money from the transaction, as the compensation was primarily in the form of paying off claims by other Indians and whites against the Osages. Conversely, the Osages never received compensation for their claims for horses and stock stolen from them or damage to the Osage villages, nor for the loss of the buffalo and other game animals killed by Indians and whites trespassing on Osage lands. In one especially egregious instance, the payment of such claims for the cession of approximately 1,200,000 acres in Arkansas and Oklahoma amounted to $54,000 or about four and one-half cents per acre. The land thus acquired by the United States was then immediately sold to the Cherokee Nation for $2,000,000. Obviously, the Osages did not receive fair value for their land in this transaction, but it also illustrates the preferential treatment that the Cherokees and the other four so-called "Civilized Tribes" received vis-à-vis the Osages who were considered to be untamed and uncivilized by the officials in Washington.[21] In the early years, the Osages did not adapt well to the white man's ways. The Osages lived by the hunt and what they were able to gain through conquest of the other Indian tribes. The Osages were not agriculturally oriented and thus had difficulty adjusting as their territory of operation became constricted.

Around 1800 random bands of the Osages from southern Missouri formed around Chief Claremore I and moved to villages on the lower Neosho/Grand and Verdigris Rivers in today's Oklahoma.[22] One of the earliest known Osage villages in Oklahoma was established by Chief Tracks Far Away (Ka-she-Se-gra or Cashegra), who around 1802 moved about half of the Missouri Osages to the Three Forks area, between the Verdigris and the Neosho/Grand, opposite where Fort Gibson was later built.[23] In June of 1802 the Spanish governor canceled Auguste Chouteau's trade monopoly with the Osages in favor of Manuel Lisa. The Chouteaus interpreted Lisa's new trading license to cover only the Missouri River and its tributary, the Osage River, and not the Arkansas River and its tributaries. About that time, perhaps induced by the Chouteaus, the faction of Osages led by Tracks Far Away left Missouri and joined Claremore's band on the Arkansas River. This allowed the Chouteaus to continue trading with several thousand Osages at their new village in the Three Forks Area. The separate Osage bands there became variously known as the Claremore bands, the Arkansas bands and the Cheniers (or Shaners).[24]

The Osage Nation did not fare well in its dealings with the United States and the American settlers. The United States failed to enforce the various treaties to prevent encroachments into the Osage lands by white settlers and the neighboring tribes. By the 1850s, the Osage Nation had been whittled down by wars with other Indian tribes, but even more so by the ravages of various diseases of the white man resulting in devastating epidemics. By 1855 or so, the population of the Osage Nation had been reduced to about 5,000 individuals and their territory was about equivalent to the current Osage reservation that is present-day Osage County, Oklahoma, the largest land area of any county in that state.

Osage Villages in Oklahoma, 1802-1840. Louis F. Burns, Osage Indian Clans and Bands, *Ciga Press, Fallbrook, CA (1983), p. 5.*

The Lure of the Arkansas River and Santa Fe

Just as the Lewis and Clark Voyage of Discovery had opened up the fur trade and settlement of the lands bordering the Missouri River, Zebulon Pike's expedition to the headwaters of the Arkansas, although much less successful, excited the imaginations of men anxious to exploit the riches of the area watered by the Arkansas and Rio Grande Rivers, including Santa Fe. Pursuant to the Louisiana Purchase, the Americans claimed all of the land north of the Arkansas. The Spanish did not accept the American conclusion and continued to claim ownership of the lands between the Arkansas, north to the Missouri. Spanish troops were even dispatched in 1805 in an unsuccessful attempt to intercept Lewis and Clark.

The early history of Santa Fe and the arrival of the Americans are covered very well in *Ciudad Santa Fe*, a 3-volume set authored by Father Stanley.[25] Father Stanley's research was undertaken between 1938 and 1965 and his bibliographies in the volumes are very comprehensive, including most of the surviving Spanish-language records. Most of this section is taken from these histories written by Father Stanley.

General James Wilkinson dispatched Pike on his mission in 1806 without the knowledge of President Jefferson. As in the case of his earlier expedition on the Mississippi, Pike's was a small and poorly equipped unit. It has been speculated that this was another of the machinations of Wilkinson and Aaron Burr to possibly establish their own empire in the Southwest, although Pike certainly denied that. He departed from St. Louis and went overland, using Osage Indians as guides for most of the way, reaching the Arkansas River in the vicinity of present-day Pueblo. It is curious that Pike erected a stockade fort on the west bank of the Rio Grande River, clearly on Spanish territory in present-day Colorado. Perhaps Pike's move was intentional and part of a scheme to get into Santa Fe to reconnoiter the area. In any event, he was captured by Spanish troops sent out from Santa Fe to take him into custody. He and his men were first taken to the jail in Santa Fe, where they were interrogated by the governor. They were subsequently taken to the prison in Chihuahua, the seat of the government that controlled Santa Fe and *Nueva Mexico*. When news of the capture of Pike and his men reached Washington, D.C., belated retroactive approval of his expedition was given, probably to avoid not only further imprisonment of Pike and his men, but also embarrassment to the United States.

Although Pike's account of his travels was not particularly impressive, it nonetheless spawned other trading expeditions to Santa Fe. Rumors persisted of vast wealth in Spanish gold and silver mines, as well as the expectation of valuable fur trapping. Some of the ensuing trading expeditions went overland from

Santa Fe, while others took the route up the Arkansas River. Frequently, the approaching trading party would be reported to the governor in Santa Fe as a large American invasion army. The Spanish troops quartered in Santa Fe would be sent out to meet the invaders. The small American trading party would be outnumbered by the Spanish and would be summarily arrested and taken to Santa Fe.

Several early travelers to Santa Fe sent out by American interests liked the town so much that they stayed and prospered. These included Baptiste La Lande, a trader sent out by William Morrison of Kaskaskia, Illinois and James Purcell, a trapper from Bardstown, Kentucky.[26]

In 1811, a small trading party was arrested on the Red River by troops sent out by the governor of Santa Fe. They were held in various prisons, including Chihuahua, for a year. After returning from prison, J. McClanahan later wrote to Missouri Governor Howard that he had noted that the views of the inhabitants of the area differed markedly from that of the Spanish and that in his opinion Americans would be welcomed in the area if the Mexicans obtained their freedom from Spain.[27]

Ten adventurers from St. Louis, including Robert McKnight, one of five brothers in a successful St. Louis mercantile business, undertook the first large trading expedition to Santa Fe. They had heard a rumor that the Spanish government had been overthrown and that New Mexico was an independent state. They set out from St. Louis in 1812 but were arrested later that year when they entered Santa Fe. Their goods were confiscated and they were incarcerated. Two men managed to escape their captors in Santa Fe. They stole a small boat when they reached the Canadian River and sailed the full length of that river east, the first Americans to do so. The remainder of the trading party were not so lucky. They were taken to Chihuahua, then on to Durango, where they remained in prison for ten years until 1822.[28]

In 1816, Auguste P. Chouteau and his partner, Julius Du Munn, led a trapping and trading party to the Upper Arkansas. They may have been the first Americans to attempt this Arkansas River corridor to Santa Fe. They received different treatment from Governor Mainez who welcomed them. Chouteau thought he would receive a license to trap beaver on the tributaries to the Rio Grande, but returned to trade with the Indians on the Arkansas before receiving the necessary approval from Chihuahua. That approval was not forthcoming and Governor Mainez was replaced in Santa Fe. Chouteau, Du Munn and 24 other Americans were arrested on the Arkansas by a large body of Spanish troops sent out from Santa Fe by the new governor. The traders' goods worth in excess of thirty thousand dollars were confiscated. The Americans were tried by a court martial in Santa Fe, at which the governor presided. Du Munn later wrote that he feared the worst at the trial as none of the six members of the court spoke English and five of them appeared to be illiterate even in Spanish. The Americans were required to kneel down to hear the sentence which did provide their release, but at the cost of the forfeiture of their valuable goods and most of their horses and mules.[29] In all, the Chouteau-Du Mann trading party was kept in Santa Fe for two years.[30] While most of the early travelers to Santa Fe were fur trappers or traders, some other visitors to the area came to explore and map the territory.

Captain Pryor and the Osage

Our first written evidence of Nathaniel Pryor's relations with the Osages is the license he was granted to trade with the Osage Nation dated November 29, 1819, which he received from Robert Crittenden, the secretary and acting governor of Arkansas Territory. This license was probably issued to Pryor shortly after the death of his first partner, Samuel Richards, and permitted him "to trade with the Osage Nation of Indians, as well as to ascend the river Arkansas with one trading boat to the six bull or Verdigris, together with all hands that may appertain thereto."[31] The "six bull" was the Osage name for the Neosho or Grand River. This license would have placed Pryor in the Three Forks area. However, Pryor must have been present and have traded in the

Three Forks area for two or three years before he obtained his 1819 trading license. It was there that he met and married his Osage wife Ah-Sin-Ka (sometimes Asinga or Osinga). Later baptismal records verify that their first child was born in September of 1818, indicating that Pryor and Ah Sin Ka were married at least a nine-month gestation period earlier.

Ah-Sin-Ka was a birth-rank name, signifying a third or later-born daughter. The Osage birth-rank name for a first daughter was Mi-na or Me-nah, and for a second daughter, We-ha or Wi-he. The Osages also had birth-rank names for their sons, with the first-born being more favored in both genders. In the Osage culture marriages with non-Osages were not desirable, although occasionally an Osage family would consent to an "outside" marriage. Most "outside" marriages were for an Ah-Sin-Ka, rarely for a first or second born daughter. Thus for the whites, the name "Ah-Sin-Ka" came to have the more general or secondary connotation of simply "an Osage woman," and the marriages recorded by the local Catholic Priests used the term frequently.

Osage Chief. © State Historical Society of Missouri, No. SHSMO 021420.

Pryor's Ah-Sin-Ka may have been a sister of Chief Claremore I. Burns has reported that this first Chief Claremore died in 1794 or early 1795, long before Pryor arrived in the area. Claremore I's successor was White Hair I (Iron Hawk or Pa-hus-ka) who probably was a brother of Claremore I. When Claremore I died, his son Claremore II was only a small boy, probably born around 1780–85, so he could not have been the father of Pryor's Ah-Sin-Ka, who was born about 1786, based upon her reported baptismal age of 55 in 1841 (see below). Claremore II was also known as "Town Maker."

As set forth above, Claremore II led his band to the Three Forks area after 1800 and established his Claremore Village near Claremore Mound, a few miles northwest of today's Claremore, OK, on the east side of the Verdigris, about 45 miles up from its mouth. This Chief Claremore II was a prominent chief among the Osages. He was the Chief of the "Great Osages" of the Missouri and Arkansas Territories. He accompanied William Clark and other Osage Chiefs when Clark took them to Washington in the summer of 1812 to meet with President Madison.[32] The Claremore Osages had been at Claremore Village for at least 15 years when Pryor arrived as a trader in the Three Forks area.[33] Pryor soon became intimately acquainted with Claremore II, from about 1816 or 1817 until Claremore II's death in 1828. Pryor was Claremore II's close friend, interpreter, and counselor. Pryor's Ah-Sin-Ka may possibly have been Claremore II's sister or the sister of his father Claremore I. Pryor also went with the Claremore Osages on several of their semi-annual buffalo hunts into what are now Western Kansas and Oklahoma. Pryor served as an unofficial and unpaid sub-agent for the Osages for several years before his official appointment in 1831. Ah-Sin-Ka's 1841 baptismal record (see below) reported that she was then 55 years old, so she would have been approximately 30 at the time of her marriage to Nat Pryor.

In 1818 and 1819, three men ventured into the Arkansas River territory for other than trapping or trading purposes. Thomas Flint was a writer who intended to write a western travel narrative for the area, as he had already done relative to the Ohio and Mississippi River Valleys.[34] Thomas Nuttall was a Philadelphia-based botanist or naturalist and Henry Rowe Schoolcraft was "an aspiring mineralogist and future ethnologist of Native American culture."[35] Flint and Schoolcraft wandered rather aimlessly from St. Louis on foot to the Ozark Plateau of Arkansas. Schoolcraft, with just one companion, was so poorly equipped that they carried fowling pieces, which were virtually useless in the wilderness, instead of rifles. They were frequently short of food and very often traveled in circles. Flint's expedition was not much better equipped and it is no wonder that the accounts of Flint and Schoolcraft were not complimentary to the area.

The eminent English naturalist, Thomas Nuttall, had resided in Philadelphia for a few years and was a member of the American Philosophical Society in Philadelphia, the same Society that had prepared Meriwether Lewis for his expedition. Nuttall intended to botanize the Southwest up the Arkansas as far as the Rocky Mountains. Flint, Schoolcraft and Nuttall demonstrated great fortitude in surviving the extreme hardships of their travels. They were each very lucky not to have encountered hostile Indians and other life-threatening experiences. Flint and Schoolcraft were not wealthy and they were strapped by financial problems. Nuttall was only slightly better off. Each man wrote of his travels and the accounts were very helpful to the Americans who followed them. Flint and Schoolcraft generally disparaged the area and its inhabitants. Nuttall's account was more enthusiastic. He had traveled at least as far West as the Verdigris on the Arkansas and had also explored south to the Canadian and Red Rivers.

In his *Journals of Travels Into the Arkansas Territory During the Year 1819*, Nuttall mentioned meeting Pryor and Richards in March of 1819 "descending the Arkansas on their way to New Orleans with cargoes of furs and peltries gotten in trade with the Osages".[36] Nuttall met Pryor again in May of 1819 at the "little trading settlement at Three Forks."[37] Pryor's partner Richards must have died before November 29, 1819, when Pryor alone received a license "to trade with the Osage Nation of Indians, as well as to ascend the river Arkansas with one trading boat to the six bull or Verdigree."[38] Richard's death in 1819 is also confirmed by a collection action brought by the partnership's former employee Samuel B. Rutherford against "Nathaniel Pryor, surviving partner of Pryor & Richards." By order of the Circuit Court for the Territory of Arkansas, County of Arkansas, dated November 1, 1819, Rutherford obtained a default judgment against Pryor.[39]

In 1819, Nuttall also met and stayed with Charles Bougie, probably the earliest trader with the Osages in the Three Forks area. A French-Canadian from Kaskaskia, Bougie became a trader at Arkansas Post in 1804 and in 1806 went up the Arkansas River with $10,000 of goods for trading with the Osages at the mouth of the Verdigris. Nuttall was ill and stayed with Bougie for over a month at Bougie's trading post in the Three Forks area, close to the falls of the Verdigris and near to that of Nathaniel Pryor.[40] Later that year, Nuttall returned to Fort Smith to observe the September 1819 council attended by Pryor, Chief Claremore II and other important Osages. That council will be discussed below.

Shirley Christian has written that a Joseph Bogy came to the Three Forks area in 1807 and established a trading post on the Verdigris, where "about thirty log houses were gradually built along a clearing by the Verdigris River opposite a waterfall," and where the government's Osage Agency was established in 1826.[41] Joseph Bogy is probably the same person as Charles Bougie. The waterfall was about four miles upstream from the mouth of the Verdigris.

Sometime after the death of Richards, Pryor entered into a trading partnership with Hugh Glenn, another of the early traders in the Three Forks area. Glenn was licensed to trade with the Osages and the Cherokees. Pryor's good reputation in the area is shown by a quote from Thoburn-Wright as: "Captain Pryor figured prominently in the affairs of the region surrounding the Three Forks, for he was especially held in high esteem by the Osages."[42]

Pryor's trading store was located a mile and a half above the mouth of the Verdigris on the west bank of that river which enters the Arkansas from the north. See Note 4. In a 1924 article in the *Chronicles of Oklahoma*, Grant Foreman wrote:

> "Several trading houses were doing business at the mouth of the Verdigris, and upon the arrival of Col. Arbuckle in 1824, it was the center of such enterprise as existed in this western wilderness and the only settlement of any importance for hundreds of miles."[43]

This location is approximately opposite present Muskogee, Oklahoma, about 130 river miles upstream from Fort Smith, Arkansas. Fort Smith was established in 1817, about 550 river miles upstream from Arkansas Post, to provide protection for traders and trappers between the Osages, who were generally upstream from Fort Smith, and the Cherokees, who were mostly downstream at that time. This accords with the information in the Journals of Thomas Nuttall and Thomas James. However, the author has discussed this several times with Mrs. Betty Lou Harper Thomas, Director of the Mayes County Historical Society at Pryor, Oklahoma. Mrs. Thomas has indicated that her research has led her to conclude that Nathaniel Pryor never had a trading post "at Three Forks," but merely in the "Three Forks Area," a broad enough area to include Pryor's trading post on Pryor Creek, some 40 miles North of Three Forks, a tributary of the Neosho (Grand) River. Mrs. Thomas has not made her research available to the author. She is also writing a biography of Nathaniel Pryor, so perhaps this apparent conflict will be clarified in the near future.

The Chouteaus from St. Louis were also involved in the trading operations in the area. The trading venture of Auguste P. Chouteau to Santa Fe was discussed above and no doubt started from the Three Forks area. The Chouteaus established a trading post about 40 miles upstream from the mouth of the Grand (Neosho) River near present Salina in Mayes County. As a result, Pryor would have resumed his friendship with Pierre and Col. A. P. Chouteau.[44]

The simmering hostilities between the Osages and Cherokees erupted in the fall of 1817. A large war party consisting of approximately 600 eastern and western Cherokees, Choctaws, Shawnees, Delawares, Caddos, Tonkawas, Comanches, Coushattas and a sizable body of white men, raided Claremore's village while the Osage warriors were away to the west on their fall buffalo hunt. The raid was especially treacherous as the Cherokees first approached the village offering to have a peace parley to discuss the tribes' differences. The Osages sent an old chief to

tell the Cherokees that a council could not be held until Claremore returned. After feeding the Osage chief, the Cherokees
killed and scalped him before attacking the village. "It was
reported they (the Cherokees) killed more than 80 old men,
women, and children, and took over 100 prisoners; as well as
firing the town and destroying provisions."[45] The Cherokees cel-
ebrated this surprise attack upon relatively defenseless Osages
as a great victory. It was not an unusual attack in the many wars
between the various Indian tribes on the Great Plains.[46] The
similarity between this Cherokee victory and the "Sand Creek
Massacre," where a predominantly volunteer force of Colorado
Militia attacked a Cheyenne encampment of mostly older men,
women and children, is inescapable.

In 1818, several Osage Chiefs traveled to St. Louis where
William Clark, Governor of the Missouri Territory, signed a
treaty with them. By this treaty, the Osages ceded to the United
States the land bounded on the south by the Arkansas River, on
the west by the Verdigris River, up to its falls, thence northeast
to the Grand Saline [where Pierre Chouteau had established a
trading post], thence east to the Cherokee settlement. Before
the Osage Chiefs returned from St. Louis, a Cherokee raiding
party stole 20 or more horses from an Osage band. Because of
this and the raid on Claremore II's village the previous year, the
Osages began preparations for an all-out war against the Cherokees. "But this time Captain Nathaniel Pryor, trader, friend, and
intermarried white citizen, counciled with them (the Osage) and
urged them to wait until he [had gone to and] returned from Fort
Smith to talk with Major Bradford." [Emphasis added].[47]

Pryor persuaded Major Bradford, the commandant at Fort
Smith, to visit Chief Claremore II's village. Bradford found the village full of Sac and Foxes, Iowas, Omahas, Otoes, Konzas (probably Kaws or Kansas), and Quapahs, all preparing to aid the
Osages in a war against the Cherokees. With Pryor's assistance,
Bradford was able to halt the war movement by promising that
he would see that the Cherokees returned the prisoners taken in
1817 by the summer of 1819.[48]

Osage Warriors. © State Historical Society of Missouri, No. SHSMO 021419.

In September of 1819, Chief Claremore II and many of his tribesmen went to Fort Smith to a council scheduled by Major Bradford to receive the Osage prisoners from the Cherokees. Claremore II was accompanied by his counselor (Tallai), his son Bad-Tempered-Buffalo [a/k/a Mad Buffalo], and Captain Nathaniel Pryor. Thomas Nuttall, the English naturalist, had returned to Fort Smith, in part because he wanted to attend and observe this scheduled council. The Cherokees stalled for twelve days and then failed to deliver all of the prisoners. As a result:

> "Nathaniel Pryor, their white friend and an <u>inter-married</u> trader, suggested that as the Cherokees had not been strictly sincere about the Osage captives, the

Osages ought to demand of the commandant at Fort
Smith that they, the Osages, take the five Cherokees
home as hostages." [Emphasis supplied].[49]

Bad-Tempered-Buffalo opposed Pryor's suggestion, saying
that the Cherokee hostages' presence in Claremore II's village
would only remind the Osage women of their loved ones who
had been murdered or were still being held by the Cherokees.
The Osages went away angered since not all of the prisoners
had been returned and the bitterness between the two tribes
continued.[50]

Establishment of the Union Mission (1819–1821)

In 1819 a young missionary, Rev. Epaphras Chapman, came
west to establish a mission among the Osages. He was probably
present at the Fort Smith council in September of 1819 where
he met Thomas Nuttall and Captain Nathaniel Pryor. Pryor
brought Chapman to the site of the proposed Union Mission,
which was a 1,000 acre tract a few miles southeast of the present town of Chouteau and just northeast of present Mazie, in
Mayes County, Oklahoma.[51] There, Pryor helped the religious
group, sponsored by the Boston Congregational Church, to settle and establish the Union Mission, which was intended to
spread Christianity among the Indians.[52]

The advance members of the missionary contingent arrived at
Union Mission in mid-November of 1820. The rest of the missionaries arrived in February of 1821 and the Union Mission opened
the first school in Oklahoma shortly after their arrival.[53] In addition to opening the first school in Oklahoma, Union Mission is
also credited with printing the first book in Oklahoma, "a little
primer in the Creek language".[54] Other firsts for Union Mission
in Oklahoma were the holding of the first Protestant wedding on
March 10, 1821, and the establishment of the first church on May
26, 1821.[55] The school at Union Mission was discontinued in
1836 and the Mission closed in 1836.[56]

Possible Reunion With Touissant Charbonneau

It is possible that Pryor was visited by Toussaint Charbonneau in about 1820. This would have been a rare reunion of members of the Lewis and Clark Expedition. A recent biography of Jean-Baptiste (Pomp) Charbonneau indicates that he probably did not travel to the Arkansas.[57] Toussaint Charbonneau was of course the husband of Sacagawea. Jean-Baptiste Charbonneau was their son, born on the Expedition. Jean-Baptiste Charbonneau had been adopted, raised and educated by William Clark in St. Louis. He was the "Little Pomp" who had been carried in a cradleboard on the back of Sacagawea for most of the Expedition. After the Expedition, Toussaint Charbonneau worked for various fur trapping companies as a guide and interpreter. Nathaniel Pryor surely would have encountered Pomp in the company of William Clark at St. Louis in 1809–1812, during Pryor's visits with Clark. One writer has written that when Pomp was about 15 years old, he and his father were trapping for a fur company along the Neosho River and that this river flowed in the area where Nathaniel Pryor's trading post was located.[58] If this is true, then it could be possible that Toussaint and Pomp may have visited Pryor's trading post at Three Forks.

A Cherokee Theft From Pryor's Trading Post (1820)

In February 1820, while hunting bear along the Poteau River, Bad-Tempered-Buffalo (also called "Mad Buffalo") became angry and let his warriors kill three Cherokees after he discovered that the Cherokee bear hunters had killed sows and cubs as well as boars, which was not the practice of the Osage. Bad-Tempered-Buffalo was the son of Claremore II. He and his braves then went to Pryor's trading post at Three Forks.[59] As they approached the store, they noted a large party of Cherokees standing about the store, but it was too late for the Osages to turn back, so they rode boldly up to the trading post. The Cherokees were out to avenge the death of their bear hunters and were led by Dutch, one of their most renowned warriors. Mathews has described the events that followed:

> Pryor noted the glee of the Cherokees when they saw that they greatly outnumbered the Bad-Tempered-Buffalo party, but he knew they would not attack them at the post; so he immediately had one of his men, David McGee, to call the leader of the Cherokees and his followers to the opposite side of the main building to show him some new shiny copper kettles which all tribes valued very highly for cooking... .
>
> While the Cherokees ... wondered about the amount of beaver or bear hides it would take to own one kettle [and] ... bring to Pryor to trade for one, Bad-Tempered-Buffalo and his warriors fled on their strong Pawnee horses, and they soon left behind the badly mounted Cherokees, who tried to overtake them.
>
> The Cherokees were angered, and they left the post scowling at Pryor, but they went only a short distance, then waited for darkness. ... then slipped into the area around the post and very quietly broke into the store and stole 150 pounds of beaver fur.
>
> ... Like white men, they [the Cherokees] didn't go to the trouble of denying the theft of Pryor's beaver, but under the aegis of the law, which recognized the fact that the Osages and the Cherokees were at war with each other and that this white man Pryor had not been neutral in the matter in which a citizen of the United States must be, but had aided the Osages. Pryor put in his claim to the War Department [in 1824], asking for redress under the guarantee made when he was given a trader's license. The War Department agreed with the Cherokee contention. Under Secretary of War John C. Calhoun, the Department was interested, with General Jackson and Governor McMinn, in keeping the Cherokees well disposed toward full migration to Arkansas. Their lands were needed by the Amer-Europeans.[60]

Capt. Pryor showing copper kettles to Dutch and the Cherokees. Drawing by Richard Florence.

The ruse of Nat Pryor and his employee had worked to deceive the Cherokees and allow the Osages sufficient time to effect their escape. When Dutch and his cohorts discovered that the Osages had left, they pursued them but were outdistanced by the better-mounted Osages.[61] Pryor's intervention to assist Bad-Tempered-Buffalo and his party was a very brave act as Dutch was probably the fiercest and most feared Cherokee warrior chief at the time. He was an implacable enemy of the Osages and was said to have killed over twenty-six Osages in his numerous confrontations with them.[62] George Catlin traveled several months with Dutch and painted his portrait in 1834, titled "Tuch-ee." McKenney & Hall probably painted Dutch's portrait a few years earlier as their portrait of him, titled "Tah-chee," was included in the portfolio published in 1836.[63] Despite his violent nature, Dutch lived a full life and died peacefully in 1848.

Nathaniel Pryor filed his claim for the property stolen from him accompanied by an affidavit dated September 11, 1824. Pryor's affidavit given before Justice of the Peace John Nicks of Crawford County, Arkansas Territory, stated as follows:

This day personally appeared before me, John Nicks, one of the Justices of the Peace in and for said County Nathaniel Pryor of the Osage Nation of Indians, who being of lawful age and duly sworn according to law, deposed and said that some time in the month of February 1820, on the Virdigris River, a branch of the Arkansas or Paune River, at said Pryor's trading house, <u>about one and a half miles above the mouth of said Virdigris</u>, this deponent had about one hundred and fifty weight of Beaver fur, and about said time a Cherokee Indian by the name of Dutch and two others, companions of his, took from the possession of this deponent the said one hundred and fifty weight of Beaver for the property of this deponent and which said Beaver fur has never been restored to him or any part thereof, nor the value or any part thereof. (Emphasis supplied).

This deponent further stated that about the month of February, 1822, the Cherokee Indians stole from his possession a large bright bay horse with a star in his fore-head and about fifteen hands high and which said horse he has never been able to recover or reclaim nor the value thereof, or any part thereof, and further this deponent said not.[64]

Pryor signed and swore to the affidavit on September 11, 1824.[65] His affidavit was supported by another affidavit from his employee, David McKee, given on the same date before Justice of the Peace Nicks. McKee's affidavit is basically identical to Pryor's, but McKee added that the fur was stolen and "this deponent verily believes by the said Cherokee Indians. The deponent further states that fur was selling at that time at two and a half per pound."[66] On April 30, 1832, Geo. Vashon, "Agt. Chers. West" (Agent for the Cherokees West) certified that the affidavits by Pryor and McKee were true copies made from the files in his office.[67]

The Cherokees opposed Pryor's claim. Major E. W. Duval, agent to the western Cherokees, submitted a statement on their behalf, explaining that at the time of this taking of Pryor's property, the Osages and the Cherokees were at open war with each other. Further, that the war party of Cherokees commanded by Dutch was more numerous than the Osages under "Mad Buffaloe, that the Osages were completely in the power of the Cherokees, who considered the Osages their prisoners and were only waiting until the Osages left the premises of Mr. Pryor to capture them."[68]

Major Duval's affidavit further stated that Dutch:

> "... was invited out on one side of Mr. Prior's [sic] house ... at the instance of Mr. Prior by a man named McKee or McGee, where he and his party were detained by amusements until the Mad Buffaloe and his party had time to escape; that he believed and still believes, their escape was contrived by Mr. Prior; ... that for this interference ... on the part of Mr. Prior, whereby he [Dutch] was prevented making prisoners of the [Osage] party and in so far weakening or injuring the enemy and rendering essential service to his own nation, he took the property for which Mr. Prior claims payment.
>
> "That Mr. Prior, a citizen of the U. States intermarried with an Osage woman ... was as it would seem to the committee bound to have preserved a perfect neutrality between the belligerent parties; and that by having aided the Osages in the manner set forth by the Dutch and admitted to by himself he ceased to maintain the character of a neutral and thereby subjected his property to seizure by the party injured."[69]

Pryor's claim was denied. Although perhaps the Cherokees' retaliation may have been justified at the time because of Pryor's assistance to the Osages, it is difficult to understand how it would justify the stealing of Pryor's horse two years later. This event not only is illustrative of Pryor's courage, but also of his resourcefulness in avoiding a very serious situation that could have inflamed the war between these tribes. It also illustrates the fine line required to be walked by traders and other white settlers on the fringes of the western frontier at the time.

John Nicks, the Justice of the Peace who took Pryor's deposition had a long association with Pryor in the area. After retiring from the Army as a Colonel, Nicks was appointed the sutler at Ft. Smith. He served in the Arkansas Territorial Legislature and later was a Congressman from the Arkansas District. He relocated to Cantonment Gibson when that post was established in 1824, where he was the sutler. Nicks was appointed a Brigadier General in command of the Arkansas Militia by President John Quincy Adams on March 27, 1827. General Nicks died at Cantonment Gibson on December 31, 1831, several months prior to the transmittal of the Pryor affidavits to the Indian Office in Washington, D.C.[70]

Assertion That Capt. Pryor Urged Osages to Destroy Fort Smith (1821)

Author Larry E. Morris has recently written that:

> "In 1821, at a government post on the Arkansas River [Fort Smith], the men were informed that 350 Osage warriors 'were on their way to kill and plunder the Cherokees.' A Captain Pryor was said to be urging the Osages to war and was also reportedly planning to lead them in destroying the post."[71]

This report apparently stems from two letters written in 1821 by Matthew Lyon, one to Major William Bradford, the Commander at Fort Smith, and the other to Secretary of War John C. Calhoun. Morris, however, finds little credence in the Lyon assertions. Morris notes that shortly after Lyon's letters four Delawares were killed by a group of Osages. "But no attack was launched on the post, and no evidence was offered that Nathaniel Pryor had instigated anything."[72] To further substantiate his conclusion that Pryor was innocent of the charges, Morris cites two letters written by Sam Houston, which will be discussed in detail later. Those letters, written to President Andrew Jackson and Secretary of War John H. Eaton, praise Pryor's efforts in pacifying the Osages and improving the Osages' relationships with the Americans as well as with the neighboring Indian tribes.

Morris wrote that, "The bad blood between Pryor and the Cherokees probably accounted for the rumors that were floated about him."[73] Accordingly, the words of Sam Houston praising Pryor carry even more weight, since Houston had been adopted into the Cherokee tribe, had married a Cherokee and maintained a trading post in the vicinity of Pryor's trading post.

Finally, in addition to Houston's two supporting letters, Colonel Matthew Arbuckle also wrote a letter to Secretary of War Eaton in support of the subagent appointment for Pryor in 1830. In his letter, dated December 19, 1830, written from Cantonment Gibson, Arbuckle wrote:

> "... I believe I am justified in saying that he (Pryor) had done more than all the agents employed in the Indian Department in restoring peace between the Indians on this Frontier, particularly in <u>restraining</u> Clermont's Band of the Osages from depredating on the neighboring Tribes, <u>as well as on our citizens,</u> which they had been in the Habit of doing for a number of years. ... Yet if he was now removed from that Band I would not be surprised if they should commence their former Habits, and thereby disturb the peace of this Frontier." (Emphasis supplied).[74]

Col. Arbuckle had been at Fort Smith and then was the post commander at Fort Gibson since April of 1824 and would certainly have had complete knowledge of Pryor's activities in the area. Like Pryor, Arbuckle had also served under Gen. Jackson at the Battle of New Orleans.[75]

As set forth above, at least by 1817 or 1818, Pryor had married Ah Sin Ka. Pryor was a trusted friend of the Osage and represented them not only in dealings with the American government and its representatives, but also with the other tribes. The Osages were constantly at war with the Choctaws and Cherokees who were continually raiding into and encroaching upon the Osage lands. Several other traders were active in the area, including Hugh Glenn and Auguste P. Chouteau, whom Pryor had met many years before in St. Louis and who had accompanied Pryor on his ill-fated journey up the Missouri River to return Chief Sheheke to his Mandan tribe.[76]

Notes

1. Generally, Mathews, John Joseph—*The Osages, Children of the Middle Waters*, U. Okla. Press, Norman, (1961, 3rd printing, 1973). Washington Irving visited the Three Forks region in 1832 and unflatteringly wrote of: "a sprinkling of trappers, hunters, half-breeds, creoles, negroes of every hue; and all that other rabble rout of nondescript beings that keep about the frontiers, between civilized and savage life ... ." Christian, *Before Lewis and Clark*, p. 312.

2. Shoemaker, *Many Faces*, p. 50; Thoburn, Joseph B. and Wright, Muriel H.—*Oklahoma a History of the State and Its People*, Lewis Hist. Pub. Co., New York, 1929, p. 86. Arkansas Post, now a national monument, was established as a fort and trading post in 1686, by a French lieutenant with the explorer LaSalle. It was the first permanent European settlement in the Mississippi Valley. In 1819 it became the territorial capital of newly created Arkansas Territory and the home of its first newspaper. In 1821 both the capital and the *Gazette* were moved to Little Rock. Arkansas became a state in 1836.

3. *Arkansas Gazette*, October 28, 1820, Vol. 1, Iss. 50, p. [4}, citing the petition of Harold Stilwell, an assignee of Richards, for partition of the property. An earlier issue of the *Arkansas Gazette* gave notice that the interests of Pryor and Sampson would be sold for taxes on November 6, 1820, and presumably that occurred. *Arkansas Gazette*, September 2, 1820, Vol. 1, Iss. 42, p. [1].

4. The author has had an on-going debate with Betty Lou Harper Thomas, Director of the Mayes County, OK Historical Society, as to

whether or not Pryor had a trading post at Three Forks prior to establishing his trading post at Pryor Creek, near Pryor, the county seat of Mayes County. The author is convinced that the mention of Pryor's trading post at Three Forks by several of the early explorers and traders who ventured through the area, such as the several citations in Thoburn-Wright, *Oklahoma*, the McKnight-James Expedition, the Glenn-Fowler Expedition, and Thomas Nuttall, discussed *infra*, clearly prove that Pryor was there from approximately 1817 until about 1821–23. In addition, Pryor gave his own affidavit on September 11, 1824, relative to depredations and losses at his trading post. Therein, Pryor stated that "some time in the month of February, 1820, on the Virdigris (sic) River, a branch of the Arkansas or Paune River, at said Pryor's trading house, about one and a half miles above the mouth of said Virdigris (sic), this deponent ... ." Douglas, Walter B.—*Documents: Captain Nathaniel Pryor*, The American Historical Review, January, 1919, p. 255. Pryor's affidavit was supported by the affidavit of his employee, David McKee, given on the same day, wherein McKee stated that "a Cherokee Indian by the name of Dutch, with two other Cherokee Indians came to Nath. Pryor's trading house on the Virdigris (sic) River, a branch of the Arkansas River, ..." *Id*, pp. 255–6. Copies of both affidavits were transmitted to Crawford County, Arkansas Territory, on April 30, 1832. George Vashon, Agent for the Western Cherokee Nation in 1832, certified that these copies were true copies of the original affidavits on file in his office and given before Justice of the Peace Jno. Nicks on September 11, 1824. *Ibid*.

5. Thoburn-Wright, *Oklahoma*, pp. 85–86.

6. Masterson, V.V.—*The Katy Railroad and the Last Frontier, U. Missouri Press, Columbia*, 1988, p. 134.

7. *Ibid*; and, Christian, *Before Lewis and Clark*, p. 302.

8. Shoemaker, *supra*, p. 50.

9. It is not the purpose of this paper to give a detailed history of the Osage Nation, but a brief overview will be presented. The author is indebted to the excellent research and writings of the eminent Osage scholar and historian, Louis F. Burns, in the following publications: *A History of the Osage People*, Ciga Press, Fallbrook, CA, 1989; *Osage Indian Customs and Myths*, Ciga Press, Fallbrook, CA, 1984; *Osage Indian Bands and Clans*, Ciga Press, Fallbrook, CA 1984; *Osage Mission Baptisms, Marriages and Interments, 1820–1886*, Ciga

Press, Fallbrook, CA, 1986. See also, Foreman, *below, Centennial of Ft. Gibson*, at p. 119.

10. Burns, *Osage People*, p. 88.

11. Although many historians omit references to General St. Clair's Defeat, it remains as the worst disaster inflicted upon the American Army by Indians during the long duration of the Indian Wars. The casualties suffered were almost triple those suffered by Custer and the Seventh Cavalry at the Battle of the Little Big Horn. The Americans under St. Clair lost 630 killed and 283 wounded. Burns, *Osage People*, p. 257.

12. Burns, *Osage People*, p. 208, citing Donald Jackson, ed., *Letters of Lewis and Clark Expedition with Related Documents, 1783–1854*, [Chicago: University of Illinois Press, 1978], pp. 109, 125.

13. *Ibid*.

14. Burns, *Osage People*, p. 18.

15. Hogan, Lawrence J.—*The Osage Indian Murders*, Amlex, Inc., Frederick, MD, 1998, at p. 10.

16. *Ibid*.

17. *Ibid*, at p. 1.

18. *Ibid*, at p. 5.

19. *Ibid*, at p. 14.

20. *Ibid*, pp. 239–242.

21. The so-called "Civilized Tribes" were the Cherokee, Chickasaw, Choctaw, Creek and Seminole Tribes.

22. Other authors have referred to this Chief Claremore as Clermont. He was also known as Tawaghe, Town Builder or Town Maker. We prefer Claremore, because it matches the present names of Claremore Mound, Claremore Village and the present town of Claremore in Oklahoma. The prominent Osage historian, Louis F. Burns, in his *A History of the Osage People*, U. Ala. Press, Tuscaloosa and London (2004), differentiates between the First Claremore (Clermont, Clermor, Gra Moh, Gra Moie, or Arrow-Going-Home), who died in 1794 or 1795, as Claremore I; his son as Claremore II (Town Maker) who died in 1828; and to the third Claremore as Claremore III (Town Maker II). We subscribe to Burns' designations.

23. Burns, *Osage People*,(1989 ed.), p. 122.

24. Christian, *Before Lewis and Clark*, pp. 103–04.

25. Stanley, F.—*Ciudad Santa Fe*, 3 volumes sub-titled Vol. I, *Spanish Domination* (1610–1821) World Press, Denver, CO, 1958; Vol. II, *Mexican Rule* (1821–1846) Pampa Print Shop, Pampa, TX, 1962 and, Vol. III, *Territorial Days* (1846–1912), Pampa Print Shop, Pampa, TX, 1965. Unfortunately, the second volume is mis-titled "Cuidad" instead of "Ciudad." Father Stanley was a Franciscan Priest and a very prolific author, self-publishing 177 titles, primarily histories of the towns and villages in New Mexico and West Texas. He was born Louis Crocchiola in New York, but after ordination was Fr. Stanley Francis Louis Crocchiola, writing under the pseudonym of "F. Stanley." Walker, Mary Jo—*The F. Stanley Story*, The Lightning Tree, Santa Fe, NM, 1985, p 23.

26. Stanley, *Mexican Rule*, p. 196.

27. Stanley, *Spanish Domination*, p. 382

28. *Ibid*, p. 381

29. *Ibid*, pp. 383–384.

30. Stanley, *Mexican Rule*, p. 198.

31. Douglas, Walter B.—*Documents*, p. 254, Item I.

32. Jones, Landon Y.—*William Clark and the Shaping of the West*, (Hill and Wong, New York, 2004), p. 207.

33. See <u>Clermont</u> in Johansen, Bruce E. and Grinde, Donald A., Jr.— *Encyclopedia of Native American Biography*, (Henry Holt & Co., 1997), p. 74. The name Clermont [Claremore] was used by a succession of Osage chiefs. See the discussion at note 22 above.

34. Lange, Lou Ann—*Travelers and Travel's "Significant Others": Three Visitors to the Arkansas Territory in 1818–1819*, Missouri Historical Review, Vol. 100, No. 1, pp. 19–39, at p. 19.

35. *Ibid*.

36. Shoemaker, *Many Faces*, at p. 50; Middlebrooks and Harper, *Ancestry of Nathaniel Pryor*, p. 302.

37. *Ibid*.

38. Douglas, Walter B.—*Documents*, p. 254. The Indian name for the Neosho River was the "Six Bulls." Rydjord, John—*Kansas Place Names*, (U. Okla. Press, Norman, 1972) p. 113.

39. *Arkansas Gazette*, December 11, 1819, Vol. 1, Iss. 4, p. [1].

40. Thoburn-Wright, *Oklahoma*, at pp. 56–58 and 85.

41. Christian, *Before Lewis and Clark*, p. 312.

42. Barry, Louise—*The Beginning of the West*, (Kan. State Hist. Soc,, Topeka, 1972), p. 78; Thoburn- Wright, *Oklahoma*, p. 86.

43. Foreman, Grant—*The Centennial of Ft. Gibson*, *The Chronicles of Oklahoma*, Okla. Hist. Soc. , Vol. 2, pp. 119–32, p. 121, (1924).

44. Thoburn-Wright, *Oklahoma*, pp.84–87.

45. Barry, *Beginning of the West*, p. 78, citing several sources. Burns, *Osage People*, (1989 ed.), at p. 268 reported the casualties as 14 old Osage men killed; 69 old women, boys and children killed; and, slightly more than 100 young children taken captive. Of the captives, only a few were returned to the Osages.

46. Hagen, Dennis E.—*Counting coup: the nature of intertribal warfare on the Great Plains considered*, *Roundup* of the Denver Posse of Westerners, Inc., Nov–Dec 2004, pp. 3–20.

47. Mathews, *The Osages*, p. 341–44; and, for this paragraph, Burns, *Osage People*, (1989 ed.), p. 351;

48. Mathews, *The Osages*, pp. 431–32.

49. Mathews, *The Osages*, p. 432–44.

50. Mathews, *The Osages*, pp. 434–35.

51. McMillan, Ethel—*Women Teachers in Oklahoma, 1820–1860*, *The Chronicles of Oklahoma*, Okla. Hist. Soc., Vol. 27, p. 3, (1949).

52. *The Chronicles of Oklahoma*, Okla. Hist. Soc., Vol. 10, pp. 461–2, (1932).

53. Variously, Thoburn-Wright, *Oklahoma*, pp. 58, n. 40, 86; Barry, *Beginning of the West*, p. 95, citing several sources.

54. Shoemaker, *Many Faces*, p. 50.

55. *Notes*, *The Chronicles of Oklahoma*, Okla. Hist. Soc., Vol. 12, No. 2, 1934, p. 221.

56. Barry, *Beginning of the West*, p. 95.

57. Colby, Susan M.—Sacagawea's Child, *The Life and Times of Jean-Baptiste (Pomp) Charbonneau*, Arther H. Clark, Co., Spokane, WA, 2005.

58. Walker, Wayne T.—*Pomp—Son of Sacajawea*, True West magazine, July, 1970, pp. 10–11, 38–42, at p. 40.

59. Mathews, *The Osages*, p. 435.

60. Matthews, *The Osages*, pp. 435–436.

61. Foreman, Carolyn Thomas—*Dutch, The Cherokee, The Chronicles of Oklahoma*, Okla. Hist. Soc., Vol. 27, p. 252–67, at p. 262 (1949); Shoemaker, *Many Faces*, p. 50.

62. Foreman, Carolyn Thomas—*Dutch.* Unfortunately, Mrs. Foreman dates the event between Pryor, Mad Buffalo and Dutch in 1836 instead of the actual year of 1820. Pryor died in 1831.

63. Catlin's portrait of Dutch (Tuch-ee) is in the collection of the Virginia Museum of Fine Arts.

64. Douglas, *Documents*; p. 255.

65. *Ibid.*

66. *Ibid*, at pp. 255–256.

67. *Ibid.* The wording of these affidavits by Pryor and his employee has led the author to conclude that Pryor had a trading post at Three Forks as late as February of 1820 and perhaps as late as February of 1822. In a footnote to Pryor's affidavit Walter B. Douglas recites that "Pryor is mentioned as living among the Osages, on the Verdigris in 1822, by James" in *Three Years among the Indians and Mexicans*, discussed below, and also in the *Missionary Herald*, XIX, 74. The *Missionary Herald* is believed to have contained information provided by the missionaries at Union Mission, but the document has not been reviewed by the author.

68. *Ibid*.

69. *Ibid*, also p. 257.

70. Foreman, Carolyn Thomas—*General John Nicks and His Wife, Sarah Perkins Nicks*, *The Chronicles of Oklahoma*, Okla. Hist. Soc., 1930, Vol. 8, pp. 389–406.

71. Morris, Larry E.—*The Fate of the Corps*, (Yale Univ. Press, New Haven & London, 2004), p. 164.

72. *Ibid*, and n. 3, p. 251, and citations therein.

73. *Ibid*, p. 164.

74. Douglas, *Documents*, p. 263.

75. Thoburn-Wright, *Oklahoma*, p. 62, n.5.

76. Ruth, Kent—*Oklahoma—A Guide To The Sooner State*, U. Okla. Press, 1941, p. 164.

9

PRYOR IN THE INDIAN TERRITORY

By the fall of 1821 parts of Mexico had won independence from Spain and had begun to encourage trade with the United States. Mexican Independence was proclaimed on September 27, 1821. Seizing upon this new trading opportunity, three trading expeditions headed for Santa Fe that year and two of them stopped at or near Nat Pryor's trading post at Three Forks.

The McKnight-James Expedition (1821–1822)

John McKnight and General Thomas James headed up the first trading party. McKnight was anxious to get to Santa Fe to look for his brother who had been in prison since 1812. James later served with distinction in the Black Hawk War and became a General in the Illinois Militia.[1] James wrote the record of his trip to Santa Fe, but it was not published until his descendants published it in 1916.[2] James had already ventured with Manuel Lisa on a fur trapping expedition up the Missouri in 1808–1810. James spelled the name as "Liza" and had nothing good to say about him. Evidently Lisa had cheated James and had not paid James his share of the profitable venture. James did write about Pryor's attempt to return Sheheke to the Mandans and was solidly of the

135

opinion that it had been Lisa who had told the Arikaras that Pryor was following with a large store of goods as well as the Mandan Chief. The depth of James's feelings against Manuel Lisa is shown by the following passage from his Journal:

"Liza we thoroughly detested and despised, both for his acts and his reputation. There were many tales afloat concerning villainies said to have been perpetrated by him on the frontiers. These may have been wholly false or greatly exaggerated, but in his looks there was no deception. Rascality sat on every feature of his dark complexioned, Mexican face—gleamed from his black Spanish eyes, and seemed enthroned in a forehead 'villainous low.' We were glad to be relieved of his presence."[3]

In referring to Pryor's ill-fated attempt to return Chief Sheheke and his family to the Mandans, James wrote:

"He (Lisa) was suspected of having invited the Ricka-rees (sic) to attack the Government troops under Capt. Prior (sic—Ensign Pryor), with Shehaka (sic) the year before for the purpose of preventing the traders and trappers who were with the troops from getting into the upper country."[4]

James also was with Expedition member George Drouillard in the spring of 1810 at a small fort near the confluence of the Madison and Jefferson Rivers in present-day Montana. James wrote that he was part of the group that recovered and buried the mutilated remains of Drouillard who had been surprised and killed by Indians, probably from the Gros Ventre Tribe.[5]

McKnight and James set out from St. Louis on May 10, 1821, with a Santa Fe-bound expedition of eleven men. They descended the Mississippi in their keelboat and then ascended the Arkansas to Three Forks. James had goods aboard valued at $10,000 and carried a Spanish passport. McKnight hoped to find his brother

Robert, who had been a prisoner of the Spanish since his ill-fated expedition to Santa Fe undertaken in 1812.[6] John and Robert McKnight were finally reunited in Santa Fe in 1822, when John was released following Mexico's independence from Spain.

In August of 1821, Thomas James arrived at Pryor's trading post with his large party. James had been told that the Arkansas River was navigable to a point sixty miles from Taos, New Mexico.[7] Pryor told James that he had been misinformed, but James ignored Pryor's advice and set off in his dugout canoes. Two days later James sent back to Pryor for help. Pryor took forty Osage braves and a sufficient supply of horses to the general who continued overland to Taos and Santa Fe. Pryor and his Indians went along with James for two days, but then left the trading party to go on the Osages' fall buffalo hunt.

Another writer reported that when: "[h]alted by low water a few miles above the mouth of the Cimarron [about 15 miles west of present Tulsa], James and two others went cross country to Clermont's village of Osages, where James bought 23 horses." Returning to the Arkansas, they cached their heavier goods, loaded pack animals and set off overland for Santa Fe, which they reached on December 1, finding the people there friendly.[8]

While James and McKnight were in Santa Fe, news of the successful revolution by the Mexicans reached that area in December of 1821. The Mexicans in Santa Fe apparently put James in charge of their Independence Celebration held in late January or February of 1822. Although James probably exaggerated his role in the proceedings it is an exciting account of the festivities. As was the case with most of the first Americans to visit Santa Fe and Taos, James was very critical of the Mexicans and their way of life, generally criticizing them as lazy and shiftless.[9]

James, Pike, Jacob Fowler and many of the early American visitors to Santa Fe were not complimentary to the local populace, especially the upper class, referred to as "ricos." This is somewhat surprising, as Santa Fe was a town of over 6,000 inhabitants in 1820, whereas St. Louis, the largest American town in the West barely had a population of 2,000. James wrote extensively and disparagingly about the habits and proclivities of the Mexicans. He was particularly critical of the extensive gambling by both men and women during the Independence Celebration, so much so, that Father Stanley thought James must have been a big loser at the gambling tables.[10] Departing from Santa Fe, James wrote that:

> "I had seen enough of Mexican society to be thoroughly disgusted with it. I had not supposed it possible for any society to be as profligate and vicious as I found all ranks of that in Santa Fe."[11]

Thomas James provided some insight into Pryor's reason for his sudden departure from military service in 1815. In a letter or report, James wrote, "On reduction of the Army after the war, he (Pryor) was discharged to make room for some parlor soldier and sunshine patriot, and turned out in his old age upon the world's wide common. I found him here among the Osages with whom he had taken refuge from his country's ingratitude, and was living as one of the tribe, where he may yet be, unless death has discharged the debt his country owed him."[12]

The Glenn-Fowler Expedition (1821–1822)

Hugh Glenn came to Fort Smith in 1817 as its first sutler, or post trader. He received a trading license for trade with the Osages and Cherokees on September 17, 1817.[13] About that time, Glenn established a trading house at Three Forks, near the mouth of the Verdigris River where it enters the Arkansas. Sometime after the death of Nat Pryor's partner, Samuel Richards, in 1819, "Col. Hugh Glenn … entered partnership with Captain Pryor in his [Pryor's] trading business on the Verdigris."[14]

Captain John R. Bell's notes indicate that his mounted party reached Hugh Glenn's trading post at the mouth of the Verdigris on September 5, 1820. Bell's party had been detached from Major Stephen H. Long's expedition while traveling eastward on the return from present Colorado.[15]

In September of 1821, a trading company led by Major Jacob Fowler left Fort Smith and reached "the trading Hous of Conl Hugh glann [Glenn] about mile up the virdegree [Verdigris]."[16] That was also the location of Pryor's trading post. It is probable that Glenn and Pryor had become trading partners by this time. Perhaps because of his partnership with Pryor, Glenn joined the Fowler party and actually became its leader. On September 25, 1821, Fowler noted: "We found our Selves 20 men in all, and under the Command of Conl Hugh glann." Among the 20 men named on the list by Fowler was "Nat Pryer." This man must have been Nathaniel Miguel Pryor, a possible son or nephew of Nathaniel Hale Pryor and not Captain Pryor himself. This confusion of names is discussed below. On that same day, the Glenn-Fowler party left Glenn's post and reached Chief Claremore's village on September 28th, finding "not one sole in or about the village" as "the Indians are all gon a buffelow Hunting."[17] Fowler's journal does not mention Nathaniel Pryor's trading post or meeting Capt. Pryor. This would verify that Pryor had joined Chief Claremore's hunting party after assisting the McKnight-James trading party.

The Glenn-Fowler party reached the vicinity of present Pueblo, Colorado, in late November. From there, Glenn and four men went on to Santa Fe and Taos, where they exchanged their trade goods for Spanish currency. Fowler and the rest of the party trapped in the Rio Grande Valley of northern New Mexico and southern Colorado for the rest of the winter and early spring.[18] While in Santa Fe, Glenn met and joined with the trading venture of Thomas James. Glenn was evidently short of funds and borrowed $100 from James, a debt that was never repaid, which James noted several times in his Journal.

In an article in *True West Magazine*, Arthur Shoemaker also wrote of this Glenn-Fowler trapping and trading expedition in 1821 and 1822 led by Jacob Fowler and assisted by Nat Pryor's partner, Hugh Glenn.[19] Shoemaker wrote that Fowler's journal of the expedition included a roster of the twenty men along on the expedition. On Fowler's list is a "Nat Pryer". The misspelling by Fowler is forgivable, but Shoemaker wrote that this man was Nathaniel Miguel Pryor, possibly the son of Nathaniel

Pryor and Peggy Patton.[20] It has been reported that Miguel was in the Verdigris area in the 1820s.[21] The first printing of Fowler's Journal was done in 1898 by the renowned researcher and author Elliott Coues. Unfortunately, Coues mistook Fowler's entry and wrote that the "Nat Pryer" listed among the twenty men on the Fowler expedition was "Nathaniel Pryor, ex-Sergeant of Lewis and Clark's Expedition." Coues added in a footnote that "the most interesting of the above names is that of Nathaniel Pryor, of whose identity with the sergeant of Lewis and Clark I have no doubt." Fowler's Journal, with Coues's notes, was re-edited and published in 1970. Therein, the authors correct the information regarding Nathaniel Pryor and clarify that the "Nat Pryer" with the Glenn-Fowler expedition was Nathaniel Miguel Pryor, possibly a nephew, son or namesake of Nathaniel Hale Pryor.[22]

In the 1970 edition of Fowler's Journal, the authors wrote that Nathaniel Miguel Pryor was born between 1798 and 1805 in Kentucky.[23] He moved to Missouri in 1820 and by 1821, when he joined the Glenn-Fowler expedition, he was living on the lower Verdigris near the trading posts. Nat Pryor, clearly Nathaniel Miguel Pryor, is mentioned four times as a member of the Fowler party between September 25, 1821 and June 16, 1822. His whereabouts for the next three years are unknown, but he must have gone back to the Three Forks area. In the summer of 1825 he and three companions left that area and went to New Mexico. In 1827, he joined the party led by James Ohio Pattie and went with them to Arizona, where they trapped along the Gila River. The Pattie group later arrived in California where they were arrested by Mexican authorities and held in jail for almost a year. Sylvester Pattie died in prison, but after being released from prison, Nathaniel Miguel Pryor settled in the Los Angeles area.[24] Shoemaker also wrote that Miguel left Fowler's group in the Rockies and went with other trappers to the Gila River country in Arizona. Miguel's later life and possible relationship to Nathaniel Hale Pryor will be discussed in Appendix C, but he died in Los Angeles in 1850. By trade, Miguel was a silversmith, clockmaker, trapper and hunter.

Fowler's journal reports that "Pryer" was with Glenn and Fowler in present Colorado during December of 1821. Entries in the *Union Mission Journal* for December 10, 29, and 30, 1821, report that Captain Pryor was present at Union Mission on the Neosho River (present Oklahoma) on those dates.[25] The "Pryer" with the Glenn-Fowler Expedition therefore could not have been Captain Nathaniel Hale Pryor and must have been Nathaniel Miguel Pryor. This conclusion is further buttressed by the later affidavit sworn to by Nathaniel Pryor, wherein he attested that he was in the Three Forks area during February of 1822 when some Cherokees stole his bay horse, as described previously in Chapter 8. In February of 1822 the "Pryer" with the Glenn-Fowler Expedition was still in New Mexico.

On June 1, 1822, the Glenn group, joined by Fowler, and the McKnight-James company started back east together from Taos, with over 140 horses and mules. James accused Glenn of cowardice when their group encountered Comanches and Pawnees on two occasions during their return to the Arkansas.[26] The two parties did not retrace their routes west, but traveled together to the area of present Great Bend, Kansas, where they parted. The Glenn-Fowler group went northeast to the Missouri River then canoed down it to St. Louis. The McKnight-James party followed an Osage trail overland generally eastward. Both parties reached St. Louis in mid-July.[27] When Glenn's party left the James party, James wrote that Glenn had "cheated me out of his debt to me, as I ought to have expected him to do after his previous cowardice and hypocrisy."[28]

The journals and records of these various trading expeditions all verify the conclusion that Nathaniel Pryor maintained a trading post near the mouth of the Verdigris during the period from about 1817 to the early 1820s.

Captain Nathaniel Pryor's New Trading Store

Sometime after August, 1821, when Thomas James arrived at Pryor's trading post near the mouth of the Verdigris, Pryor

moved his trading store to a new location on the west side of the
Neosho (Grand) River, some 35 miles to the north of the
Arkansas. His new location was thus between the Union Mission
and the Chouteau Trading Post near the Grand Saline, present
Salina, Oklahoma. Pryor's new trading store was located on or
near the mouth of Pryor Creek, bearing his name. The present
town of Pryor, the county seat of Mayes County, is located on
Pryor Creek, seven miles northwest of where Pryor's trading
store was located. The town was originally named Pryor Creek,
but the name was later shortened to Pryor. The town "was
named for the redoubtable Nathaniel Pryor, pioneer Indian
trader and subagent to the warlike Osages".[29]

Inset from painting of Captain Nathaniel Pryor at Trading Post on Pryor
Creek, *by Nick Calcagno, at Coo-y-yah Museum, Pryor, OK © Betty Lou
Harper Thomas.*

Erroneous Report of the Death of Nathaniel Pryor (1822)

In early 1822, many eastern newspapers reported the death of Nathaniel Pryor in articles similar to the following "Extract of a letter from Arkansas to a gentleman in Congress."

> "We have just received information that the Cherokees lately made an incursion into the Osage county, and killed some white people who were trading there. Nathaniel Pryor, we understand, was killed. They likewise killed and took prisoners many Osages, and carried away seventy horses.
>
> Nathaniel Pryor accompanied Lewis & Clark in their expedition to the Pacific, and more recently bore the commission of captain in the regular army."[30]

Massacre of White Traders by Osage Indians (November 1823)

On November 17, 1823, some 200 Osages, probably led by Bad-Tempered-Buffalo, also known as Mad Buffalo, one of the sons of Chief Claremore II, attacked a camp of Arkansas hunters on the Blue River in present Bryan County, Oklahoma, near the Texas border. The Arkansans were trespassing in the area in violation of an 1822 treaty with the Osages. Five hunters were killed, including Major Curtis Welborn, a U.S. Army Officer, who was either retired or on leave. The Osages also plundered the camp and took thirty horses from the hunters.[31] This attack probably would not have resulted in serious consequences had the Osages not killed and decapitated Major Welborn. Because of this, however, the army and the settlers in the area were outraged and were pressuring Colonel Arbuckle, the commanding officer at Fort Smith, to demand surrender of the "murderers" or to take them by force.[32]

With the army and the Osages on the verge of war, Captain Nathaniel Pryor, Chief Claremore II and his counselor, Tallai, went to Fort Smith in December of 1823 to discuss the matter with Col. Arbuckle. As Mathews has written: "Capt. Pryor, a trader friend of the Osages, wanted the matter of the white hunters settled so there would be peace. ..."[33]

Col. Arbuckle conveyed his fears of an Osage attack to his superior, General Winfield Scott, in command of the Army's Western Division at New Orleans.[34] Scott ordered Arbuckle to move five of his companies from Fort Smith to the Three Forks area. Col. Arbuckle did so and moved his five companies of soldiers to a site that was selected on April 20, 1824, for the new Cantonment Gibson. Capt. Nathaniel Pryor assisted Col. Arbuckle in selecting the site for the military post that became Fort Gibson.[35] The site was on the east side of the Neosho (Grand) River, about three miles from where that river enters the Arkansas, near present day Muskogee. Another purpose for the establishment of the new fort was to keep peace between the Osage Indians and the new immigrant tribes that were being resettled to the area from the southeast United States.

On June 7, 1824, some 500 Osages came to Fort Gibson and delivered six of their tribesmen to Col. Arbuckle as the leaders and perpetrators of the "massacre" of the white trespassers. The Osage leaders had been urged to turn over the six by: "Nathaniel Pryor and their new agent, David Barber." The six leaders of the attack were ready to accept a possible verdict of death, by command of their tribal elders and the Grand Hunkah, Chief Claremore II. The six men included Chief Claremore's son, Bad-Tempered-Buffalo, Wa-Na-Sha-Shi'n (Little-Eagle-That-Gets-What-He-Wants), of the Eagle Clan, and four others. The missionaries from Union Mission canoed down the Neosho (Grand) to witness the surrender of the six Osages. Mathews wrote that the missionaries were deeply impressed and quoted the following from the Union Mission Journal:

> "... to see six brave men come forward, and voluntarily submit to become prisoners; to be put in irons; and sent away to be tried for their lives; to see this done

with firmness and decision, by the unanimous consent of the Nation, and without a single sign from their affectionate wives ... to see the senses of honor manifested on the part of the criminals, and the desire to do justice in the Nation, was indeed affecting to every spectator."[36]

One of the six Osages escaped while the group was being taken to Little Rock under a military guard. The remaining five were tried there in November. Three of them were acquitted, but Bad-Tempered-Buffalo and Little-Eagle-That-Gets-What-He-Wants were convicted of the murder of Major Welborn and sentenced to be hanged in December. Their executions were postponed, however, and President John Quincy Adams pardoned the two men on March 21, 1825, one of his first acts as President after being inaugurated on March 4, 1825. The Osages were set free in May. This incident again serves to illustrate the valuable services that Nathaniel Pryor performed on behalf of the Osages and the whites as a spokesman, peacemaker and conciliator.

Establishment of Hopefield Mission (December 1823)

In December of 1823, Missionaries Chapman and Requa of Union Mission established a new Osage mission station, named Hopefield, about four miles up the Neosho (Grand) River from the Union Mission. This Hopefield Mission was just across the river from Pryor's trading post on Pryor Creek.[37] Subsequently, because of floods, cholera and other troubles, Hopefield Mission was moved first to a site near present Pensecola, Oklahoma in 1830 and then to Labette County, Kansas in 1837.[38]

One of these missionaries to the Osages wrote about another time where they had trouble with Cherokee raiders. Pryor had advised the missionaries and their Osage converts to remove themselves from Hopefield and go to Union Mission for their safety. Pryor then helped to facilitate a solution with the Cherokees so that the missionaries and their flock were able to return to Hopefield.[39] It has not been determined as to whether this incident occurred at Hopefield Mission #1, before 1830, or at Hopefield Mission #2.

The Osage Treaties of 1825

The United States and the Osages entered into two important treaties in 1825. The first treaty signed in St. Louis, ceded additional Osage lands to the United States. It also sought to establish a neutral buffer zone between the Osage villages in Kansas and the western border of Missouri. Known as the Osage Neutral Lands, the zone was 25 miles wide, east to west and fifty miles long, north to south.[40] Although theoretically a good idea, in practice this experiment never worked. Intruders quickly settled in the lands illegally and the United States did not enforce the terms of the treaty. A final insult to the Osages was that although the Osage Neutral Lands were created from land donated by the Osages, the zone was later given to the Cherokees by the United States without compensation to the Osages.

In addition to the large cession of Osage lands to the United States, Article Six of the Treaty did set aside 54 sections of Osage land to be sold to establish an education fund to be used to educate the Osages. Unfortunately, this good idea also resulted in dilatory application by the United States and even malfeasance on the part of some of the American officials administering the fund.

Article Four of the Treaty sought to provide livestock and agricultural implements to the Osages, but the Osages were not yet interested in those pursuits. As Louis Burns noted, it was still possible for an Osage to trade one buffalo skin for a year's supply of corn. Articles Seven, Eight and Nine basically dealt with claims against the Osages and resolved them in the claimants' favor. Article Ten did away with the Harmony and Union Missions, replacing them with a smaller Osage Mission on the Osage lands in Kansas.

Osage Treaty of 1825. © Michael Wimmer, courtesy of the artist.

It does not appear that Nat Pryor participated in negotiating the Treaty of 1825. Claremore II was one of the Osage Chiefs who signed the Treaty with William Clark as Superintendent of Indian Affairs. Pierre Chouteau, the Osage Indian Agent, was also present at the signing.

The second Osage Treaty of 1825 is known as the Council Grove Treaty and basically provided for the opening of the Santa Fe Trail. It does not appear that any of the Osage Chiefs from the Arkansas Territory participated in this treaty.[41]

Pryor's Gold-Seeking Expedition (Circa 1826)

Another article in *The Chronicles of Oklahoma* described an expedition led by Nathaniel Pryor to look for gold along the Arkansas River in what is now eastern Oklahoma and southern Kansas in 1826. The following is an excerpt from the article: "Led by Nathaniel Pryor, a member of the Lewis and Clark expedition and then a trader near Gibson, the party searched for several weeks without luck and finally returned home empty handed …

He [Jesse Chisholm] joined a group of 20 white frontiersmen and military men on a gold seeking expedition up the Arkansas into Kansas—country dominated by roving bands of Osages and Pawnees—still unknown and dangerous."[42] This unsuccessful expedition was no doubt pursuing the myth of lost gold mines and treasure supposedly buried by the earlier Spaniards under attack by the Indians. Despite the perilous presence of the Indians, many frontiersmen persisted in looking for the rumored treasures of lost Spanish gold mines in the southwest.

Jesse Chisholm (1805–1868) is the important cattleman for whom the Chisholm Trail was named. Chisholm's mother was a Cherokee. He came to the Indian Territory at least by 1826, at the age of 21. The first mention of him is at Cantonment Gibson

Osage Chief Black Dog, Drawing by Richard Florence from illustrations in Tracing the Ancient Paths, Kansas City Star Magazine, *April 16, 2006, by Terri Baumgardner.*

and he established a trading post near that area in the 1830s prior to getting into the ranching and cattle business. The presence of Jesse Chisholm with Pryor on this gold-seeking expedition adds another illustrious personage with whom Nathaniel Pryor had contact.[43]

Capt. Nathaniel Pryor Helps Settle a Dispute Between Osages and Cherokees

In late 1826 or early 1827, a raiding party of the Osages had killed several Cherokees. The Cherokees sent a party of about twenty-five warriors to even the score and they arrived near Union Mission. The war party was intercepted near Fort Gibson and Walter Webber, "with the influence of Captain Nathaniel Pryor, succeeded in preventing them from making the attack."[44] Later, the Cherokees "prevailed upon their mutual friend Captain Nathaniel Pryor to go to the Osage Nation to counsel with them" on peace negotiations between the tribes.[45] The Cherokees had Pryor convey that "they wished to come to a lasting peace, to bury the tomahawk and become neighbors and friends—'that when we meet, we can smoke together and shake hands as Brothers.'"[46] Presumably this was accomplished.

Capt. Pryor Helps Retrieve Osage Prisoners From the Choctaws

There had been long-standing hostility between the Osage and Choctaw tribes. At some time during the mid-1820s, Pryor was able to work out the differences between the tribes by working with William L. McClellan, the Indian Agent for the Choctaws. At the time, McClellan reported that some of the Choctaws had crossed the Mississippi River and located along the Red River where they had taken some Osage prisoners. McClellan recommended that Pryor be appointed as the agent for the Osage and that Pryor and some Osage chiefs accompany him to the Red

River to obtain the release of the captives. Pryor and McClellan were evidently successful in these peace negotiations, which greatly facilitated the westward migration of the Choctaws.[47]

Fort Gibson Celebrates Independence Day (1827)

An interesting episode in Pryor's life was the celebration of the 4th of July in 1827, at nearby Fort Gibson. The Commandant's wife described the mood and life of the times as follows:

> "The 4th of July was celebrated at Fort Gibson with a banquet at which thirteen toasts were drunk. Many men celebrated in this section responded to toasts: among them, Colonel Nicks, Captain Nathaniel Pryor, ... and Col. A. P. Chouteau. Life was very monotonous at this western post but there were a few diversions, which included a race track at Fort Gibson. Colonel Chouteau had a private track at his baronial estate on Grand River (the Neosho) where races were run and he entertained the army officers lavishly. Poker parties were frequent and betting was high."[48]

Osage Conflicts With Nearby Tribes

There was continual strife between the Osage Indians and the eastern tribes being resettled into the land of the Osage. Understandably, the Osage resented these intrusions into their lands. In an article about the history of Fort Gibson, Charles W. Sasser enumerated several serious fights between the Osages on one hand and the Choctaws, Cherokees, Delawares, Pawnees and/or Comanches on the other.[49] Thus Sasser mentions the killing of several Osage warriors by a force of Cherokees and Delawares near the Red River in January of 1827. Pawnees threatened the area in the summer of 1828 when they killed and scalped two soldiers. The soldiers retaliated by tracking the Pawnee war party

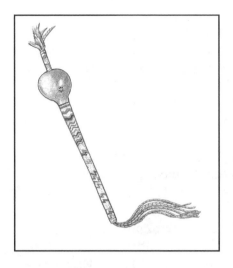

Osage Peyote Gourd Rattle, Drawing by Richard Florence from photo in Art of the Osage, St. Louis Art Museum and Univ. of Washington Press, 2004.

and killing seven of their braves. In that same summer, it was reported that 1,500 Comanche warriors threatened to drive the whites away from the area. A major battle between the Pawnees and the Osages occurred in the autumn of 1830 when the Osages killed eighteen Pawnee warriors, suffering the loss of only two Osage braves. The Pawnees returned in force the following spring forcing the Osages to seek the protection of Fort Gibson. Although Nat Pryor is not mentioned in the Sasser article, it may be assumed that Pryor's services in negotiating on behalf of the Osages were required frequently.

Pryor Visits the Osages on the Kansas Neosho (1828)

On August 25, 1828, Chief White Hair II (Pa-hu-ska) and three other Osage leaders signed a letter at White Hair's Town requesting the removal of the Rev. Benton Pixley from the Osage Mission on the Kansas Neosho. Louis Burns has provided a full copy of this letter, showing that it was: "Signed in presence of P.L. Chouteau, sub-agent, N. Pryor, sub-agent, and B. Morgan, interpreter."[50]

At the time of this 1828 letter (and from 1822 to 1833), White Hair's Town was across the Neosho River just west of the present town of Shaw, in Neosho County, Kansas, about 110 miles up the Neosho from its mouth in the Three Forks area.[51] White Hair's Town was the beginning reference point for the eastern boundary of the Osage Reservation that was created by the

Treaty of 1825. By 1827, the headquarters of Osage Agent John F. Hamtramck, the first resident agent of the Osages, was on the right bank a half-mile from the Neosho at the site of White Hair's Town.[52]

P.L. Chouteau was Paul Ligueste Chouteau, the youngest son of Pierre Chouteau. Paul had obtained an Osage trading license in 1816; had since lived among the Osages; had been an Osage sub-agent since 1818; and in 1828 established his trading house at White Hair's Town. In 1830, Hamtramck was dismissed as the Osage Agent and Paul Ligueste Chouteau was appointed to replace him.[53]

"B. Morgan" in the 1828 letter was Baptiste Mogray or Monrain (a/k/a Jean Baptiste Mongrain), a grandson of White Hair I. Baptiste subsequently moved to a second White Hair's Town established six miles south of the first one. In April 1827 Baptiste Mongrain was hired as the interpreter at the Osage Agency on the Kansas Neosho. He continued as the appointed interpreter there for many years, and by 1840 was a major Osage chief at the second White Hair's Town.[54] Baptiste Mongrain's daughter Mary later married Nathaniel Pryor's Osage son, William (Quiver) Pryor.

Notes

1. Stanley, *Spanish Domination*, p. 394.
2. James, Thomas S.—*Three Years Among the Mexicans and Indians*, Missouri Historical Society, 1916, on-line at: http://www.xmission.com/~drudy/mtman/html/Jamesint.html.
3. *Ibid*, Ch, 1.
4. *Ibid*.
5. Crosby, Mike—*Joined by a Journey*, pp. 81–84.
6. Barry, *Beginning of the West*, pp. 96, 98, 68–69; Shoemaker, *Many Faces*, p. 50. Gen. Thomas James had been a member of the St. Louis Missouri Fur Company expedition up the Missouri River in

1809 that safely returned Chief Sheheke to his Mandan village. James then continued up the Missouri and spent the winter of 1809–10 trapping beaver near Three Forks, Montana, with Manuel Lisa and John Colter. From 1812–14, James was engaged in river trade and transport between St. Louis and Pittsburgh. Colter-Frick, *Courageous Colter*, pp. 10–14, 220–246; Christian, *Before Lewis and Clark*, p. 167.

7. Shoemaker, *Many Faces*, p. 50 (this and following information about the James expedition).

8. Barry, *Beginning of the West*, pp. 96–97.

9. Stanley, *Spanish Domination*, pp. 391–398, and *Mexican Rule*, pp. 32–35.

10. Stanley, *Mexican Rule*, p. 34.

11. James, *Three Years*, on-line, Ch. 4.

12. *Ibid*, on-line, Ch. 3.

13. Thoburn-Wright, *Oklahoma*, p. 86, n.35; Barry, *Beginning of the West*, p. 78.

14. Thoburn-Wright, *Oklahoma*, p. 86.

15. Barry, *Beginning of the West*, pp. 92–93.

16. Barry, *Beginning of the West*, pp. 97–98, citing Elliot Coues, *The Journal of Jacob Fowler*, (New York, 1898) and later edition (U. of Nebraska Press, Lincoln, 1970), pp. 3–4.

17. Coues, Elliott, ed., *The Journal of Jacob Fowler*, with additional notes by Raymond W. and Mary Lund Settle and Harry R. Stevens, U Nebraska Press, Lincoln, (1970), pp. 16–17.

18. Barry, *Beginning of the West*, p. 98; Smith, *supra*, pp. 403–04.

19. Shoemaker, *Many Faces*, pp. 50–51.

20. Unfortunately, the Shoemaker article in *True West* magazine does not contain citations. In 1999, I attempted to obtain clarification of this passage and wrote to Mr. Shoemaker c/o *True West* and c/o the Mayes County, Oklahoma Historical Society, but did not receive a reply.

21. Letter from Mrs. William (Betty Lou) Thomas, of the Mayes County, Oklahoma Historical Society, to author, dated September 28, 1999.

22. Coues, *Jacob Fowler*, pp. 17–18.

23. *Ibid*, at p. 18, for this and the subsequent information here about Nathaniel Miguel Pryor.

24. An interesting account of the Patties and their travels has been written by Dennis Goodman, in the Westerners section of *Wild West* magazine, June 2005, pp. 12, 67–68.

25. Coues, *Jacob Fowler*, at note 193, at p.62, citing the "Union Mission Journal," *American Missionary Register, II*, [May 1822}, 431, 432.

26. James, *Three Years*, on-line, Ch. 5.

27. Barry, *Beginning of the West*, p. 404; Smith, *supra*, p. 404.

28. *Ibid*.

29. Masterson, *supra*, p. 114, n.3.

30. *Baltimore Patriot*, February 6, 1822, Vol. XIX, Iss. 29, p. [3].

31. Barry, *Beginning of the West*, p. 113; Mathews, *The Osages*, pp. 434, 502.

32. Mathews, *The Osages*, pp. 504–06.

33. Mathews, *The Osages*, pp. 432–33, 506. This meeting at Fort Smith was in December of 1823, not 1824, as mistakenly written by Mathews.

34. This and subsequent information about this incident from: Mathews, *The Osages*, pp. 507–10; Thoburn-Wright, *Oklahoma*, p. 86; and, Barry, *Beginning of the West*, p. 113. Gen. Winfield Scott was later one of the heroes of the War with Mexico and later the Commanding General of the U.S. Army, when he was known as "Old Fuss 'N Feathers."

35. Frazier, Robert W.—*Forts of the West*, (U. Okla. Press, Norman, 1965), pp. 119–20; Thoburn-Wright, *Oklahoma*, p. 86.

36. Mathews, *The Osages*, p. 509.

37. Barry, *Beginning of the West*, pp. 113–4, citing several sources.

38. Barry, *Beginning of the West*, pp. 171, 184; Burns, *Osage People*, pp. 171, 300, 319–20.

39. Foreman, Carolyn Thomas—*Hopefield Mission in Osage Nation, 1823–1837, The Chronicles of Oklahoma*, Vol. 28, p. 198, 1950.

40. Burns, *Osage People*, (2nd ed.), pp. 160–164. The material set forth in the text is from these cited pages.

41. *Ibid*, p. 165.

42. *The Chronicles of Oklahoma*, Vol. 66, p. 354, 1988.

43. *Ibid.*

44. Foreman, Carolyn Thomas—*Early History of Webbers Falls, The Chronicles of Oklahoma*, Vol. 29, p. 444, 1951.

45. *Ibid.*

46. *Ibid.*

47. Pickett, Ben Collins—*William L. McClellan, Choctaw Indian Agent, West, The Chronicles of Oklahoma*, Vol. 39, p. 48, 1961–62.

48. *Celebrating the 4th of July at Ft. Gibson, 1827, The Chronicles of Oklahoma*, Vol. 46, p. 206, 1968. Col. John Nicks was the sutler at Cantonment Gibson. See discussion at note 4 of Chapter 8.

49. Sasser, Charles W.—*Fort Gibson—Graveyard of the Army*, Old West, Winter, 1984, pp. 38–43.

50. Burns *Osage People* (1989 ed.), p. 303; Burns *Osage People* (2004 ed.), p. 224.

51. Burns, *Osage People* (2004 ed.), p. 58.

52. Barry, *Beginning of the West*, pp. 120, 139.

53. Barry, *Beginning of the West*, pp. 75–76, 95, 107–108, 138; Christian, *Before Lewis and Clark*, pp. 315–16.

54. Burns, *Osage People* (2004 ed.), pp. 54, 58, 156, 325; Barry, *Beginning of the West*, pp. 120, 138, 221, 245; Christian, *Before Lewis and Clark* pp. 160–161.

10

THE LAST DAYS OF CAPTAIN NATHANIEL HALE PRYOR

During the early 1820s, Nat Pryor served without pay as the unofficial agent or subagent of the Osages. Several of his influential friends, besides the Choctaw Agent McMillan, attempted to get him appointed as the official agent for the Osages. William Clark wrote a recommendation letter on his behalf.[1] In a letter to Secretary of War James Barbour dated August 4, 1827, in support of Pryor's possible appointment to the Osage sub-agency, Clark mentioned that: "As the situation of the [Osage] Band requires a Sub Agent of respectability and influence, I have employed Capt'n Nathaniel Pryor, at the rate of $500 pr ann. and given him a temporary appointment of Sub Agent."[2] We do not know if this payment to Pryor continued until his death, or just during periods in which the sub-agency was vacant. In 1830 the government began moving eastern Indians to eastern Oklahoma areas in ever-increasing numbers. On May 28, 1830, President Jackson signed the controversial Indian Removal Act, which passed the House by the narrow margin of 102 to 97. This Act authorized the President to exchange public land to the West of Missouri and Arkansas Territory for Indian lands in the East, with

Osage Owl Fan by Julia Pryor Mongrain Lookout, Drawing by Richard Florence from photo in Art of the Osage, *St. Louis Art Museum and Univ. of Washington Press, 2004.*

the consequent removal of the Eastern Indian tribes to the Western lands.

On September 27, 1830, by the Treaty of Dancing Rabbit Creek, the Choctaws ceded all of their land east of the Mississippi, consisting of 10,423,130 acres, and agreed to move more than 5,000 of their people to lands in eastern Oklahoma. This was the first removal negotiated with one of the so-called "Five Civilized Tribes," the Cherokee, Chickasaw, Choctaw, Creek and Seminole Tribes.[3]

Nat Pryor developed a friendship with Sam Houston, whom he may have known during their military service in the War of 1812. Houston had been an U.S. Congressman from Tennessee (1823–27); the Governor of Tennessee (1827–29); and later would become President of the Republic of Texas (1836–38 and 1841–44). In April 1829 Houston resigned as Governor of Tennessee, shortly after the dissolution of his marriage, and sought refuge in the Three Forks area with his adoptive father from his teen years, Cherokee Chief John Jolly. Houston reached Fort Gibson by May 29 and built his "Wigwam Neosho" trading post midway between the Grand/Neosho and Verdigris Rivers, about three miles from Fort Gibson and about 30 miles from Pryor's trading post that was at Pryor Creek by that time. Except for trips to Washington in aid of his Indian friends, Houston remained in the Three Forks area until 1832, when President Jackson sent him to Texas [then a province of Mexico] to negotiate Indian treaties for the protection of U.S. traders near the Mexican border.

While living in the Three Forks area, Houston wrote a poignant letter to President Andrew Jackson, dated December 15, 1830, in which he wrote:

Sam Houston and Nathaniel Pryor at Three Forks. © Michael Wimmer, courtesy of the artist.

"I have the honor to address you upon the subject of one of your old soldiers at the Battle of New Orleans. I allude to Capt. Nathaniel Pryor, who has for several years past, resided with the Osages as a sub-agent, by appointment of Gov. Clark, but without any permanent appointment from the Government ... He was the first man who volunteered to accompany Lewis and Clark on their tour to the Pacific Ocean ... at the commencement of the last war entered the Army again and was a Captain in the 44th Regiment under you at New Orleans; and a *braver* man never fought under the wings of your Eagles. [Emphasis is Houston's]. He has done more to tame and pacificate the dispositions of the Osages to the whites, and surrounding tribes of Indians than all other men and has done more in promoting the authority of the

U. States and compelling the Osages to comply with
demands from Colonel Arbuckle [the commander of Fort
Gibson] than any person could have supposed. Capt.
Pryor is a man of amiable character and disposition—
of fine sense, strict honor—perfectly temperate in his
habits—and unremitting in his attention to business".[4]

That is very high praise indeed for Nathaniel Pryor from one
of America's greatest heroes.

Also on December 15, 1830, Sam Houston wrote a letter on
Pryor's behalf to General John H. Eaton, the Secretary of War. In
it, he wrote:

"It is impossible for me ever to wish or solicit any
patronage from the Government for myself or anyone
connected with me, but when I see a *brave, honest, hon-*
orable and faithful servant of that country which I once
claimed as my own, in poverty with spirit half broken
by neglect, I must be permitted to ask something in his
behalf! [Emphasis is Houston's].

Could any just man know him as I do, who had
power to offer reparation for what he has done for
his country, what he has suffered, I am sure he would
not be allowed to languish in circumstances hardly
comfortable. I trust in God that he will be no longer
neglected by his country."[5]

Obviously seeing Pryor as neglected and unrewarded by his
country, Houston almost saw Pryor as a victim. Perhaps it was
seeing Pryor in such circumstances that convinced Houston not
to play out the rest of his life as a trader at an Indian trading post
on the Cherokee Reservation. We have no way of knowing
whether Pryor viewed himself as a victim or was in any way bitter toward the government in Washington. Nathaniel Pryor certainly viewed the Osages as victims. He wrote a touching letter to
his former Expedition Captain, William Clark, dated January 22,

1831.[6] Pryor was still just the unofficial subagent for the Osages and Clark was his reporting superior as the Superintendent of Indian Affairs. In regard to the Osage villages on the Verdigris (in present Oklahoma), Pryor perceptively reported that:

> "... the Osages appear to be a very unhappy people, and I think it is altogether attributable to the emigration of so many Red People to the West. The Game is entirely destroyed and they see that they must now cultivate the soil for a subsistence. They are extremely poor and they feel their inability to do any thing for themselves without the assistance of the Govt who, they are anxious would enable them to commence farming by furnishing them with the necessary means, and would like to have among them persons to instruct their young to spin and weave."[7]

When he wrote this letter, Pryor had an Osage wife and four half-Osage, minor children, ages about 6, 8, 10 and 12. Pryor had been trading with and living among the Osages for at least fourteen years, during which time he had participated with and counseled the Osage chiefs and leaders in all of their important decision-making councils. He had never been compensated by the U.S. Government for his many efforts on behalf of the United States and the Osage Nation.

Pryor's assessment of the dire situation facing the Osages was very accurate. In a letter to Clark written two days before Pryor's letter, Osage Agent Paul Liguest Chouteau requested that the principal Osage Agency on the Kansas Neosho be moved, for the most remarkably stated reason that:

> "The Agency at present is surrounded by Indian villages, some within half a mile, consequently the crying of the Indians for lost relations the morning and evening (which is a religious ceremony amongst them) makes it very unpleasant to myself and my family."[8]

Of this time in the beginning of the removal of Indians to the West, author Landon Jones has written that:

> "The Indian agents were overwhelmed by the scale of the tragedy unfolding around them. Clark pleaded for budgetary relief from Washington but instead was told to cut his expenses."[9]

During the winter of 1830–31, Nathaniel Pryor contracted some sort of illness, probably a form of pneumonia. In a letter to P.L. Chouteau, then the official U.S. Osage Agent, dated February 6, 1831, written from Cantonment Gibson, Pryor wrote: "I have been confined by sickness at this post for five or six weeks and am not yet sufficiently recovered to return home."[10] In a second letter to Chouteau, written on February 19, 1831, from Union Mission, Pryor wrote: "When I last wrote you I expected to return home before this time … . This has been prevented by the continuance of my bad health. I am now somewhat recovered, hope soon to be restored to good health."[11]

It is very possible that Nathaniel Pryor's illness may have been a severe case of Influenza. Louis Burns noted that the Osages suffered a severe flu epidemic during 1829–1831 from which hundreds died.[12] Perhaps Nathaniel Pryor was one of the unfortunate victims.

In a letter to "Capt. N. Pryor" dated 4 April 1831, Chouteau informed Pryor that the letter would be delivered by Major D.D. McNair, Sub Agent for the Osages, "who visits your post by my directions in order to obtain information relative to the present State of existing difficulties between Clermont's Band of Osages and the Cherokees, and to make the necessary arrangements for contemplated meeting of those tribes at Cantonment Gibson on the 1st and 5th of May next."[13]

On May 7, 1831, Nathaniel Pryor, "stationed at Cantonment Gibson," was officially appointed as the permanent sub-agent for the Osages of the Verdigris (Clermont's band, i.e., Claremore's), and attached to the Osage agency under P.L. Chouteau, at an annual salary of $500.[14] It is unclear whether this $500 was to be an annual salary or a one-time payment, or if Pryor or his heirs ever received any part of the salary.

On May 10, 1831, Captain Pryor, as a witness, signed a treaty between the Creeks and all bands of the Osage Nation, at Cantonment Gibson.[15] The *Arkansas Gazette* credited Nathaniel Pryor, among others, for their "zeal and industry" in reconciling the differences between the tribes.

Pryor was in failing health, however, and died on June 9, 1831. He was buried without ceremony on his own land near his trading post on Pryor Creek, about seven miles southeast of the town of Pryor, in present Mayes County, Oklahoma. Similar to the burial of his cousin, Sergeant Charles Floyd, Pryor's original grave marker was evidently lost and his grave was forgotten. The Oklahoma Historical Society appointed a committee to locate the grave, which was done on April 10, 1934. The committee reported that it:

> "... proceeded to the old home site occupied by
> Nathaniel Pryor, at which he died and was buried ...
> The remains of the old log cabin once occupied by him
> can be identified. There was nothing to mark the grave,
> but it was in a cultivated field which had been plowed
> over ... Mr. George W. Mayes lived on the place with
> his father in his boyhood and knew the location of the
> grave. ... He located the spot for us and we put up a
> post and had some stones placed around it so as not
> to lose the location."[16]

After locating the grave, the Oklahoma Historical Society was directed to apply to the War Department for a permanent marker for the grave of Nathaniel Pryor, which was done. In 1982, his remains were exhumed and reburied under a beautiful granite memorial slab in the Fairview Cemetery at his namesake town of Pryor, Mayes County, Oklahoma. The War Department's 1934 marker from the original grave is also a part of the monument.

Pryor's probate estate may have been filed initially at Fort Smith, then the County Seat of Crawford County, Arkansas Terri-

Grave and Monument of Nathaniel Hale Pryor, Fairview Cemetery, Pryor, OK. Photo by James C. Mordy, November, 2004.

tory. If so, those records were no doubt lost when the Crawford County Court House was destroyed by fire in 1878.[17] Larry Morris wrote that Pryor's estate probate proceedings began in St. Louis in December of 1831.[18] Shoemaker wrote that the proceedings listed Pryor's still pending claim for his losses of $5,216.25 at his Galena lead smelter and trading house as the major portion of his estate. Also that Pryor's heirs received notice a year after his death that the claim had been disallowed.[19] The author has reviewed the probate papers, filed in St. Louis, which state only that Pryor died intestate, without a will, had no known heirs and had no real or personal property except as listed in the Inventory. No real or personal property was listed. Thomas Ingram, Jr. was originally appointed as the Administrator of the Estate, but he was later replaced by John P. Reily.[20] Each Administrator filed basically identical Inventories. The only asset listed was a cash payment of $215.46 received from "Gen'l W. Clark." A claim was filed by Abraham Gallatin in the amount of $5,750, evidently for the cost of merchandise furnished to Pryor in 1811 and lost when the Winnebagos attacked Pryor' trading post and lead smelter at Toledo Mort.[21]

There is no explanation for the payment from William Clark listed in Pryor's probate records. It may be that the payment was a prorated amount of Pryor's sub-agency salary of $500 per year, but that would mean that Pryor's appointment as the Osage sub-agent just a month before his death was retroactively effective to almost the first of the year, or that Clark had continued to pay Pryor as an unofficial sub-agent. It is also curious that no heirs or real or personal property are listed. Clark should have known that Pryor did have heirs, as well as real and personal property at his trading post on Pryor Creek. It may be conjecture, but the author believes that Clark and Gallatin knew that Pryor's damage claim was still pending and they thought that if the claim were allowed, Gallatin would be able to recoup some of his investment. There remains the possibility that there was another probate of Pryor's real and personal property at Ft. Smith, Arkansas that would have had jurisdiction over Pryor's real and personal property at Pryor Creek. If there was another probate filed at Ft. Smith, those records apparently were lost in the fire of 1878.

Nathaniel Pryor's Osage Wife, Children and Descendants

By 1817, Nathaniel Pryor had married Ah Sin Ka, who, as discussed above, was either the sister or aunt of Chief Claremore II.[22] Nat and Ah Sin Ka were the parents of three daughters and a son: Marie, born in 1818; Wa Hula Sha, born in 1820; William (Quiver), born in 1822; and Mary Jane, born in 1824.[23] Although the Osage genealogy on the lines of descent from Nathaniel and Ah-Sin-Ka are not complete at this time, it appears that there are no surviving descendants from Marie and Mary Jane Pryor, although both married. There are strong lines of descent from William (Quiver) Pryor and his sister, Wa Hula Sha Pryor. Those lines are set forth in the attached pages of exhibits in Appendix A.[24]

Claremore III, Drawing by Richard Florence from painting by George Catlin of Clermont, son of Claremore II, the Town Maker, original at the Missouri Historical Society, St. Louis, Missouri.

Some ten years after his death in 1831, Pryor's widow and two of his daughters were baptized at St. Mary's Mission, near Marmaton, Kansas, probably in present Bourbon County, Kansas.[25] This would have been about 120 miles north of Nathaniel's Pryor Creek trading house. Church baptismal records record the baptisms of: "Mary Jane, daughter of Capt. Pryor and Osage woman" on November 11, 1841, aged 17 years; of "Capt. Pryor's Osinga" on the same date, aged 55 years; and of "Marie Prior" [sic] on September 1, 1842, age 24.[26] These dates and ages have been used to approximate the birth years for Marie and Mary Jane and to put the marriage of Nathaniel to Asinga at least by early December, 1817, after allowance of a nine month gestation period.

Six days after her baptism, Mary Jane Pryor married Francis St. Michel. Father Herman G. Aelen, S.J., "near Marmiton (now

Marmaton) River," consecrated the marriage on November 17, 1841, again probably in present Bourbon County, Kansas.[27] Four years later, on June 20, 1845, Pelagie, a daughter of "Francois Michel" and "Marie Jeanne Prior", born on October 13, 1844, was baptized by Father Felix L. Verreydt, S.J.[28] We have no further definite information regarding Pelagie Michel.

Two other marriages occurred on the same date as the marriage of Mary Jane Pryor to Francis St. Michel in 1841. That day, Father Aelen also performed the marriages of Louis Peltier to Angelique Osinga and of Charles Cardinal to Angelique Wot-Sing-a. One is tempted to conjecture that one of these brides may have been Asinga [Ah-Sin-Ka], the widow of Nathaniel Pryor. Another explanation is that "Osinga" and "Wot-Sing-a" were just the Catholic Priests' practice of identifying the Indian brides by the white men's generic term for "Osage Woman."[29] "Angelique" (little angel in French) was simply a generic term of endearment, not a given birth name.

Nathaniel's oldest daughter, Marie Pryor married a Charles Mongrain, probably a son of Noel Mongrain, but to date no records have been found regarding their marriage. The date of the marriage of Marie Pryor to Charles Mongrain is unknown. Nothing further is known about Marie Pryor and Charles Mongrain.

The Mongrain family had been traders and settlers in the area of the Missouri-Kansas Osage for many years. The Mongrains became closely associated with the Pryors. Nathaniel Pryor's only son, William (Quiver) Pryor, married Mary Mongrain. Mary's Grandfather, Noel Mongrain, served as an interpreter for Pierre Chouteau when Chouteau first came to the Osage area in Missouri. Noel Mongrain's wife was Pa Hu Shan, a daughter of the famous Chief Pawhuska (also known as "White Hair") of the Osage. As discussed above, Mary Mongrain's father, Jean Baptiste Mongrain, one of the older sons of Noel Mongrain, was an interpreter at the Osage Agency on the Kansas Neosho between 1827 and 1833, and was an Osage chief by 1840. William (Quiver) Pryor's daughter, Mary Pryor, married Steve Mongrain, so the relationship between the two families continued for some time. The line from this marriage has continued to the present day.

Space does not permit a complete listing of the accomplishments of the Osage descendants of Nathaniel Pryor but a few notable achievements will be presented. Chief James Bigheart (1837–1908) was a grandson of Nathaniel Pryor, a son of Wa Hula Sha Pryor and James Bigheart, Sr. The second James Bigheart was a very prominent Osage Chief in the late 1800s. In 1881, at a convention held at Pawhuska, Oklahoma Territory, the Osage Nation adopted a constitution for the organization of their tribal government, with a legislative council and a principal chief to be elected by the people, and a supreme court to be chosen by the council. James Bigheart served as president of this convention and was later elected a principal chief of the Osage.[30]

Under the General Indian Allotment Act of 1887 the Osages were exempt from its provisions regarding the division and allotment of common tribal lands to individual tribal members in severalty (permitting individual ownership with a fee simple title). The Osages were also exempt from the opening of surplus lands on the reservations to white settlement, which called instead for a special agreement between the United States and the Osage Nation. During June of 1893 members of the Cherokee Commission met at the Osage tribal "Round House" near Pawhuska and sought to extract such an agreement from the Osage. Chief James Bigheart and Black Dog, the heads of a committee representing the full-blooded members of the tribe, presented their objections, asserting that they could not consent

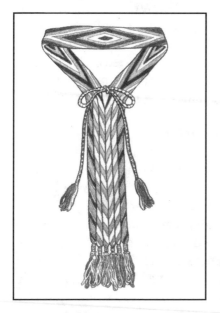

Osage Belt by Julia Pryor Mongrain Lookout, Drawing by Richard Florence from photo in Art of the Osage, *St. Louis Art Museum and Univ. of Washington Press, 2004.*

to the allotment and division of tribal lands on the basis of the existing tribal roll, since it contained the names of a number of persons who had no right to be on that roll.[31] The Osage Nation successfully resisted this realignment and in March 1896 an oil and gas lease covering the entire Osage Reservation was signed by Edwin B. Foster of the Osage Council and by Chief James Bigheart. As a result of the consequent oil exploration and production, the Osage were probably the wealthiest Indian Tribe prior to the advent of casinos.

In 2004, the Saint Louis Art Museum displayed a major special exhibit entitled "Art of the Osage." The Museum also published a book by that name containing excellent articles describing Osage history, customs, art, dances and religion, with beautiful color photographs of the numerous items in the exhibit.[32] Just inside the entrance to this exhibit, the first poster panel included a photograph of Rose Pryor and her husband, Henry Red Eagle. Another photograph of several Osage women included Julia Pryor Mongrain Lookout. Rose Pryor and Julia Pryor Mongrain Lookout were grandchildren of Nathaniel Pryor.

The very first item of the St. Louis Osage exhibit was a marvelous pair of beaded moccasins made about 1915 by Julia Pryor Mongrain Lookout. She was described in the exhibit caption and in the accompanying book as "one of the most prominent Osage artists of the twentieth century." Julia wore these moccasins in 1924 during special ceremonies at Pawhuska that recognized Osage participation in World War I and

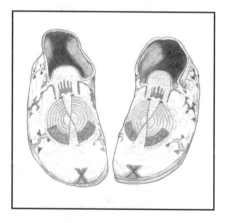

Moccasins made by Julia Pryor Mongrain Lookout for a special ceremony in 1924 honoring the participation of the Osages in World War I. Drawing by Richard Florence from photo in Art of the Osage, *St. Louis Art Museum and Univ. of Washington Press, 2004.*

included the presentation of a certificate of appreciation signed by President Coolidge.[33] Other items in the exhibit associated with Julia Lookout were a beaded and feathered bonnet worn by her at the beginning of Soldier Dance ceremonies; a playcoat made by her for her grandson; a beaded belt she made for her husband; a peyote gourd rattle; and an Owl fan used by the Osage Black Bear Clan priest, Steven Mongrain, the husband of Nat Pryor's daughter Mary.

The author has not discovered much "family lore" about Nathaniel Pryor, but one of the author's Osage cousins has told him that it was known that Pryor supposedly preferred the meat of a dog to that of other choices available to him and the Osages. It is true that the beloved canines had played an important role in both native and American history. Before the introduction of the horse, the dog was the only domesticated animal known to the Plains Indians. The dogs were trained to pull small travois, which would carry the food and implements necessary for the daily life of the nomadic tribes. The Indians also held spiritual ceremonies where the dogs were sometimes sacrificed and consumed. Perhaps Nathaniel Pryor acquired this taste when, at his first meeting with the Yankton Sioux, they dined on a fat dog. Many of the members of the Lewis and Clark Corps of Discovery acquired a taste for dog meat and traded the Indians for it when little game was available. Many of the men evidently preferred it to elk, deer, beaver, buffalo, and other wild game. It was said that only Clark himself abstained from eating dog meat. This is an interesting reflection as the author's great-grandfather, Martin V.B. Floyd, recalled "Osages, on the Black Dog Trail, trying to barter for 'doggie-meat,'" as they came through Sedan, Kansas during annual ritual migrations in the late 1800s.[34]This was of course prior to the discovery of oil, not to mention the advent of casinos. It is unfortunate that the author's Floyd family at Sedan, Kansas, about forty miles north of Pawhuska, did not discover their relationship to the Osage Pryors until 2004.

In recent years, the Red Eagle family descended from Nathaniel Hale Pryor has been prominent in the affairs and governance of the Osages. Henry Red Eagle was a principal chief in the early 1900s. His son Edward Red Eagle was an assistant chief until his death in 1999. His son, Edward Red Eagle, Jr., is the Director of the Osage Cultural Heritage Center. In the summer of 2004, the author was contacted by Edward Red Eagle, Jr. and another Osage cousin, Linda Thiry. This led to an exchange of correspondence and emails and finally a small reunion between the Pryor and Floyd family cousins in Bartlesville, OK, in November of 2004. We thought that this might have been the first reunion of these branches of the Pryor and Floyd families since at least 1815 at the Battle of New Orleans, or perhaps in 1804 at the death of Sgt. Floyd.

Reunion of Pryor and Floyd Descendants, Bartlesville, OK, November 2004. (left to right) James C. Mordy, Linda Thiry, Edward Red Eagle, Jr., John C. Floyd, Lawrence R. Reno. Author's photo.

Notes

1. Shoemaker, *Many Faces*, p. 51.

2. Douglas, *Documents*, pp. 260–261.

3. The infamous Trail of Tears, when the U.S. Army rounded up some 17,000 Cherokees in Georgia and Tennessee and marched them on foot to eastern Oklahoma, losing some 4,000 of them by death, occurred eight years later, during the winter of 1838–39.

4. Foreman, Grant, *Nathaniel Pryor*, at pp. 162–163. Clark was Governor of the Missouri Territory from 1813 to 1820 when Missouri became a state. Clark was defeated when he ran for Governor in the first state election held in Missouri.

5. *Ibid*, at p. 163.

6. Jones, *supra*, pp. 305–06; William Clark Papers, KSHS, 6:104.

7. *Ibid*.

8. Jones, *supra*, p. 306, citing letter from Paul Liquest Chouteau to Clark dated 20 Jan 1831; William Clark Papers, KHSS, 6-100-01.

9. Jones, *supra*, p. 306.

10. Douglas, *Documents*, p. 264.

11. *Ibid*.

12. Burns, *Osage People*, (2nd ed.), p. 239.

13. *Ibid*.

14. Douglas, *Documents*, p. 265.

15. *Ibid*.

16. Minutes, Board of Directors, October 25, 1934, *Chronicles of Oklahoma*, Vol. 12, p. 490 (1934).

17. Information from Col. Billy T. Cox of the Arkansas Society, Sons of the Revolution, on April 10, 2006, verified that there are no probate records for Nathaniel Pryor in the Arkansas State Archives at Little Rock, AR.

18. Morris, *Fate of the Corps*, p. 198, citing *Nathaniel Pryor documents, Meriwether Lewis papers, Missouri Historical Society*. The probate record located at the Missouri State Archives is referenced at Note 20, below.

19. Shoemaker, *Many Faces*, at p. 50; Foreman, Grant, *Nathaniel Pryor*, at p. 164.

20. Missouri State Archives, St. Louis County Case No. 00927, filed in 1833, #C27476.

21. *Ibid.* At the side of the claim is the notation of "1811, Dec. 31st," the day before the Winnebago raid. If Gallatin was trying to establish the date of his loss, perhaps he had the wrong date of the raid, or maybe the Winnebagos arrived on New Year's Eve instead of New Year's Day.

22. Asinga's name has been written as Ah Sin ka, Osinga, Osage Woman and Angelique. Some authors have written that the name means "Osage Woman", while others have written that the name means the "third" or "later daughter." See also notes 23 and 25 below.

23. Genealogical information furnished by Edward Red Eagle, Jr. and Linda Thiry, both of whom are Osage descendants of Nathaniel Pryor. Also, Middlebrooks and Harper, *Ancestry*, at p.303, citing church baptismal records from the St. Mary's Mission, Marmeton, Kansas, of the baptisms of "*Mary Jane*, daughter of Capt. Pryor and Osage woman" on November 11, 1841, aged 17 years; of "(Capt. Pryor's) Osinga, on the same date, aged 55 years; and of "*Marie Prior*" (sic) on September 1, 1842, aged 24. Also, *The Lewis & Clark Corps of Discovery, Their Lives and Their Lineage*, Clatsop County Genealogical Society (2004), Vol. I, pp. 496–509.

24. The author acknowledges the assistance and cooperation of Pryor Osage descendants Edward Red Eagle, Jr. and Linda Thiry in providing information regarding the Osage descendants of Nathaniel Pryor.

25. Surviving records of some births of part Osage children were kept by Jesuit and other Roman Catholic priests, who began traveling into the Indian country of western Missouri and eastern Kansas in 1822. Most of the white settlers in the area were Catholic holdovers of French or Spanish heritage, so they took their children by Indian women to the priests to be baptized. At times the priests would record the births as being illegitimate but more often than not they simply stated the names of the father and god-father. Unless the mother was part French and had a European first name, she was usually not identified, or was identified only as "Achinga," meaning Osage woman. Christian, *supra*, p. 307. Another Osage historian wrote that "Ah senka" was the Osage name for the third

daughter. Burns, Louis F.—*A History of the Osage People*, (Ciga Press, Fallbrook, CA, 1989), p. 426. Of course both of these spellings are additional variations of Asinga.

26. Middlebrooks and Harper, *Ancestry*, at p. 303, citing baptismal records from "the St. Mary's Mission, Marmeton, Kansas."

27. Barry, Louise—*The Beginning of the West*, (Kan. State Hist. Soc., Topeka, 1972), pp. 439–40, citing Pottawatomie Marriage Register (microfilm in K SHS).

28. Barry, *Beginning of the West*, p. 440. It is obvious that these are misspellings of the names of Francois St. Michel and Mary Jane Prior. It is also interesting to note that "Pelagie" was the first name of both a sister and of the mother of three Chouteau brothers with whom Nat Pryor had numerous contacts: Auguste Pierre (A.P.) Chouteau; Pierre (Cadet) Chouteau, Jr.; and, Paul Liguest Chouteau.

29. See p. 32, and notes 235 and 238, above.

30. Wright, *supra*, pp. 194–5.

31. Wright, *supra*, p. 195; Bailey and Swan, *below*, p. 138.

32. Bailey, Garrick and Swan, Daniel C.—*Art of the Osage*, (St. Louis Art Museum and U. of Wash. Press, Seattle, 2004).

33. Bailey and Swan, *Art of the Osage*, p. 187.

34. Kinnaman, *Ancestry*, pp. 8–9.

11

CONCLUSION

As discussed above, Nathaniel Pryor died on June 9, 1831, and was buried first on his property about seven miles southeast of Pryor, Oklahoma. Similar to his cousin, Sgt. Charles Floyd, Pryor was dug up and reburied at least once, the last time in 1982. A monument and marker have now been placed in his honor at his reburial in Pryor, Mayes County, Oklahoma. At the reburial of Pryor and the dedication of his Monument in 1982, three generations of his Osage descendants were reportedly present. They were: Margaret Spurrier Avant (a granddaughter of Chief James Bigheart, a grandson of Pryor); Margaret Iron, of Pawhuska, OK (the Tribal headquarters of the Osage); and Edward Red Eagle, Jr., of Tulsa, OK.[1] Margaret Avant stated that Nathaniel Pryor and the Osage woman Asinga (Ah Sin Ka) had three daughters, naming them as "Chief Bigheart's mother, Rosa Pryor Red Eagle and Julia Pryor Lookout." Rosa and Julia were probably grandchildren of Nat Pryor and Asinga [Ah-Sin-Ka], instead of being their children.[2] As shown above, Ms. Avant was somewhat in error as Nat and Asinga had three daughters and one son.[3] Ms. Avant omitted mention of Nathaniel Pryor's son, William (Quiver) Pryor.

Nathaniel Hale Pryor's Legacy and Place in History

One may consider various events that might have changed the course of history. For example, John Adams, as President, might have taken the United States into a war with France, as he was urged to do by many people. Without much doubt, such a war might have prevented Jefferson and Napoleon from arriving at the Louisiana Purchase deal and the western part of the United States might have remained part of a foreign power for a considerably longer time.

Considering Nathaniel Pryor's legacy and "what might have been" without him, we can review several chapters in his life, and rely primarily on the evidence of those men who knew him well. There were a hundred ways that the Lewis and Clark Voyage of Discovery might have failed or been aborted but for the courage and persistence of the young men who endured that trip. It is ironic that a 100-foot obelisk monument was built to the memory of Sgt. Charles Floyd although others such as Floyd's cousin Nathaniel Pryor received no such recognition. Floyd is remembered primarily for the fact that he was the only man that died on the trip, in contrast to Pryor's significant participation and contributions at almost every important point on the arduous trip to the Pacific Ocean and back. Pryor's performance on the Expedition was presumably best judged and confirmed by William Clark, who later selected him to escort Chief Sheheke in 1807 and still later selected him to spy on the camp of Tecumseh and The Prophet.

During the War of 1812, Lieutenant Pryor was part of Andrew Jackson's army. His promotion to Captain in 1814 serves to illustrate that he continued to be held in high regard by his superiors. Three months later the skills of the American frontiersmen were perhaps displayed most convincingly at the Battle of New Orleans. We do not know the specific details of Pryor's service during the battle and have to rely on the assessment of Sam Houston, who wrote in his letter to President Andrew Jackson that: "a *braver* man never fought under the wings of your eagles."

Pryor's legacy later, during his years with the Osages, is simply that, in the absence of Pryor, the Osage might have continued their warlike ways longer and more aggressively. Almost certainly there would have been more difficult confrontations between the Osages ant the Cherokees and other tribes relocated into the lands and former lands of the Osages. Similarly, the Osages would most likely have had more serious confrontations and conflicts with the white settlers, as well as with the troops of Colonel Arbuckle and Major Bradford at Forts Smith and Gibson. Who is to say whether or not this would have changed the pattern of removal of eastern Indian tribes to Oklahoma? One can easily visualize the possible development of a scenario more like the events surrounding the Apaches under the leadership of Geronimo.

It is said that some 67 Indian tribes ended up in Oklahoma, many of them occupying land that had been Osage land. Among them were some 50,000 Indians that were removed from their eastern domains. Of course there were conflicts with the Osages. What can be said is that whenever there was a conflict in the Arkansas/Oklahoma area during Pryor's residence, Pryor was participating in the negotiations between and among the U.S. military and various Indian tribes, counseling patience, moderation and peace. Amazingly, Pryor became respected by all of the parties in these negotiations. Even the Cherokees reached the point where they considered Pryor to be their friend, although he had undoubtedly sided with the Osage in many discussions and in many conversations between these two important Indian Nations.

As to how Pryor managed his delicate balancing act among the parties, there could hardly be a better judgement than that of Colonel Arbuckle in his assessment a few months before Pryor's death. Arbuckle praised Pryor as having done more than all the agents employed in the Indian Department with respect to restraining the warlike Osages and restoring peace among the Indians.

Pryor left Osage children, grandchildren and descendants who became leaders of the tribe. Today, Nathaniel Pryor is remembered and respected by many of his proud Osage descendants. It can be said that Pryor merged the white culture and the Indian culture on a personal level and contributed mightily to a successful merging of the two civilizations over a long period of years.

Perhaps no other member of the Lewis and Clark Expedition has had more places named for him, other than the captains themselves. Pryor was the namesake for the town of Pryor, the Pryor Mountains, Pryor Creek, and the Pryor Mountain Wild Horse Preserve, all in Montana. The town of Pryor and another Pryor Creek were also named for him in Mayes County, Oklahoma.

It is astonishing to think of all of the famous men and women encountered by Nathaniel Hale Pryor during his lifetime odyssey. How many other men at any time in history had the opportunity to associate with, be involved with, or to spend time with the likes of Lewis, Clark, the other men of the Expedition, Sacagawea, Pomp, various Indian chiefs, including Sheheke, Claremore II and Dutch, General George Rogers Clark, Abraham (Albert) Gallatin, William Henry Harrison, Tecumseh, The Prophet, Andrew Jackson, Sam Houston, Davy Crockett, Thomas Nuttall, Thomas James, Jesse Chisholm and many others. It is also important to mention the momentous events in which he was involved, such as the Voyage of Discovery, the Battles of Tippecanoe and New Orleans, and finally the opening of the American frontier. It may easily be concluded that no other member of the Voyage of Discovery, other than William Clark himself, made as significant a contribution to the exploration, settlement and pacification of the Western Frontier as did Nathaniel Hale Pryor.

One of these days we expect that Nathaniel Pryor will be honored by the National Cowboy Hall of Fame and Western Heritage Museum in Oklahoma City, along with William Clark, Meriwether Lewis, Sacagawea and York, all companions of Pryor on the famous Voyage of Discovery. Pryor's service on the Expedition alone would justify recognition for him, even without his later extensive activities among the Indians along the Missouri, Mississippi and Arkansas Rivers. Others who are already honored as "Great Westerners" in the Museum include Sam Houston, Kit Carson, and Buffalo Bill Cody along with numerous cattlemen, railroad men and others.[4]

Nathaniel Hale Pryor, explorer, soldier, trader, frontiersman, and the valued spokesman and sub-agent for the Osages, did indeed lead a very full and eventful, albeit under-appreciated life, but left his strong and forceful imprint on the settlement of the West.

Notes

1. Undated article in the *Tulsa (Oklahoma) Tribune*, by Joseph E. Howell, about the reburial of Nathaniel Pryor in 1982. The article is presumed to be contemporaneous with the reburial.

2. The article by Middlebrooks and Harper, *Ancestry*, at p. 304, notes the presence of two sisters, Rosie and Julia, in the household of Allottee No. 460, William Pryor, a son of "William Pryor (Quiver) and his wife Mary".

3. The author is greatly indebted to Linda Thiry and Edward Red Eagle, Jr. of the Osage Nation for genealogical information about the descendants of Nathaniel Pryor and Asinga.

4. The author's maternal grandfather, Calvin Walker Floyd, a relative of both Nathaniel Pryor and Sgt. Charles Floyd, was honored as a "Great Westerner" from the State of Kansas in 1958 by the National Cowboy Hall of Fame and Western heritage Museum.

A

FLOYD AND PRYOR—
FAMILY GENEALOGY

O ver the years, a great deal of genealogical information has been compiled relative to the author's maternal ancestral family, the Floyds of Virginia and Kentucky. The first published work was by N. J. Floyd in 1912.[1] The Floyd family owes a debt of gratitude to N.J. Floyd for this very early genealogical effort. However, his work contributed to errors in other following books and articles, because it hopelessly muddled the families of brothers Charles Floyd and Robert Clark Floyd. N.J. Floyd must have been a very loyal Confederate. He had been a Captain in General Cadmus Wilcox's Alabamians, but his volume did not accurately follow any of the Floyd relatives who went north or fought for the Union. Thus, he dealt generously with the Floyds who were Governors of Virginia, or were officers in the Confederate Army. He extolled the virtues of John Buchanan Floyd, the former Governor of Virginia, who was Secretary of War under President Buchanan. The northern view was that John Buchanan Floyd committed treason by transferring arms and munitions to the Southern armories prior to the outbreak of the Civil War. That transfer was certainly helpful to the Confederacy as it entered the war.

The Floyd family has been unable to trace its genealogical roots definitively to ancestors in England or Wales.[2] It is known that the earliest Floyds arrived in the Virginia Colony during the middle of the Seventeenth Century, probably from Wales. So far, the family has been able to definitively trace its lineage only to William Floyd, born about 1720 in Accomac County, Virginia, although his forbears had already been in Virginia for at least fifty years. William Floyd married Abadiah Davis in 1747 in what later became Amherst County, Virginia. Abadiah Davis was the daughter of Robert Davis. Abadiah definitely was of Indian heritage and a family tradition holds that Abadiah Davis was a granddaughter of Nicketti, whose mother may have been "Cleopatra", a sister of Pocahontas, although there is no definite proof of this. This would tie the family into the family of Powhatan.

William Floyd is known to have been in Albemarle County, Virginia by 1745; in Amherst County, Virginia by 1761; and then in Jefferson County, Virginia (which was Kentucky Territory at the time) prior to 1786. He was the county surveyor for Amherst County in the 1760s and 1770s, as well as being a colonel in the militia. Among the ten known children of William and Abadiah Floyd were Robert Clark Floyd, the father of Sergeant Charles Floyd, and Nancy Floyd, the mother of Sergeant Nathaniel Hale Pryor, both of the key figures in this study. To establish a Revolutionary War ancestor, N.J. Floyd traced his descent through his Grandfather, Charles Floyd (1760–1828), who is the author's greatgreatgreatgrandfather and his wife, Mary Stewart Floyd (1764–1850). However, even though N.J. Floyd's grandmother, Mary Stewart Floyd, died at the home of her son, the author's greatgreatgrandfather, Charles Stewart Floyd, in Bond County, Illinois, N.J. Floyd did not so much as mention the name of Charles Stewart Floyd.[3] Moreover, Charles Stewart Floyd was an older brother of N.J. Floyd's father, Nathaniel Wilson Floyd, so N.J. Floyd must surely have known about Charles Stewart Floyd.

Anna Cartlidge, of Baltimore, Maryland, another descendant of Charles Floyd (1760–1828), did meticulous, accurate research into the genealogy of the Floyd family and filed over 1,500 pages of her research with the DAR in Washington, D. C. One of her papers con-

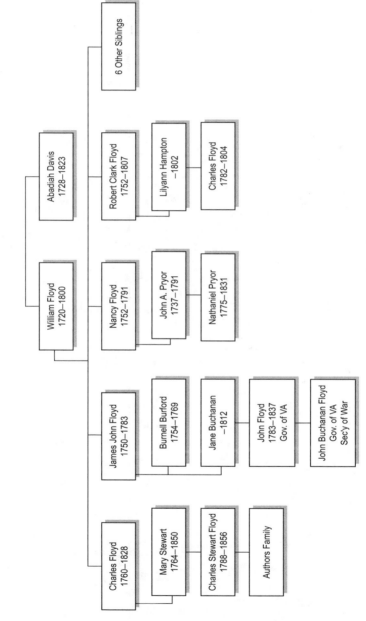

Descendents of William Floyd (Abbreviated)

Children of John A. Pryor and Nancy Floyd

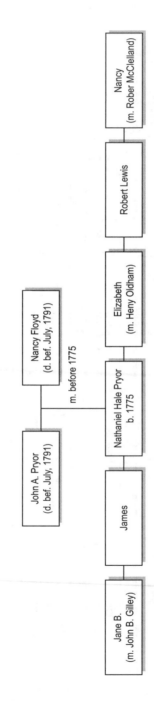

Descendents of Nathaniel Hale Pryor (Abbreviated)

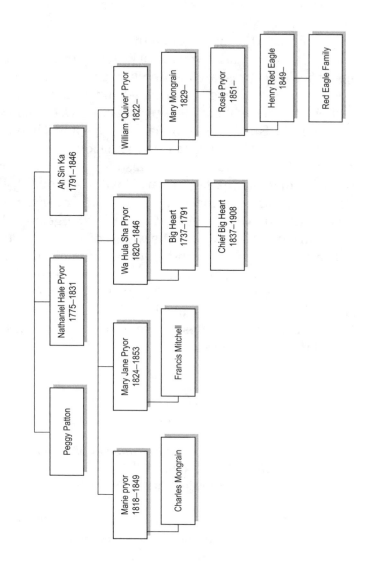

tained the first mention encountered by the author that Nathaniel Pryor was one of his Floyd relatives.[4] We had previously known that Sergeant Charles Floyd, of the Lewis and Clark Voyage of Discovery, was a close relative, but we had not heard of the relationship to Pryor. Then, in 1967, another cousin, Thad Kinnaman, of Sedan, Kansas, a Marine veteran of Iwo Jima, distributed copies of his genealogical research to family members. Drawing heavily upon the earlier works of N. J. Floyd and Anna Cartlidge, Thad's compilation brought our family's lineage down to Thad's and our generation.[5] The works of Anna Cartlidge and Thad Kinnaman both verified that Sergeants Pryor and Floyd were not only first cousins of each other, but were also first cousins of our great-greatgrandfather, Charles Stewart Floyd. The Floyd/Pryor family acquired another connection to the Corps of Discovery when Woodford Floyd, another first cousin of Sergeants Floyd and Pryor, married Mary Myrtle, the widow of Reuben Field in 1824.[6]

The early genealogy of the Pryor family is discussed in Chapter 3 of the text and will not be repeated here. Abbreviated charts of the descendants of William Floyd, of John A. Pryor and Nancy Floyd, and of Nathaniel Hale Pryor are shown. It is hoped that enough information is shown to permit other descendants to add their lines of descent.

Notes

1. Floyd, N.J.—*Bibliographical Genealogies of the Virginia-Kentucky Floyd Families*, Williams and Wilkins Co., Baltimore, MD, 1912; other early family genealogists who made significant contributions were Anna Margaret Cartlidge and Thad Kinnaman, both with unpublished manuscripts in the 1960s that are cited below.

2. Information relative to the genealogy of the Floyd family is primarily from *Children and Grandchildren of William and Abadiah (Davis) Floyd*, by Anna Margaret Cartlidge, unpublished manuscript, 1966 and from *Ancestry and Posterity of M.V. Floyd*, by Thad Kinnaman, unpublished manuscript, Sedan, KS, 1967. Anna M. Cartlidge was

the genealogist for her DAR Chapter in Baltimore, MD, and filed approximately 5,000 pages of genealogical information and articles with the DAR Library in Washington, D.C. Ms. Cartlidge was a third cousin, once removed of the author. Thad Kinnaman was a Marine veteran of the battle of Iwo Jima and a first cousin, once removed of the author.

3. Charles Stewart Floyd, his wife Caziah, and his mother, Mary Stewart Floyd are buried together in a plot at the Wisetown Cemetery, Beaver Creek, Bond County, IL.

4. Cartlidge—*These, Too, Are our Ancestors*, pp. 3–6.

5. Kinnaman—*Ancestry and Posterity*, p. 3–33.

6. Woodford Floyd married Mary Myrtle Field on March 1, 1824, pursuant to a marriage license issued February 24, 1824. Woodford must have died shortly thereafter, as Mary was married again to Robert Gailbreath on August 11, 1825. No child was born to Woodford and Mary. Foregoing data is from Cartlidge, *Children and Grandchildren*, at pp. 21 and 25.

B

A PURPORTED SON OF
NATHANIEL HALE PRYOR

An article in 1970 by Glenna Parker Middlebrooks and Elizabeth Pryor Harper in *The Chronicles of Oklahoma* is very informative, but creates confusion in the line of descent from Nathaniel Hale Pryor.[1] Unfortunately, the Pryor family from Georgia has maintained a family myth that Nathaniel Pryor went to Georgia in 1810 and married Nancy Sally Melton on February 12, 1811. However, the Melton/Pryors admit that the marriage certificate of the parties clearly indicates that the groom's name was "William H. Pryor." Middlebrooks and Harper circumvent this by alleging that the middle initial was in error and should have been "N" and, further, that the man went by the name of "Nathaniel." Nancy Melton was born July 16, 1779, and was the daughter of William Alexander Melton, Sr., and Lucy Daniel Allen. Nancy may have been married earlier but by 1811 she was either divorced or widowed, presumably the latter. According to Middlebrooks and Harper, William Melton was supposedly a very strict Baptist and a meddlesome man. The Melton/Pryor family story is that Nathaniel Pryor could not take William Melton's interference and left his wife shortly after their marriage, ostensibly to return to Kentucky to obtain fine race horses to be brought back to Georgia. Pryor never returned to Georgia and Nancy gave birth to a son, William Stokes Pryor, on November 15, 1811. The cited article states that members of the family referred to Pryor's disappearance as "a family legend which pride has hushed for more that a century and a half." Nancy subsequently procured a divorce from Pryor, which required an Act of the Georgia Legislature [*Georgia State Journal,* December 18, 1818], and it is important to note that the Georgia Act also names Nancy's husband as "William H. Pryor."

The Melton/Pryors in Georgia apparently lost track of Nancy's husband. In any event, they did not know of Nathaniel Hale Pryor's procurement of a trading license in 1810; the building and operation of his trading post and smelter at Toledo Mort in 1810–12; his services for William Clark and William Henry Harrison; of his narrow escape from the Winnebagos; of his reentry into the Army as an officer; his service under Andrew Jackson; or of his later location among and assistance to the Osage Nation. In the author's opinion, the fact that Nathaniel Pryor was definitely in St. Louis in July of 1810, plus the fact that he was negotiating with William Clark for the trading license and with Abraham Gallatin for funds to establish his trading post and lead smelter operation, and was joined by George Hunt at Toledo Mort in September of 1810, conclusively proves that this Nathaniel Hale Pryor was not down in Georgia courting Nancy Melton.

Middlebrooks and Harper explain the position of the Melton/Pryors in detail in the cited article. Nonetheless, the repetition of these assertions is a serious blot upon the character and reputation of Nathaniel Hale Pryor. Ms. Harper was a "fifth generation descendant" of Nathaniel Stokes Pryor. A later genealogist in the Nathaniel Stokes Pryor family tried for a number of years to connect to Nathaniel Hale Pryor, but was unsuccessful. This was Ms. Bettye Bean of Arlington, TX. In two letters to a "Paula" in November of 1989 (copies of which are in the author's possession), Ms. Bean admitted her inability to tie her Pryor line to that of Nathaniel Hale Pryor, though she had diligently tried to do so for over twenty years. Ms. Bean and her sister, Nina McMillen, also of Arlington, TX, attended the dedication of the Pryor Monument at Pryor, OK, in 1982. It is believed that the Pryors of Georgia are probably related to the Pryors of Virginia and Kentucky, but it is the author's conclusion that they are not descended from Nathaniel Hale Pryor, nor from John Pryor and his wife, Nancy Floyd, the parents of Nathaniel Hale Pryor.

One of the more interesting parts of the article by Middlebrooks and Harper is the general description of members of the family. They note correctly that no physical description or contemporary illustrations of Nathaniel Hale Pryor exist. Despite his service in the Army on at least three occasions, the spaces opposite his physical description on his military records are blank. Ms. Harper fills part of this void by stating: "I never saw a man in the Pryor branch of my family who was not rather handsome. They were gentlemen, too, always kind and thoughtful toward everyone. While family characteristics and physical features are not always identifiable in offspring, the following description of Nathaniel's uncle, Colonel John Floyd, brother of Nathaniel Pryor's mother, Nancy (Floyd) Pryor, is interesting; 'Colonel Floyd was over six feet high, very military in his bearing, of beautiful appearance, exceedingly agreeable ... an impressive manner gave him great influence.'"[2]

Although any relationship of Ms. Middlebrooks and Ms. Harper to Nathaniel Pryor has not been proven, their description accords with contemporary descriptions of the Pryor and Floyd families in Kentucky. The description of Colonel John Floyd would also be very similar to descriptions of the author's Great-GreatGreatGrandfather Charles Floyd, another uncle of Nathaniel Pryor. Charles Floyd was riding with his brother, Colonel John Floyd, when they were ambushed by Shawnees in 1783. Col. Floyd received a fatal wound in that ambush.[3] The foregoing physical description is also very similar to descriptions of the author's GreatGreatGrandfather Charles Stewart Floyd, another first cousin of Nat Pryor, who was described as being over six feet tall and very erect in bearing. The description also accords with the recent forensic reconstruction of Pryor's first cousin, Sgt. Charles Floyd, who died on the Expedition, where reconstructions have been installed at the Floyd Museum and at the

Lewis and Clark Interpretive Center, both in Sioux City, Iowa. Recently installed manikins of Sgt. Floyd in full uniform at the Sioux City Museum and Interpretive Center, as well as at the Carnegie Museum in New Albany, Indiana, are very similar in appearance to the foregoing description.

Notes

1. Middlebrooks and Harper, *Ancestry,* at note 35.

2. *Ibid,* p. 296, and citing a statement by Elizabeth Pryor Harper at Shreveport, Louisiana.

3. The son of Col. John Floyd born shortly after his death became a prominent physician and the Governor of Virginia. His son, John Buchanan Floyd (i. e., Col. John Floyd's grandson) became a U.S. Congressman, the Governor of Virginia and finally Secretary of War under President Buchanan. John Buchanan Floyd was accused in the press of treason for transferring substantial stores of arms and ammunition to U. S. armories in the South prior to the Civil War, making it easier for the Confederacy to arm itself. He became a General in the Confederate Army, but withdrew his forces when Grant attacked Fort Donelson in 1862. As a result, Floyd was removed from command. He died in the fall of 1863.

C

A POSSIBLE SON OF NATHANIEL HALE PRYOR

I t is possible that Nathaniel Hale Pryor had a son, variously called "Nathaniel Miguel Pryor" or "Louis Nathaniel Pryor" or other variations [hereinafter referred to as "Miguel Pryor"]. This putative descendant is alleged to be the son of Nathaniel Hale Pryor and his first wife, Peggy Patton, born about 1798, at or near Louisville, Kentucky. This author is open to the possibility of such a son, but to date has not seen sufficient proof of the relationship. Anna Cartlidge knew of the existence of Nathaniel Miguel Pryor, but thought that he was a nephew rather than a son, as she had been unable to locate any proof of his descent from Nathaniel Hale Pryor. However, the descendants of Nat's siblings are known and none of them have names even close to "Nathaniel Miguel Pryor." Therefore, if not Nat's son, Miguel would probably be another cousin of some degree. The author assumes that this Pryor acquired the name of "Miguel" after his arrival in either Santa Fe or California, although it may have been "Michael" originally.

The LDS International Genealogical Index [IGI] lists a "Miguel Luis Nathaniel Pryor" born about 1806 in Louisville, Kentucky. His parents are listed as Miguel Nathaniel Pryor and Mary Davis.

The author has been unable to locate any "Miguel Nathaniel Pryor" in the Louisville area at any time, but especially during the period of 1795–1810. Nor has the author been able to determine the identity of "Mary Davis." Miguel Pryor married Maria Theresa Sepulveda on February 2, 1838 at San Gabriel, Los Angeles, California, which of course was a part of Mexico at the time. The IGI does not list any children of this marriage. Maria Theresa evidently predeceased Miguel Pryor, as he married Maria Paula de Jesus Romero on August 10, 1848, at the Los Angeles Plaza Church, Los Angeles, California. The IGI shows a son of that marriage, Daniel Juan Pryor, christened October 29, 1848, at the Los Angeles Plaza Church, Los Angeles, California. The IGI lists that Miguel Pryor died in May of 1850 and was buried on May 11, 1850, at the Los Angeles Plaza Church, Los Angeles, California. No source information is shown for the IGI entries.

Betty Lou Harper Thomas, the Director of the Mayes Co., OK Museum and Historical Society, is convinced that Miguel Pryor was the son of Nathaniel Hale Pryor.[1] Ms. Thomas informed the author that she had corresponded and conversed with descendants of Miguel Pryor's first marriage, who had provided Ms. Thomas with photographs, baptismal certificates and other genealogical evidence of their descent from Miguel Pryor. Unfortunately, Ms. Thomas has not provided any of that documentation to the author. Nor has she provided the names and addresses of those descendants.

The 1806 birth date and the names of the parents set forth in the IGI record would seem to preclude that Miguel Pryor is the son of Nat Pryor. However, the undocumented IGI records are known to contain many errors. More favorable to a finding of descent is the following passage:

> "Nathaniel Pryor—sometimes known as Don Miguel
> N. Pryor or Prior—is the pioneer referred to by Keller.
> At the age of thirty, it is said, <u>in 1828</u>, he came here, and
> fifteen or twenty years later, about the time that he was
> a *Regidor* or Councilman, was one of eight or ten East-
> erners who had farms within the pueblo district … .

Pryor was twice married, having a son, Charles, by his first wife, and a son, Nathaniel, Jr., by his second. Pablo Pryor of San Juan was another son. The first Mrs. Pryor died about 1840. The second Mrs. Pryor, who inherited [Pryor's] property, died about 1857. Mrs. Lottie Pryor, is a surviving member of this family."[2] [Emphasis supplied].

The foregoing passage would indicate a birth of about 1798 or so, which would have been more in accord with Nathaniel Hale Pryor's marriage to Peggy Patton in that year.

Arguing against the finding of descent would be the original instructions from Lewis to Clark to basically select single, unencumbered men for the Expedition. The genealogy of the family of Nat Pryor's first wife, Margaret (Peggy) Patton, is well known. She is listed as having married Nathaniel Pryor, but no child is listed from that marriage, although her sisters, their husbands, and their descendants are traced for several generations, whereas there is no information about Peggy except the date of her marriage to Nathaniel Pryor.[3] Peggy's father's Will, probated in 1815, does not list Peggy, or any child of Peggy's. If Peggy had had a child with Nat Pryor, surely one of her siblings would have had some record or knowledge of the child and the child probably would have been mentioned in his grandfather's will.

Betty Lou Harper Thomas of the Mayes County Historical Society has asserted that Nathaniel Hale Pryor returned to Louisville after he was discharged from the Army following the Battle of New Orleans. She then indicates that he retrieved this son, Miguel Pryor, and also acquired some fine racehorses. According to Ms. Thomas, Nat Pryor then took Miguel and the horses to the Arkansas Territory in the vicinity of Fort Smith. As justification for this, Ms. Thomas has stated that this would be normal for a soldier returning from the War to collect his child. However, there is no record that Nat Pryor made any effort to collect his child after his three-year absence on the Expedition in 1806. Nor is there any evidence that Nat Pryor returned to Louisville or took any child to his operations at Toledo Mort after his discharge from the Army in 1810. Nor is there any mention of him having a child with him in the early years when he was at Arkansas Post and then at the Three Forks area. Although there was a considerable amount of horse racing in the areas where Nat Pryor was located, the story about him bringing racehorses from Kentucky appears to this author to be too much like the similar story from the Georgia Melton/Pryors detailed above.[4]

The first mention of Miguel Pryor being in the Three Forks area indicates that he was with the Glenn-Fowler expedition that left that area in September 1821. Ms. Middlebrooks and Ms. Harper wrote that Nathaniel Miguel Pryor was in the area of the Verdigris River by at least April 4, 1824. They mention an entry of that date in the diary of Colonel Auguste Pierre Chouteau that reads: "Young Pryor came by the place a few days later."[5] Col. Chouteau was born in 1786 and thus was about eleven years younger than Captain Pryor, who was about 49 at the time of this 1824 diary entry. Chouteau would not have referred to his 49-year old elder as "Young Pryor." At least we know that there was a younger Pryor present in the area at that time.

In 1919, Walter B. Douglas wrote the following:

> It appears from Bancroft's <u>History of California</u> (Vol. III, p. 163), that among the company that arrived in California, under the leadership of the Patties, in March <u>1828</u>, was a man whose name is given as Nathaniel Pryor or Nathaniel Miguel Pryor. It is said of him that he was then <u>twenty-three years old</u>, and that he had lived four years in New Mexico. This man was a silversmith and clock-maker, and became known as Miguel el Platero [Spanish for Michael the Silversmith]. He married a Mexican woman, raised a family, and died in 1850.[6] [Emphasis supplied].

Don Tryon of the San Juan Capistrano (CA) Historical Society has recently verified that Miguel Pryor came to California with the expedition of Sylvester Pattie in 1828.[7] The Patties had gone to the Rocky Mountains and Santa Fe on a beaver trapping and trading expedition. After encountering many misfortunes, including having their furs and horses stolen by Indians, Tryon wrote that

"...they walked across the desert toward Calif. In 1828 Nathaniel Pryor and 7 other survivors arrived in San Diego, preceded only by Jedediah Smith's trapping party in blazing a trail overland to Calif. The Calif. Governor put the Americans in an adobe jail in San Diego to discourage other Americans from an overland invasion of Calif.

Nathaniel Pryor, then 30 years old, was sent to San Luis Rey Mission to repair and make silver altar pieces for their chapel. Thereafter he was called 'El Platero,' silversmith.

A severe smallpox epidemic swept Calif. The Pattie party carried a vial of smallpox vaccine. James Pattie negotiated to vaccinate Californians in return for the liberation of the Americans. Upon their release most of the Americans remained as permanent residents of Calif.

Nathaniel Pryor became a silversmith in the Pueblo of Los Angeles, and profitably engaged in otter hunting for furs. The Californians called him 'El Platero,' and gave him a Spanish name, 'Don Miguel.'

Nathaniel and Maria Teresa Sepulveda of Rancho Palos Verde were married about 1836. Nathaniel purchased a farm within the Pueblo of Los Angeles, which extended from the Los Angeles River west to Jackson Street, on which he had a grape vinyard [sic] and an orange orchard. The Pryors lived in an adobe home facing Jackson Street. Nathaniel 'Don Miguel' Pryor served as a Councilman for the Pueblo of Los Angeles.

Nathaniel and Maria Teresa's son, Pablo Pryor, was born in the Pueblo of Los Angeles, Alta Calif., in 1837. Three years later Maria Teresa died in childbirth and was buried in the old Plaza Catholic Church.

When Pablo was old enough to attend school his father sent him East to Boston to attend American

schools. When Pablo returned to Calif. A young man
he had forgotten early Calif. cultures and the Spanish
language. He soon resumed his earlier Calif. ways. He
dressed handsomely and was a young gentleman. When
Nathaniel Pryor died in 1850 his son Pablo inherited his
farm within the Pueblo."

We have recently discovered several census entries regarding
Miguel Pryor and his family. An 1850 city census for Los Angeles,
evidently taken before Miguel Pryor's death in May of 1850, lists
Miguel Pryor as being from Louisiana.[8] It does not appear to
show his age. Unfortunately, it is difficult to read the on-line transcription. The 1850 U.S. Census for Los Angeles was taken after
Miguel's death. It does not enumerate Miguel and it is therefore
not helpful as to his parentage or place of birth.

Miguel Pryor fathered at least two sons by his first wife, Maria
Teresa Dolores Sepulveda. Those sons were Pablo Pryor, born on
8 February 1839[9] and Manuel Pryor, born in June 1840, both born
at Los Angeles, California, a part of Mexico at the time. Manuel
may have died at the time of birth with his mother. We have not
found a listing for Pablo Pryor in the 1850 U.S. Census. Nor have
we found any information to verify that Pablo Pryor was
schooled in Boston. We have not found any listing of Pablo Pryor
having debarked from a ship in Boston, which would probably
have been required before the completion of the transcontinental
railroads, although overland travel to the east was possible.

Pablo Pryor evidently chose to be known as Paul Pryor in his
later years. Paul Pryor is listed in the 1860 U.S. Census for San
Juan Township, Los Angeles County, which was enumerated on
23 July 1860. He is listed in the household of John Forsten [sic -
usually shown as Don Juan Forster], who had bought the Mission of San Juan Capistrano in 1845. Paul Pryor is listed as being
21 years old, with his real estate valued at $12,000 and his per-
sonal estate at $500. This would verify that he was born in 1839
instead of 1837, and that he inherited the land from his father.

Paul Pryor married Rosa Modesta Avila on January 14, 1864,
and died at San Juan Capistrano, California on August 1, 1878,

where he is buried. Pablo and Rosa were the parents of three sons and four daughters, although one of the daughters died an infant. The 1870 U.S. Census enumerated on 13 June 1870 lists Paul Pryor, head of household, family #15, age 31. The value of his real estate is shown as $10,000, with his personal estate of $800. Others in the household were Rosa, age 34, Miguel, age 5, Teresa, age 3, Reginaldo, age 2. Daughter Dolores, born 6 March 1879 is not shown, and the later children, Paul and Soledad were born after this census.

The home of Pablo Pryor in San Juan Capistrano was an adobe home and is thought to be one of the oldest adobe houses in California still standing.[10] Built by at least 1792, the building and the ranch property belonged to Juan Avila. When his daughter Rosa married Pablo Pryor, Avila gave the property to Rosa. Unfortunately, Paul Pryor died a very mysterious death on 1 August 1878. That morning, he drank his usual morning eggnog but noted a strange taste. His wife Rosa tasted it and noticed the same thing. She collapsed and all attention was devoted to her. Attendants forced olive oil down her throat, which saved her. When the attendants turned to Paul Pryor, he was already dead. The cause of the death was determined to be strychnine poisoning. Don Tryon indicated that no one was ever charged with the murder of Paul Pryor, but that many years later Mrs. Pryor received a letter from someone who was dying and wanted to unburden his soul by confessing to the murder. Rosa Pryor never married again and died at San Juan Capistrano in 1915.

Miguel Pryor also had two sons by his second wife, Daniel Juan Pryor born 14 October 1848 and Nathaniel Pryor born in September 1850. We have not found any subsequent information relative to Daniel. The 1880 U.S. Census for Los Angeles City lists Nathaniel Pryor, the son of Miguel Pryor and his second wife, together with his wife, two daughters and his widowed mother. This Nathaniel Pryor listed his father (i.e., Miguel Pryor) as having been born in England.[11] The English birth place for Nathaniel (listed as Natanel) Pryor's father (who was Miguel Pryor) is repeated in the 1900 U.S. Census.[12]

Descendents of Nathaniel Miguel Pryor

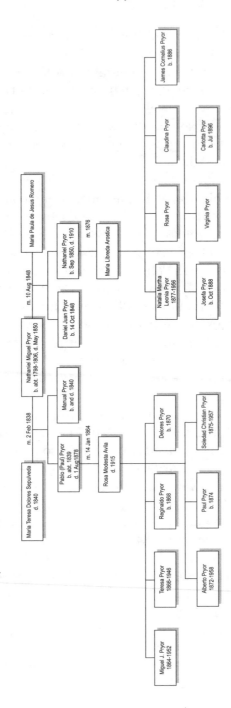

There are lines of descent from Pablo Pryor's children, Pablo being Miguel Pryor's son from his first marriage. There is also a line of descent from Nathaniel Pryor, a son of Miguel's second marriage. We have not presumed to trace those lines of descent down to the present.

In summary, the IGI lists Miguel Pryor's birthdate in 1806; *Sixty Years in California* indicates 1798, which would be more likely if he was Nathaniel Hale Pryor's son; and Bancroft's *History of California*, puts the date at 1805, more in line with the IGI. The city census for Los Angeles in 1850 lists Miguel as being from Louisiana and then the 1880 and 1900 U.S. Censuses for one of his sons indicates that he was born in England. This would seem to negate the possibility that Miguel Pryor was the son of Nathaniel Hale Pryor.

Additional genealogical research and more information are obviously required before we can determine if, in fact, Miguel Pryor was the son of Nathaniel Hale Pryor. It is hoped that the book being written by Ms. Thomas may clarify this genealogy.

Notes

1. Conversations between Ms. Thomas and the author during 2004 and 2005.

2. *Sixty Years in Southern California, 1853–1913, containing the reminiscences of Harris Newmark*, Chapter XX, p. 293.

3. *Kentucky Genealogy*, Kentucky Historical Society, Vol. II, pp. 51–61, 63, 64, 73, 80. ["Captain James Patton of Augusta County, Virginia, and Louisville, Kentucky, Ancestors and Descendants"].

4. As noted in the quotation at page 150 above, there were racecourses maintained at least at Fort Gibson and at "Colonel A.P. Chouteau's baronial estate" during the 1820s.

5. Middlebrooks and Harper, *Ancestry*, p. 296, citing the Grant Foreman *Frontier Days* book above at p. 210.

6. Douglas, Walter B.—*Documents: Captain Nathaniel Pryor* [The American Historical Review, Vol. 24, Jan. 1919], at pp. 253–54.

7. Handwritten information received from Don Tryon by mail on May 1, 2006.

8. *Los Angeles City and County Census*, 1850 [database online]. Orem, Utah: Ancestry.com, Inc., 1997. Original data: Alliot, Hector. Census of City and County of Los Angeles 1850, Los Angeles: Times Mirror Press, 1929.

9. This date differs from the information of Don Tryon, but is taken from later Census information for Pablo [Paul} Pryor. Don Tryon also furnished a genealogy sheet showing "Pablo Pryor's list of his children and their birth dates, recorded on a page of his business ledger." Don Tryon shows the date of the marriage between Miguel Pryor and Maria Teresa Sepulveda as "about 1836." Pablo Pryor's own list indicates his birth in 1837. As set forth above, the IGI lists the marriage as being in 1838 and the Census records indicate that Pablo was born in about 1839.

10. Undated article from the *Capistrano (CA) Dispatch*, probably in 2000.

11. 1880 U.S. Census for Los Angeles City, Los Angeles County, Dist. 22, p. 155.

12. 1900 U.S. Census for Los Angeles Township, Los Angeles City.

D

---◄►---

DOCUMENTS[1]

I. Affidavit of Nathaniel Pryor, September 11, 1824.

U.S. of America
  Arkansas Territory
    Crawford County
This day, personally appeared before me, John Nicks, one of
the Justices of the Peace in and for said County, Nathaniel Pryor
of the Osage Nation of Indians, who being of lawful age and duly
sworn according to law, deposed and said that some time in the
month of February 1820, on the Virdigris [sic] River, a branch of
the Arkansas or Paune River, at said Pryor's trading house,[2]
about one and a half miles above the mouth of said Virdigris
[sic], this deponent had about one hundred and fifty weight of
Beaver fur, and about said time a Cherokee Indian by the name of
Dutch and two others, companions of his, took from the possession of this deponent the said one hundred and fifty weight of
Beaver fur the property of this deponent and which said Beaver
fur has never been restored to him or any part thereof, not the
value or any part thereof.

This deponent further stated that about the month of February, 1822, the Cherokee Indians stole from his possession a large
bright bay horse, with a star in his forehead, and about fifteen

hands high and which said horse he has never been able to recover or reclaim not the value thereof, or any part thereof, and further this deponent said not.

Sworn and subscribed to before me this 11th
Day of September, 1824.   Nathl. Pryor

Jno. Nicks
J. Peace

I certify the above to be a true copy from file in this office.

Geo. Vashon
Agt. Chers. West.

West'n Cherokee Nation
Agents Office April 30th, 1832

II.   Affidavit of David McKee, September 11, 1824.

United States of America
    Arkansas Territory
        Crawford County

This day personally appeared before me John Nicks one of the Justices of the Peace in and for said County, David McKee of said County who being of lawful age and duly sworn according to law deposith and saith that in the month of February 1820 a Cherokee Indian by the name of Dutch, with two other Cherokee Indians came to Nath. Pryor's trading house on the Virdigris River, a branch of the Arkansas River, and at that time the said Nathaniel Pryor had in deposit at said place about one hundred and fifty weight of furs, well secured under lock, and that on the evening of the morning on which said Indians left the trading house, he, the said deponent discovered that the lock which secured the fur, had been forced, and the sa[I]d one hundred and fifty weight of fur were stolen, and as this deponent verily believes by the said Cherokee Indians.

The deponent further states that fur was selling at that time at two dollars and a half per pound and further this deponent saith not.

David [X] McKee

Sworn and subscribed to before me this
11th day of September 1824

Jno Nicks

Justice Peace

I certify the above to be a true copy from file in this office.

Geo. Vashon

Agt. Chers. West

West'n Cherokee Nation
Agents Office April 30th, 1832

III.   Deposition of Maurice Blondeau, June 27, 1825.[3]

State of Missouri

Be it remembered, that on the day of the date hereof, before me, Thompson Douglass, a Notary Public, within and for the State aforesaid, duly commissioned and sworn, residing in the city of St. Louis, personally came Maurice Blondeau, who being duly sworn according to law, deposeth and saith: That, on the night of the 1st of January, 1812, a party of the Winnebago Indians came to the trading house occupied by a Mr. Nathaniel Pryor, the acting Agent for himself and Abraham Gallatin, and burnt the house with a large quantity of goods, lead and furs and peltries, to the amount, deponent believes of between 4 and 5000 dollars; that, after the attack by the Indians, N. Pryor made his escape to the house of deponent; who informed him, deponent, that they were just from the battle Teppecanoe, (sic) where they had lost some relations and friends; that they had destroyed Pryor's house and property, in revenge for the death of their relatives and friends; and that he, deponent, saw a quantity of goods, tobacco, and furs, &c.&c. burnt, and, from appearance of the quantity, he supposes that their value might be from 4 to 5,000 dollars—that Pryor's establishment was near Fevre River, on the Upper Mississippi. There was also a large quantity of lead destroyed by the burning of the house, not included in the above estimate.

In witness whereof, I have hereunto set my Notarial Seal, at St. Louis aforesaid, the 27th day of June in the year of our Lord, 1825, and of American Independence, the fiftieth year.
Thompson Douglass

IV. Statement of E.W. DuVal.[4]

The taking of the property is not denied by the individual charged with it, but he alleges as the cause and justification of the act, or acts, that he met at Mr. Prior's [sic] Trading house, at the time mentioned, a War party of Osages, under the Chief called Mad Buffaloe, that at that time the Osage and Cherokee Nations were at open War with each other, that he the Dutch (the Individual referred to) commanded and then had with him a War party of Cherokees, that his party was more numerous than that of the Mad Buffaloe and that the latter were completely in his power, that he considered them as his prisoners and was waiting only until they should leave the premises of Mr. Prior to capture and secure them. That during this time he was invited out on one side of Mr. Priors' House as he believes at the instance of Mr. Prior by a man named McKee or McGee, where he and his party were detained by amusements until the Mad Buffaloe and his party had time to escape; that he believed and still believes, their escape was contrived by Mr. Prior; that on discovering they (the Osages) were gone he immediately pursued but could not overtake them; that for this interference, as he considered it, on the part of Mr. Prior, whereby he was prevented making prisoners of the party and in so far weakening or injuring the enemy and rendering essential service to his own nation, he took the property for which Mr. Prior claims payment.

Mr. Prior having admitted to the agent the material facts set forth by the Dutch as to the aid and assistance he gave to the Osages to make their escape, The Committee desire that the case may be su[b]mitted to the consideration of the Secretary of War, for his decision. They would refer it to him on these grounds. That the Osages and Cherokees were relatively to each other independent Nations with whom the U.S. were on terms of amity and friendship. That Mr. Prior, a citizen of U. States inter-married with an Osage Woman, carrying on trade and inter-course with that nation and was as it would seem to the commit-tee bound to have preserved a perfect neutrality between the belligerent parties; and that by having aided the Osages in the manner set forth by the Dutch and admitted by himself he ceased to maintain the character of a neutral and thereby sub-jected his property to seizure by the party injured.

I certify that Mr. Prior admitted to me that he did interfere in the manner stated to secure the escape of the Osages from the Cherokees.

Signed   E. W. duVal

A true copy from the original on file this office.

Geo. Vashon
Agt. Chers. West

West'n Cherokee Nation
Agent's Office April 30th, 1832

V.   Letter from Franklin Wharton to Secretary of War James Barbour.[5]

Crawford Court House, A. Terr.
Feby. 28th, 1826

Secy. of War:
    Sir:
Capt. N. Pryor of this Territory has requested me to use means towards obtaining a liquidation of a just claim, which he supposes he has against the U.S. Will you allow me to represent its nature and solicit your answer to certain inquiries.

Capt. Pryor was the first person who volunteered his services in Lewis and Clark's expedition. He accompanied them through all their excursions and was finally sent in command of the party, to take back the Mandan chief and family to their homes. Of the event of this, you are aware. From that time to the period, when he derives his claim, he was engaged in extensive and dangerous business among the Indian Tribes.

About eighteen months before the late war, he was licensed by the Gov. of Missouri, as a trader among the Weenibagoes (sic) or Puans on the Eastern Mississippi,. Ter. of Missouri, at a place called DeBuque's Mines. At that place he was transacting a profitable business, had buildings erected as well as a smelting furnace, and was rapidly distributing through the Tribes the comforts and conveniences of civilization. About six months before the War, he received a letter from Gov. Clarke, (sic) requesting him to endeavour to find out Tecumseh or the Prophet. The execution of this duty, a duty performed at the wish of the Government—a duty delicate and hazardous in the extreme, rendered Capt. P. an object of hostility and enmity with the natives. From receiving the letter of the Gov. the Captain had heard nothing of a war likely to ensue. He was actively and industriously engaged in his occupation. On Christmas day and even after of the year '12 the Winbagoes (sic) were trading peaceably with him. On the 1st of Jany. 13 about 12 O'clock in the day, eight of the tribe came to his house, with their war accoutrements and offered violence.[6] They would not let him leave his dwelling. About sundown of same day, sixty arrived, shooting down the oxen in the yard and killing two of his men. They rushed on him, and was in the act of putting him to death, when by the politic dissimulation of a female in the house, they were averted for the moment from their intention. They then placed him in the house with a sentinel over him, intending to burn him in it. While they were plundering his stores and ravaging his premises, with the greatest difficulty, he made his escape. After crossing the Mississippi on the cakes of ice, he was still the object of pursuit to the hostile Indians. They were not so soon to forget his endavorous for Tecumseh. They robbed him of all they [he] had in the world: they entirely destroyed every article of his property. Capt. P. only claims the original amount of his goods, amounting to

5,216$ 25 cents (sic). He asks not the freight on them; he asks not what they were actually worth to him—he asks nothing for his buildings, his furnaces, his cttle, save two, which were shot down before his face. He, in fact, asks for less than what he conceives to be his just claim. And his reason is: for that which he seeks a remuneration he can positively swear to the amount. He will not add more, as he cannot remember certainly the value.

Capt. Pryor is a man of real, solid, innate worth. His genuine modesty conceals the peculiar traits of his character. He was a brave and persevering officer in the attack on New Orleans. He has the most thorough knowledge of the Western country; has been on considerable service to the U.S. and the benefit he has conferred on the Indian Tribes is gratefully acknowledged by them. He has been frequently urged by Gov. Clarke (sic) the Supt. Of Ind. Aff. and by Gen. Miller, the late Gov. Of this Territory to forward this claim. But he has refused. His own exertions have hitherto been his support. Again robbed and plundered by the savages, viz. Cherokees; he is left in a situation, where the money would be of service to him. His want drives him to that, which hitherto his conscious pride prevented. You will observe, that it was six months after the declaration of war, this transaction occurred. Yet had the traders no knowledge of it. The British Indian allies received it first through their emissaries. It was not known at St. Louis 'til months after it took place. And does not Capt. P's claim derive additional support, from the fact that Gov. Clark was bound to give notice of the war, and at the time, such notice had not been given.[7] The Capt. was trading under the license and protection of the U.S.; by an act of the U.S. of which he was ignorant, he was deprived of his property and his home. You will also please to remember that, the tribe was allied with the English troops. I am not aware, Sir, that this claim falls under your cognizance, of this much, I am certain, that, if you cannot *officially* interest yourself in it, its details will ensure your warm and generous support. The eloquent advocate of the abstract rights of man, will not lend a cold and feeble support, to what has connection, with the more kind and gentle feelings of humanity. If not inconsistent with your duty, would you be pleased to answer these inquiries.

Does this demand come within the scope of those, which have hitherto been termed just and equitable by the U.S.? If it bear no analogy to former claims allowed, is it your opinion, that it is a fair one against the U.S.? What measures are necessary to place it before the proper authority, and what is that authority?

During the spring Gen. Clark has promised to have the necessary depositions taken ... .

A letter will reach me, directed to "Dardanelle", Crawford Co. A.T. I have the honour to be

Yr. Obt. Servt.
Franklin Wharton

To James Barbour Esq'r
    Sec. Of War
        City of Washington,
            D.C.

VI.   Letter from Maj. William McClellan to Gen. William Clark.[8]

Little Rock, (A.T.) May 28, 1827

Gen. William Clark
    Superintendant of Indian Affairs
        Sir

I am happy to hear from Capt. Pryor that he is willing to serve, if appointed Sub-Agent to the Osage Indians; <u>no man can render the same services to the United States than Capt. Pryor can with those Indians. He can speak their language, and they have every confidence in his counsul and advice...</u>. [Emphasis supplied].

Respectfully,
Your Obdt. Servant
Wm. McClellan
C.A.W.M.[9]

VII. Letter from Lieut. J.F. Hamtramck[10] to William Clark.

St. Louis, June 18, 1827

Sir:

... Capt. Pryor possesses every necessary qualification and would accept the office. I therefore have the honor respectfully to suggest the propriety of such a measure and ask your attention to it.

very respectfully
your obt. Servt.
J.F. Hamtramck,
U.S. Ind'n Agt. For Osages

To Gen'l Wm. Clark
Supt. of Ind'n Affairs

VIII. Letter from William Clark to Secretary of War James Barbour, August 4, 1827.

Superintendency of Ind's Affairs
St. Louis, Aug. 4th, 1827

Sir,

Since the death of the Sub Agent of the Arkansas Band of Osages, no appointment has been made to fill the vacancy. As the situation of that Band requires a Sub Agent of respectability and influence, I have employed Capt'n Nathaniel Pryor, at the rate of $500 pr ann. and given him a temporary appointment of Sub Agent. His influence among the Indians generally, in that quarter, his capacity to act and be serviceable, added to his knowledge of, the Osage language, would it is believed justify his receiving the appointment and pay of Sub Agent and Interpreter, which would enable him to perform those duties which Col. Arbuckle, and the Choctaw and Osage Agents have suggested in their letters which I have the honor to enclose. Capt. Pryor served with me, on an expedition to the Pacific ocean in 1803, 4, 5, and 6 in the capacity of 1st Sergeant; after which he served as an officer in the Army, and was disbanded after the last war. When out of Service, he has pursued the Indian trade, in which he has been unfortunate, first by the Winnebagoes, who took every article he had and for which he has a claim before Congress, and since by casual occurrences in his commercial pursuit on the Arkansas.

Capt. Pryor's long and faithful services and his being disabled by a dislocation of his shoulder when in the execution of his duty under my command, produces an interest in his favor and much solicitude for bettering his situation by an office which he is every way capable of filling with credit to himself and usefulness to his government.

I have the honor to be

> With high respect
> Your most obt. servt.
> Wm. Clark

The Hon.
    James Barbour
      Secy. of War.

IX.   Letter from Sam Houston to Secretary of War John Eaton

> Wigwam Neosho
> 15th Dec. 1830

Gen'l Jno. H. Eaton
   Sir:

I have the honor to address you on the subject of Capt. N. Pryor's claims to the appointment of Sub Agent to the Osage nation of Indians, which I had the pleasure of mentioning to you, when I was last in the City. You then took down his name, as an applicant, and assured me, tho you "would give no pledge, yet his claims should be considered of". Mr. Carr, who has recently deceased was appointed, and Capt. Pryor passed by. His claims I have taken leave to state to the President, and do most earnestly hope that they may be met by the well deserved patronage of the Government.

It is impossible for me ever to wish, or solicit, any patronage from the Government for myself, or any one connected with me, but when I *see a brave, honest, honorable and faithful servant of that country, which I once claimed as my own, in poverty with spirit half broken by neglect, I must be permitted to ask something in his behalf!*

Could any just man know him as I do, who had *power* to offer reparations for what he has done for his country, what he has suffered, I am sure he would not be allowed to languish in circumstances hardly comfortable. [Emphasis in the foregoing is Houston's].

I trust in God, that he will be no longer neglected by his country.

With high respect,

I am your mo ob sert

Sam Houston

X.   Letter from Sam Houston to President Andrew Jackson

Wigwam Neosho,
15 Dec 1830

To Genl. Jackson
    Sir,
I have the honor to address you upon the subject of one of your old soldiers at the "Battle of Orleans." I allude to Capt. Nathaniel Pryor, who has for several years past resided with the Osages as a sub agent, by appointment of Gov. Clark but without any permanent appointment from the Government. A vacancy has lately occurred by the decease of Mr. Carr, sub agent for the Osages; and I do most *earnestly* solicit the appointment for him. When you were elected President of the U. States, I assured you that I would not annoy you with recommendations in favor of persons who might wish to obtain office, or patronage from you. But as I regard the claims of Capt. Pryor as peculiar and paramount to those of any man within my knowledge, I can not withhold a joint tribute of regard.

He was the first man who volunteered to accompany Lewis and Clark on their tour to the Pacific Ocean. He was then in the Army some four or five years, resigned, and at the commencement of the last war entered the Army again, and was a Captain in the 44th Regt., under you, at New Orleans; and a *braver* man never fought under the wings of your Eagles. [Emphasis is Houston's]. He has done more to tame and pacificate the dispositions of the Osages to the whites, and surrounding Tribes of Indians than all other men, and has done more in promoting the authority of the U. States and compelling the Osages to comply with demands from Colonel Arbuckle than any person could have supposed.

Capt. Pryor is a man of amiable character and disposition—of fine sense strict honor—perfectly temperate, in his habits—and unremitting in his attention to business.

The Secretary of War assured me when I was last at Washington, that his "claim should be considered of", yet another was appointed, and he was passed by. He is poor, having been twice robbed by Indians of Furs and merchandise, some ten years since. For better information, in relation to Capt. Pryor, I will beg leave to refer you to Gen. Campbell, Col. Benton, and Gov. Floyd of Va, who is his first cousin.[11]

With every wish for your Glory and Happiness, I have the honor to be your most obt. servt.

Sam Houston

[Endorsed:] Refer[r]ed to the Secretary of War

A.J.

XI.   Letter from Col. Mathew Arbuckle to Secretary of War Eaton

Head Qrs 7th Inf'try
Cantonment Gibson[12]
19th Dec'r, 1830

To the Honbl. John H. Eaton,
   Secretary of War.
      Sir,

Capt. Nathaniel Pryor, who has been acting as sub-agent to the Osage Nation of Indians for several years, was not a little disappointed, and mortified, when Mr. L. Choteau (sic) was appointed the agent to that Tribe,[13] in not receiving from the Government the appointment of sub-agent. That office is again vacant, and he is anxious of receiving it.

In relation to the pretentions of Capt. Pryor, I believe I am justified in saying that he had done more than all the agents employed in the Indian Department in restoring peace between the Indians on this Frontier particularly in restraining Clermont's Band of the Osages from depredating on the neighboring Tribes, as well as on our citizens. Much of this service was rendered by Captain Pryor before he was authorized to act as sub-agent to that Band, and since he has been acting by authority, except in one or two cases, soon after his appointment, the conduct of the Osages under his particular charge has been as good as that of any Indians in this country. Yet if he was now removed from that Band I would not be surprised if they should commence their former Habits, and thereby disturb the peace of this Frontier.

The high standing of Capt. Pryor for Honesty and Worth together with the service he has rendered to the public, and the call (as I judge) there is for his continuance, I hope will insure to him the appointment he desires.

I have the honor to be, Sir,
With Highest Respect
Yr Obt. Servt

M. Arbuckle
Colo. 7th Inf'try

VII. Claim filed on behalf of Abraham Gallatin in Pryor's Probate
      Estate

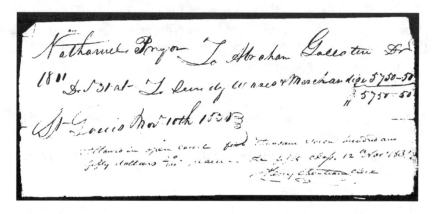

Transcription of Above Document

Nathaniel Pryor

                              To Abraham Gallatin Dr
1811
        Decr 31 [st?] To sundry wares & Merchandise <u>5750-50</u>
                                                $5750-50
St Louis Nov 10th 1831
    Allowed in open court five thousand seven hundred and
    fifty dollars 50/100 [plain ?]-- the fifth chap. 12th Novr 1831
                        Henry Chouteau, clerk

Notes

1. These documents, other than the affidavit of Maurice Blondeau, are from Walter B. Douglas, *Documents: Captain Nathaniel Pryor*, The American Hist. Review, American Historical Association, Vol. 24, January, 1919, pp. 253–265. We have tried to be faithful to the spelling, punctuation, printing and italics set forth in the Douglas volume.

2. [Footnote from source]. Pryor is mentioned as living among the Osages, on the Verdigris in 1821, by James, *Three Years among the Indians and Mexicans* (St. Louis, 1916), p. 108, and the *Missionary Herald*, XIX, 74.

3. This document is from L. R. Colter-Frick—*Courageous Colter and Companions*, Video Proof, Washington, MO, 1997, p. 487. [Printed in Italics in the Colter-Frick volume].

4. This document is not dated, but is presumed to be at or about the date of the affidavits by Pryor and McKee. Major duVal [as he usually signed his name] was agent to the Western Cherokees for some years, from 1822.

5. Douglas notes that this letter is in a folder marked "1826, Arkansas—Franklin Wharton—Claim of N. Pryor for Depredations". Franklin Wharton (1804–1847) was a son of Lieutenant Col. Franklin Wharton (1767–1818), U.S.M.C. and a younger brother of Col. Clifton Wharton, U.S.A. Dardanelle, which he gives as his address, is on the south bank of the Arkansas, about half-way up from Little Rock to Fort Smith.

6. Barbour's confusion relative to the date of the attack, on January 1, 1812, is explained in the text.

7. Again, Barbour is one year off on his dating, as the raid on Pryor's trading post occurred about six months prior to the War of 1812.

8. Douglas notes that this letter and the documents at VII and VIII, below, are in a folder marked "1827, Osages (sub-agency)—Wm. Clark— Appointment of N. Pryor sub-agent." Douglas also noted that "Governor George Izard of Arkansas Territory writes to the Secretary of War on June 6, 1827, from Little Rock: 'On my way

from New Orleans I became acquainted with Capt. Nath. Pryor, a very intelligent man, who accompanied Mess. Lewis and Clark to the Pacific Ocean, and has since that time been much among the Indians, particularly the Osages. I learned from him that he was directed by Gen. Clark the Superintendent at St. Louis to speak to me relative to the advantage of having a sub-agent appointed to reside with the band of Osages who are designated as Clermo's, and to ask my co-operation in recommending the measure to the Government.... . I am induced by these motives to join Gen. Clark in proposing the appointment of Capt. Prior [sic] to the sub-agency in question.'" [Citing *Publications of the Arkansas Historical Association, I. 445.*]

9. Choctaw Agent, West of the Mississippi.

10. John Francis Hamtramck the younger (1798–1858), who had resigned from the army as Second Lieutenant, and later was a Colonel in the Mexican War. [From Douglas].

11. Douglas used the N.J. Floyd genealogy book to correctly note that Pryor's mother was a sister of Col. John Floyd (d. 1783) and of Capt. Charles Floyd. Also that the Governor Floyd in Houston's letter was a son of Col. John Floyd. However, relying upon the misinformation in N.J. Floyd's book, Douglas mistakenly ascribed the parentage of Sgt. Charles Floyd of the Expedition to Capt. Charles Floyd, instead of to his actual father, Robert Clark Floyd.

12. Later, Fort Gibson.

13. Douglas noted that this was actually "Paul Ligueste Choteau (1792–1851), son of Jean Pierre Choteau of St. Louis, and younger brother of Auguste Pierre Chouteau who was a companion of Pryor on the voyage up the Missouri on the occasion of the unsuccessful attempt to return the Mandan chief to his home in 1807." Except as indicated, Douglas used the incorrect spelling of "Choteau," instead of Chouteau.

NATHANIEL PRYOR–BIBLIOGRAPHY

Ambrose, Stephen E.—*Lewis and Clark, Voyage of Discovery*, [Bicentennial Edition: The Filming of an Epic] National Council, Lewis & Clark Bicentennial, ISBN 0-7922-6473-8. —*Undaunted Courage*, Simon & Schuster, 1996, also Touchstone Press Edition, 1997.

Ambler, Charles H.—*Life and Diary of John Floyd, Governor of Virginia, An Apostle of Secession, and the Father of the Oregon Country*, Richmond Press, Richmond, VA, 1918,Ch. XX, republished.

American Heritage—*The History of the Great West*, American Heritage Pub. Co., 1965. —*The Pioneer Spirit*, American Heritage Pub. Co., 1959.

Appleman, Roy E.—*Lewis and Clark*, U.S. National Park Service, Washington, D.C., 1975.

Arkansas Gazette—Various editions, 1819–1920.

Bailey, Garrick and Swan, Daniel C.—*Art of the Osage*, St. Louis Art Museum and U. Washington Press, Seattle, WA, 2004.

Bakeless, John—*The Journals of Lewis and Clark*, NAL Penguin, Inc., New York, 1964.

Baltimore Patriot—February 6, 1822.

Barry, Louise—*The Beginning of the West*, Kansas State Hist. Soc., Topeka, KS, 1972.

Burns, Louis F.—*A History of the Osage People*, Ciga Press, Fallbrook, CA, 1989, (republished U. Alabama Press, 2004).

—*Osage Indians Bands and Clans*, Ciga Press, Fallbrook, CA, 1984.

—*Osage Indians Customs and Myths*, Ciga Press, Fallbrook, CA, 1984.

—*Osage Mission Baptisms, Marriages and Interments, 1820–1886*, Ciga Press, Fallbrook, CA, 1986.

Burns, Ruth S.—*Descendants of Lewis and Clark's Horses Run Wild in Pryor Mountains, We Proceeded On,* Lewis and Clark Trail Heritage Foundation, August, 1987, Vol. 13, No. 3, 1987.

Capps, Benjamin ed.—*The Indians, The Old West Series*, Time-Life, Alexandria, VA, 1973.

Captain James Patton of Augusta County, Virginia and Louisville, Kentucky—Ancestors and Descendants, Genealogy Pub. Co., Baltimore, MD, 1981.

Carter, Clarence Edwin, ed.—*Territorial Papers of the United States*, 28 vols., (GPO. Washington, D.C., 1934–75), 14:534.

Cartlidge, Anna Margaret—*Children and Grandchildren of William and Abadiah (Davis) Floyd*, unpublished manuscript, 1966, filed with DAR, Washington, D.C.
—Anna M.—*Colonel John Floyd, Reluctant Adventure,* Register of the Kentucky Historical Society, 66 (October, 1968), pp. 317–366.
—Anna M.—*Marriages of People Named Floyd*, The Maryland Genealogical Soc., Baltimore, MD, 1982.
—Anna—*These, Too, Are Our Ancestors*, unpublished, undated manuscript received by the author in 1968, filed with DAR, Washington, D.C.
—Anna M.—*Trouble at Toledo Mort*, The Filson Club Quarterly, Louisville, KY, April, 1971.

Celebrating the 4th of July at Ft. Gibson, 1827—The Chronicles of Oklahoma, Oklahoma Historical Society, Vol. 46, 1968.

Chittenden, H.M.—*The American Fur Trade of the Far West*, New York, 1902, Vol. 2.

Christian, Shirley—*Before Lewis and Clark*, Farrar Strauss and Giroux, New York, 2004.

Chuinard, E.G., M.D.—*Only One Man Died, The Medical Aspects of the Lewis and Clark Expedition*, Lewis and Clark Trail Heritage Foundation, Ye Galleon Press, Fairfield, WA, 1979 (reprinted 1999).

Clarke, Charles G.—*The Men of the Lewis & Clark Expedition*, U. Nebraska Press, Lincoln, 2002.

Cleary, Rita—*River Walk*, Dorchester Pub. Co., 2001.

Colby, Susan M.—*Sacagawea's Child, The Life and Times of Jean-Baptiste (Pomp) Charbonneau*, Arthur H. Clark Co., Spokane, WA, 2005.

Collin, Milton—*What Most People Don't Know About New Mexico*, The Denver Westerners 1966 Brand Book, Johnson Publishing Co., Boulder, CO, 1967.

Colter-Frick, L.R.—*Courageous Colter and Companions*, Video Proof, Washington, MO, 1997.

Coues, Elliott, ed.—*The Journal of Jacob Fowler*, with additional notes by Mary Lund Settle and Harry R. Stevens, U. Nebraska Press, Lincoln, 1970.

Cox, Isaac J.—*The Burr Conspiracy in Indiana*, Indiana Magazine of History, Vol. XXV, Dec. 1929.

Crosby, Mike—*Joined by a Journey, The Lives of the Lewis and Clark Corps of Discovery*, No ISBN, Library of Congress, or Copyright. Published by the Bureau of Land Management in 2004 and available from the BLM and the Sacajawea Center, 200 Main St., Salmon, ID 83467.

Dayton, Ruth Ward—*Pioneers and Their Homes on the Upper Kanawha*.

De Gruyter, Julius A.—*The Kanawha Spectator*, Beckley, WV.

De Voto, Bernard—*The Journals of Lewis and Clark*, Houghton Mifflin Co., Boston, 1953.

Dictionary of American Biography, Chas. Scribner's Sons, New York, 1934, supplemented and updated.

Dillon, Richard—*Meriwether Lewis*, Western Tanager Press, Santa Cruz, CA, 1988 reprint.

Douglas, Walter B.—*Documents: Captain Nathaniel Pryor*, The American Historical Review, Jan. 1919, vol. 24.

Draper, Lyman C.—*The Life of Daniel Boone*, (Ted Franklin Belue, ed.), Stackpole Books, Mechanicsburg, PA, 1998

Duboc, Jessie L.—*Yellowstone Adventure*, Montana Magazine, Montana Hist Soc., Helena, MT Vol. 5, No. 3, July, 1955.

Eckert, Allan W.—*A Sorrow in our Heart—The Life of Tecumseh*, Bantam Books, 1992.
—*That Dark and Bloody River*, Bantam Books, 1995.

Fiske, Thomas S.—*The Mystery of Nathaniel Pryor*, undated, unpublished manuscript available on-line.

Floyd, N.J.—*Biographical Genealogies of the Virginia-Kentucky Floyd Families*, Williams and Wilkins Co., Baltimore, MD, 1912.

Foreman, Carolyn Thomas—*General John Nicks and His Wife, Sarah Perkins Nicks, The Chronicles of Oklahoma*, Vol. 8, 1930.
— *Dutch, The Chronicles of Oklahoma*, Vol. 27, 1949.
—*Early History of Webbers Falls, The Chronicles of Oklahoma*, Vol. 46, 1968.
—*Hopefield Mission in Osage Nation, The Chronicles of Oklahoma*, Vol. 28, 1950.

Foreman, Grant—*Nathaniel Pryor, The Chronicles of Oklahoma*, Vol. 7.
—*The Centennial of Ft. Gibson, The Chronicles of Oklahoma*, Vol. 2, 1924.
—*The Three Forks, The Chronicles of Oklahoma*, Vol. 2, No. 1, 1924.

Frazier, Robert W.—*Forts of the West*, U. Okla. Press, Norman, 1965.

Genealogies of Virginia Families, Genealogy Pub. Co., Baltimore, MD, 1981.

George Rogers Clark Papers, 1781–1784, Collections of the Illinois State Hist. Library.

Gilbert, Bil ed.—*The Trailblazers, The Old West Series*, Time-Life, Alexandria, VA, 1973.

Goodman, Dennis—*Westerners, Wild West,* June, 2005, pp. 12, 67–68.

Grinde, Jr., Donald A. and Johansen, Bruce E.—*Encyclopedia of Native American Biography,* Henry Holt & Co., 1997.

Hagen, Dennis E.—*Counting Coup: the Nature of Intertribal Warfare on the Great Plains Considered, Roundup* of the Posse of the Denver Westerners, Inc. Nov–Dec, 2004.

Hagen, William T.—*The Sac and Fox Indians,* U. Okla. Press, 1988.

Harper, Elizabeth Pryor—"Twenty-one Southern Families: Notes and Genealogies", Patricia Freeman Compiler and Editor, 1985.
—and Middlebrooks, Glenna Parker—*Ancestry of Captain Nathaniel Pryor, The Chronicles of Oklahoma,* Vol. 48, pp. 295–306.
—*Pryor Family Notes,* (collected by Ben Pryor, Griffin, Georgia), Albuquerque, 1987.

Hogan, Lawrence J.—*The Osage Indian Murders,* Amlex, Inc., Frederick, MD, 1998.

Hoig, Stan—*Jesse Chisholm: Peace-maker, Trader, Forgotten Frontiersman, The Chronicles of Oklahoma,* Vol. 66, No. 4, 1988.

Holmberg, James J.—*Dear Brother—Letters of William Clark to Jonathan Clark,* Yale Univ. Press, 2002.
—*Exploring with Lewis and Clark—The 1804 Journal of Charles Floyd,* U. Okla. Press, Norman, 2005.

Huser, Verne—*On the River with Lewis and Clark,* Texas A & M Univ. Press, College Station, 2004.

Hutchins, John M.—*Lieutenant Zebulon Montgomery Pike Climbs His First Peak: The Army Expedition to the Sources of the Mississippi, 1803–1806,* privately published, Applewood, CO, 2005.

IGI Files—Records of the Latter Day Saints, Salt Lake City, UT.

Jackson, Donald ed.—*Letters of the Lewis and Clark Expedition, with Related Documents: 1783–1854,* 2nd Edition, U. Illinois Press, Urbana, IL, 1978.

James, Thomas—*Three Years Among the Indians and Mexicans,* Waterloo, IL, 1846.

Jennings, Kathleen—*Louisville's First Families,* Standard Printing Co., Louisville, KY, 1920, pp. 153–176.

Johansen, Bruce E and Grinde, Jr., Donald A.—*Encyclopedia of Native American Biography,* Henry Holt & Co., 1997.

Jones, Landon Y.—*Clark on the Yellowstone, We Proceeded On,* Vol. 32, No. 1, February, 2006, pp. 24–34.
—*Sergeant Floyd and Me, We Proceeded On,* Vol. 32, No. 1, February, 2006, p. 48.
—*William Clark and the Shaping of the West,* Hill and Wong, New York, 2004.

Kentucky Genealogy, Kentucky Hist. Soc., Vol. II.

Kinnaman, Thad—*Ancestry and Posterity of M.V. Floyd,* unpublished manuscript, Sedan, KS, 1967.

Lamar, Howard R.—*The American West,* Thomas Y. Crowell Co., New York, 1977.

Lange, Lou Ann—*Travelers and Travel's "Significant Others"— Three Visitors to the Arkansas Territory in 1818–1819, Missouri Historical Review,* Vol. 100, #1, October, 2005, pp. 19–39.

Masterson, V.V.—*The Katy Railroad and the Last Frontier,* U. Missouri Press, Columbia, MO, 1988.

Matthews, John Joseph—*The Osages, Children of the Middle Waters,* U. Okla. Press, Norman (1961, 3rd printing, 1973).

McMillan, Ethel—*Women Teachers in Oklahoma, 1820–1860, The Chronicles of Oklahoma,* Vol. 27.

Members of the Corps of Discovery, (Text by Deaton Museum Services, Minneapolis, MN), North Dakota Lewis & Clark Bicentennial Foundation, Washburn, ND, 1999.

Merritt, J. I. Editor—*Reubin vs. Reuben Field, We Proceeded On,* Lewis and Clark Trail Heritage Foundation, November, 2005.

Middlebrooks, Glenna Parker and Harper, Elizabeth Pryor— *Ancestry of Captain Nathaniel Pryor, The Chronicles of Oklahoma,* Vol. 48, pp. 295–306.

Military Warrants, Kentucky, 1782–1793.

Mordy, James C.—*The Paternity of Sgt. Charles Floyd of the Lewis and Clark Expedition and the Children of Robert Clark Floyd (1752–1807) and Charles Floyd (1760–1828),* unpublished typed manuscript, 2000. Copy on file at the Filson Historical Society, Louisville, KY.

Morison, Samuel Eliot—*The Oxford History of the American People,* New York, Oxford University Press, 1965.

Morris, Larry E.—*The Fate of the Corps,* Yale Univ. Press, New Haven, 2004.

Moulton, Gary E.—*The Journals of the Lewis and Clark Expedition,* 13 volumes and maps, U. Nebraska Press, Lincoln, 1986–.

Musselman, Joseph—website at: www.Lewis-Clark.org/Clark-YellowstonePryor/.

Newmark, Harris—*Sixty Years in Southern California, 1853–1913,* 4th ed., Zeitlin & Van Brugge, Los Angeles, CA, 1970.

O'Neil, Paul ed.—*The Frontiersmen, The Old West Series,* Time-Life, Alexandria, VA, 1977.
—*The Rivermen, The Old West Series,* Time-Life, Alexandria, VA, 1975.

Perrin, William Henry—*History of Bond and Montgomery Counties, Illinois,* O.L. Baskin, Chicago, IL, 1882.

Pickett, Ben Collins—*William L. McClellan, Choctaw Indian Agent, West, The Chronicles of Oklahoma,* Vol. 39, 1961–62.

Potter, Tracy—*Sheheke, Mandan Indian Diplomat, The Story of White Coyote, Thomas Jefferson and Lewis and Clark,* Farcountry Press, Helena, MT and Ft. Mandan Press, Washburn, ND, 2003.

Remini, Robert V.—*The Life of Andrew Jackson,* First Perennial Classics ed., Harper Collins, New York, 2001.

Ruth, Kent (Compiler)—*Oklahoma, A Guide to the Sooner State,* U. Okla. Press, Norman, 1941, reprinted, 1957.

Rydjord, John—*Kansas Place Names,* U. Okla. Press, Norman, 1972.

Sasser, Charles W.—*Fort Gibson—Graveyard of the Army*, <u>*Old West*</u>, Winter, 1984.

Schmidt, Thomas—*Guide To The Lewis & Clark Trail*, <u>*National Geographic*</u>, [Bicentennial Edition] undated.

Settle, Raymond W.—*The Mountain Men and the Fur Trade of the Far West*, Arthur H. Clark Co., Glendale, CA, 1965, Vol. II (Nathaniel Pryor chapter).

Shoemaker, Arthur—*The Many Faces of Nathaniel Pryor*, <u>*True West*</u>, September, 1988, pp. 48–51.

Stefaff, Rebecca—*Tecumseh and the Shawnee Federation*, Library of American Indian History, 1998.

Sugden, John—*Tecumseh—A Life*, Henry Holt & Co., New York, 1997.

Summers, Louis Preston—*History of Southwest Virginia, 1746–1786*, J.I. Hill Printing Co., Richmond, VA 1903.

Stanley, F. (Fr. Francis L. Stanley Crocchiola)—*Ciudad Santa Fe, Spanish Domination, 1610–1821*, The World Press, Inc., Denver, CO, 1958.
—*Ciudad Santa Fe, Mexican Rule, 1821–1846*, Pampa Print Shop, Pampa, TX, 1962.

Swan, Daniel C. and Bailey, Garrick—*Art of the Osage*, St. Louis Art Museum and U. Washington Press, Seattle, WA 2004.

<u>*The Chronicles of Oklahoma*</u>, Oklahoma Historical Society, untitled Notes and Documents in various issues, Vols. 10, 27, etc.

The Lewis and Clark Corps of Discovery, Their Lives and Their Lineage, Clatsop County (OR) Genealogical Soc., Vols. I and II, 2004.

Thoburn, Joseph B. and Wright, Muriel H.—*Oklahoma, A History of the State and its People*, Lewis Hist. Pub. Co., New York, 1929.

Tulsa (OK) Tribune, undated article, probably July, 1982, after the reburial of Nathaniel Pryor.

Van Doren, Charles, ed.—*Webster's American Biographies*, G. & C. Merriam Co., Springfield, MA, 1974.

Walker, Mary Jo—*The F. Stanley Story*, The Lightning Tree, Santa Fe, NM, 1985.

Walker, Wayne T.—*Pomp—Son of Sacagawea, True West*, July, 1970.

We Proceeded On, Lewis and Clark Trail Heritage Foundation, various issues between 1980–2006.

Wharton, Franklin—*Letter* to Secretary of War James Barbour, February 28, 1826, excerpts at *Discovering Lewis &Clark at*: http://www.lewis-clark.org, *1998*.

William Clark Papers, Kansas State Hist. Soc., Topeka, KS, 6:104.

Wright, Muriel H. and Thoburn, Joseph B.—*Oklahoma, A History of the State and its People*, Lewis Hist. Pub. Co., New York, 1929,

Yater, George H.—*Nine Young Men From Kentucky, We Proceeded On*, Lewis and Clark Trail Heritage Foundation, WPO Publication No. 11, May, 1992.

INDEX

ABOUT THE AUTHOR

Lawrence R. Reno is a third generation Coloradan with a long-time interest in the history of the Westward movement in America, military history and the genealogy of his family. Larry is a collateral relative of both Sgt. Floyd and Sgt. Pryor from the Lewis & Clark Voyage of Discovery, as his great-great-grand-father was a first cousin to each of them. Larry received his early schooling in Denver Public Schools and then graduated from Phillips Academy at Andover and Yale University, receiving a degree in Industrial Administration from Yale.

After graduation from Yale, Larry served two years in Germany as a Lieutenant in the Army Field Artillery. Returning to Denver he was employed as a systems test engineer for The Martin Company for three years, involved in the early stages of the Titan Missile program. Larry then obtained his law degree from the University of Colorado, where he graduated with the Honor of Order of the Coif. He has practiced law in Denver for over 40 years, specializing in real estate, estate planning, wills, trusts and probate.

Larry is the current *Roundup Foreman* for the Denver Posse of Westerners, Inc, an international group devoted to the history of the American West. He was the first male President of the Denver Childrens' Hospital Board of Directors; was a director and the national legal counsel for Trout Unlimited for 25 years during the early years of the environmental movement; has been the President of Denver's University Club and of the Rotary Club of Denver Mile High; is the current Chancellor of the Colorado Society of the Sons of the Revolution; and, is a current member of the Boards of the Trout and Salmon Foundation and the Western Outlaw-Lawman History Association.